From NYC
Lower East Side
To
NASA Satellite
Operations Manager

Dear Shay,

Here is a great book
to learn about your ancestors/
relatives, THE EAST COAST
CHILDREN of RUSSIAN IMMIGRANTS.

I always enjoy seeing
you.

310-880-6555 — Love,
your brother
David
Shro

From NYC Lower East Side To NASA Satellite Operations Manager

Nimbus satellite flying over Planet Earth.

RALPH SHAPIRO

To order additional copies of this book, contact:
Xlibris Corporation
1-888-795-4274
www.Xlibris.com
Orders@Xlibris.com
Book ID 116904

CONTENTS

Preface..11

Chapter 1   Humble Background 21
  Family Background 22
  Growing Up on NYC's Lower East Side 29
    Family Living Style...31
    Integrated Community..32
    Commercial Retail Businesses Available 34
    Factories and Commercial Businesses.....................35
    Unlawful Businesses...37
    Density of the Population 40
    Street Sport Activities 41
    Facility Sports 44
    Summer and Winter Fun 45
    Depression-Era Games 46
    Patriotic Activities..47
    Halloween 48
    Community-wide Entertainment............................48
    Educational Alliance Activities..............................49
    Coping with the Great Depression.........................49
  Religious Education 51
    Reflections on Religion 54
  Early Taste for Mechanics 56
  Whiz Kid at Elementary School 56
  Interest in Professional Sports....................................57
  High School Experience 58
  College Experience...60
  Family Development 63

Special Personal Experiences..70
    Experience Impacting My Political Perspective.......................70
    Experience Impacting My Religious Perspective.....................72
Religious Affiliations 74
Interest in Zionism...79
Society Payback—Volunteerism 80
Society Support—Charity Giving...87
Caught In the Lower East Side Web 88
Escaping from the Lower East Side Web................................90
    Cultural Exposure in My Senior Years.............................105
    Visit to National Memorial Sites....................................106
    Elderhostel Trip 107
    Visit to the Richmond Museum of the Confederacy...........108
Unusual Family Event at Book Completion 110
Chapter 2   Professional Experience 112
General Electric Company Employment 112
    Schenectady, New York...112
    Lynn, Massachusetts 114
    Erie, Pennsylvania...117
    Pittsfield, Massachusetts 118
    Bridgeport, Connecticut...120
    Bloomfield, New Jersey..122
    Schenectady, New York...123
Markwell Manufacturing Company Employment 124
Frankford Arsenal Employment...127
Channel Masters Employment 133
US Industries Employment 143
Transitioning to NASA Goddard Space
Flight Center Employment...147
STX Employment 148
QSS Employment 152
Postretirement Independent Consultancy..............................155
Chapter 3   Working for NASA 157
Joining NASA Beats the Odds..157
Initial Nimbus Program Role 159
Nimbus Spacecraft Operations Manager Role 163

Spacecraft Problem Management Role 166
Preparation for the Next Nimbus Spacecraft Operations 167
Managing the Second Nimbus Spacecraft
Assembly and Testing Effort...168
Operational Software Development Coordination....................171
Unofficial Use of Nimbus Data to
Support Government and Commercial Operations...................171
Supporting Other GSFC Satellite Programs 174
Helping Initiate the Earth Observing
System (EOS) Replacement to Nimbus....................................176
NASA Space Station Concept
Development Team Participation 178
Retirement from NASA...180
Chapter 4   Nimbus Satellite Program Benefits 182
Nimbus Benefits to Society 183
Nimbus Contribution to Science..184
Weather Forecasting Revolution 184
Climatology 185
Environmental Protection 186
Oil Spill Control 186
Reacting to Disruptive Volcanoes 187
Hurricane Warnings 187
Oceanographic Studies...187
Technology Transfer 188
Chapter 5   Satellite Systems Basic Tutorial 189
Understanding Scientific Satellites and Their Operations 189
Satellite Design Concept: Satellite Overview 193
Nimbus Satellite Design 194
Power System..195
Command and Data Handling System 195
Attitude Control Spacecraft
Stabilization and Pointing System..196
Communication System 196
Thermal Control System 197
Payload...197
Satellite Earth Science Basics 197

Measuring Earth's Behavior from Satellites 198
    Electromagnetic Spectrum 198
    Frequency of Radiation 199
Who Builds Satellites 200
How Satellites Are Tested 200
Satellite Operations 201
Ground System Operations 202
Control Center Operations 202
Chapter 6   Nimbus Satellite Program Overview 204
Nimbus Satellite Program Heritage 205
NASA Headquarters Program Management 205
Project Management 206
Project Staff 207
Spacecraft Developers 208
Scientist Organization 209
Center Recognition 211
Nimbus Ground System 212
    Nimbus Control Center 212
    Meteorological Data Handling System 215
    STDN Tracking and Data Network 215
Chapter 7   Nimbus Program Satellite Operations 216
Nimbus-1 Satellite: Twenty-Eight-Day
Operation Kick-Starts Satellite Earth Science 216
    Remembrances of Exciting Nimbus Activation 219
    Lessons Learned 220
    Nimbus-1 Press Conference 220
    Other Remembrances Associated with Nimbus-1 ...221
    Personal Reprimands Received 222
Nimbus B-1 Satellite Launch Failure 223
Nimbus-2 Satellite: Author's Cradle-to-Grave Responsibility 224
Nimbus-3 Satellite Revolutionizes Weather Forecasting 225
Nimbus-4 Satellite: Breakthrough in
Earth's Upper-Atmosphere Knowledge 228
Nimbus-5 Satellite Initiates New
Technology for Earth Remote Sensing 230

Nimbus-6 Satellite: Profound Impact
on Meteorology and the International
Search and Rescue Program....................................232
Nimbus-7 Satellite: Program Climax with
Many Earth Science Accomplishments........................236

Footnotes, credits/references...................................241
Index..243

Preface

The National Museum of American Jewish History (NMAJH) opened in Philadelphia in November 2010. Prior to its opening, the museum solicited input from members of the American Jewish community that described a person's special achievements under unusual background circumstances and that illustrated special accomplishments relating to the American community or highlighted opportunities the United States offered to Jewish people. I provided a brief story describing how I advanced from my heritage of an immigrant family with a humble background living in New York City's Lower East Side to serving as the spacecraft operations manager of the NASA satellite system called Nimbus. This was the first NASA research satellite system that measured Earth's atmospheric, land, and oceanic behavior and accomplished many technological advances. Seven Nimbus satellites operated over a thirty-year period, with many societal and commercial benefits. NMAJH accepted my story for display in the museum and also included an abstract of my story on their website (called *reflections*) to solicit additional stories from the Jewish community.

The NMAJH's favorable assessment of my brief personal story encouraged me to assume that an exposure to New York City's Lower East Side's distinctive lifestyle in the 1930s compared to the rest of the country could make interesting reading from a historical perspective. A reader's comparison of their personal heritage and growing-up experience to my experience could also be interesting. The East Side community's lifestyle characterization is woven in with my personal development, starting from my early childhood in the late 1920s (born in May 1924). That is followed by my elementary and high school experience during the 1930s' Depression period, a time when the young and the old in the community had to cope with the bad economic times. I was exposed to the Zionist movement, which instilled a lifelong interest and concern about the State of Israel, horrified by Hitler's ranting against the Jews heard on the radio, and disturbed by the rising isolationism and anti-Semitic speeches in this country before Pearl Harbor. I started college as a fifteen-and-a-half-year-old youth, mature somewhat intellectually but not socially. This City College of New York (CCNY) experience, starting prior to World War II, was maturing to me in many ways. I started my professional career with the General Electric Company in 1944, being kept out of serving in the armed forces due to bad vision. Learning about the Holocaust was the big shock of that period. The news of the victory against Germany and later Japan were the great excitements. How I later escaped from that proverbial Lower East Side web that confined my view of this country to seeing the beauty of our country and its heritage can be another measure of comparison for the reader.

As a youngster I had no problem deciding what career I wanted to pursue—it was engineering. I had an unusual engineering career, which I enjoyed over my long lifetime. I graduated from CCNY in May 1944 with a bachelor of mechanical engineering degree at the age of twenty. The school offered little career guidance. With their military production activity requiring more engineers, the prestigious General Electric Company recruited engineers at CCNY for the first time, and I accepted a position as a test engineer. Unhappy with the next position GE offered me and the thought of living in Schenectady, NY, I took a product/machine design position with the Markwell Manufacturing Company in New York City, a vendor of office equipment and staplers. That job ended four years later during a mild recession period. I was fortunate to get a job six months later conducting military ordnance equipment research at the army's Frankford Arsenal in Philadelphia. In anticipation of the facility closure, which did occur two years later, I took another product/machine design position with the Channel Master Corporation, makers of home television antennas, located in the small town of Ellenville, NY, where I got married and raised my new young family. Seven years later I joined US Industries in Silver Spring, MD, a company starting a new venture of developing small robotic equipment for manufacturing applications. After this job terminated in two years, with essentially no relevant experience, I fortuitously got the opportunity to work for NASA at the Goddard Space Flight Center (GSFC) in Greenbelt, MD, where I had a most rewarding twenty-four-year aerospace engineering position, mainly as the NASA Satellite Operations Manager of the Nimbus meteorological satellites. As

I started my civil service retirement in 1986, I put my energy to work constructively at the Hughes STX Corporation, an aerospace contracting company, where I worked almost ten years before another retirement. I became a workaholic. Since then I have been working as an independent proposal consultant for several companies vying for NASA, Coast Guard, NOAA, and Navy technical support services contracts, still being productive in my eighty-eighth year. This work was part-time, and it enabled me to also get much personal satisfaction performing community services, such as Meals on Wheels and miscellaneous volunteer services for the Hebrew Home of Greater Washington.

My long lifespan exposed me to many lifestyle and societal cultural changes. I grew up living in NYC's Lower East Side apartment houses with coal stoves in the kitchen for cooking, gas stoves for heating, ice boxes in the kitchen for keeping food cold, horse and wagons in the city streets for commerce, and trolleys in the streets for public conveyance. Home radio ownership was just becoming common, private telephone ownership was a rarity, car ownership was very limited, electronics for TV and computers had not been invented, and teeth braces for children unheard of devices. Medical procedures were basic, with high infant and child mortality rates, little cancer control, and periodic polio epidemics that ravaged children and adults. Childbirth in the home aided by midwives was still common, and living past the early seventies uncommon. I was exposed to the horrors of the Great Depression and witnessed the behavioral oddities of the Prohibition. During my youth, anti-Semitism and bigotry toward blacks was common, homosexual behavior exposure was very confined, and mixed racial marriages were almost unheard of. Such attitudes have fortunately changed considerably; others, like the large economic policy differences between Republicans and Democrats, have not. The horrible Nazi genocide of the Jewish people has been replaced by black genocide against other blacks in Africa. The Arabian attempt to destroy the State of Israel has been replaced by the Iranian threat to wipe out the State of Israel.

My brief NMAJH story ended with only the highlighting of my experience with NASA as a NASA spacecraft operations manager. This book fills in the details. It provides the story of how my eighteen-year industrial engineering professional career evolved, only to abruptly end when the company I worked for decided to move. The way I got my job at NASA and the Nimbus spacecraft operations manager role I inherited and served as for twenty years is almost stranger than fiction. The Nimbus program that I worked on revolutionized weather forecasting. Its success was due to the dedication of so many talented government and industry scientists, who had the vision to create the new science objectives, especially the initial early Project Manager, Harry Press, and Project Scientist, Dr. William Nordberg. Credit is due to the later project managers and the engineers and support personnel who managed the contractor design and development of the seven satellites in the Nimbus program, each advancing meteorology and Earth science. As the Nimbus Operations Manager I am especially indebted to the General Electric Team under the leadership of Bennie Palmer that operated the Nimbus Control Center flawlessly over the thirty-year Nimbus satellite operational lifetime. With the short, twenty-eight-day lifetime of Nimbus-1, I took on the caretaker role of managing the GE contractor rapid and low-cost development of the second Nimbus spacecraft, for which I was awarded the NASA Headquarters Exceptional Service Medal. As operations manager, independent of supervisory oversight I essentially planned the spacecraft operations support systems for the seven Nimbus satellites, each with essentially different advanced instruments making new measurements of Earth's atmosphere, oceans, and land resources. I managed the General Electric Company staff that conducted the Nimbus Control Center orbital operations. I also coordinated the data collection and scientific data processing with the Nimbus program scientists who developed the scientific processes (algorithms) to convert the instrument measurements into Earth component measurement information (e.g., air, ocean, and land chemistry; air and ocean temperature; energy coming in from the sun and radiating out to space). This data was applied to develop improved weather forecasting techniques, conduct climate change analysis, develop pollution analysis and control, and institute a worldwide safety system. The technologies associated with the continuously improved array of Nimbus instrumentation were essentially transferred to the National Oceanic and Atmospheric Administration (NOAA) operational satellite instrumentation that provides the input to our national weather forecasting system. It was especially personally rewarding to have creatively established immediate practical applications of Nimbus data. A system was developed to transmit to the National Weather Service Nimbus raw and processed data in near real time for operational weather forecasting in parallel with the traditional method, to the navy's Arctic Ocean ship-routing operations, to commercial fisheries to help locate schools of tuna and other large fish, and to worldwide weather forecasting systems learning how to use new types of atmospheric measurements taken by satellite to improve the weather forecasting accuracy and to extend the forecast accuracy to several days. The operational procedures I helped the control center develop and the management practices I applied that contributed to conducting the Nimbus satellite's thirty-year operations successfully are described in this book to serve as lessons learned for the reader to apply to their own endeavors.

Before I was stimulated to write this book based upon NMAJH's interest in my brief personal story, I had unsuccessfully explored with NASA's public relations offices ways of publicizing the many societal benefits derived from the Nimbus program that I had worked on. Nimbus was the first and major NASA Earth-resources research satellite program that measured Earth's atmospheric, oceanographic, and terrestrial performance. Seven Nimbus satellites collected this type of information over a thirty-year period. The first Nimbus in 1964 took high-quality daylight pictures and nighttime cloud pictures around the world, observing five hurricanes and two typhoons in its short one-month lifetime. It also provided local cloud pictures in real time to small ground stations that were then broadcast over local TV. The third Nimbus spacecraft revolutionized weather forecasting. It collected the first worldwide numerical air temperature data, the forerunner of today's accurate long-term weather forecasting system methodology. Later Nimbus spacecraft instrumentation made new types of measurements that enhanced the quality of the weather forecasts and provided the basis for accurate hurricane and cyclone forecasting. Nimbus-6 flew a device to track high-flying balloons worldwide for studying upper-atmosphere wind motion patterns. After being used on an emergency basis to locate two balloonists trying to cross the Atlantic, who were downed and lost in the Atlantic off Newfoundland, and to locate an adventurer lost in a Northern Canada crevice on his way solo to the North Pole by dogsled, this system technology became the basis of the universal satellite search and rescue system that locates downed/lost small aircraft or boats involved in an accident in remote regions. It is the technique used these days to track animals and large fish migration that receive publicity. Starting with Nimbus-7, the daily upper atmosphere's ozone content has been measured globally to supplement the sparse ground ozone measurement system. Ozone in the ground air is a pollutant, but ozone in the upper atmosphere protects people from being exposed to the sun's ultraviolet rays that cause skin cancer and cataracts. Knowledge of upper-atmospheric ozone is so important to the world that there has been an international agreement to always have the equivalent of the Nimbus-7 Total Ozone Measuring System (TOMS) on an operational satellite taking these daily measurements. Climate studies and current related climate-warming claims are derived from computer software climate models that apply atmospheric, oceanic, ice, and solar energy radiation measurements initiated by Nimbus developmental instrumentation.

NASA public relations offices never encouraged the news media to publicize these societal benefits and technological advancements accomplished by the seven Nimbus satellites, each with different instrumentation and scientific objectives; manned flight and star-gazing satellites took precedence. Writing this book enabled me to achieve some Nimbus publicity by exposing the readers to the many Nimbus program benefits to society—a payback to NASA for the exciting, rewarding experience NASA provided me. This book essentially enabled me to fulfill my role as the unofficial Nimbus project historian.

Inasmuch as the book readers will be exposed to the realm of satellites in relation to my life story, I assumed that some readers would then be curious to understand the basics of how satellites function and how satellite operations and programs are conducted. I therefore included brief, simplified tutorial descriptions of these subjects in the Nimbus program context for the benefit of this category of readers.

At age eleven, I received the Jewish history book *Stranger than Fiction* as an award for proficiency in Hebrew education. At thirteen, I received another such award, the book *In Those Days*, about an old man telling tales from his youth at age eleven until his twenties. These two books presaged my own experience. Ten years ago I wrote my own book on Jewish history, *Jewish History: 4,000 Years of Accomplishment, Agony, and Survival*, and with this book I am an old man telling tales from my youth at age four until my twenties and beyond into my senior years.

My hope is that this book will inspire readers to persevere at achieving their personal livelihood objectives and to find ways of performing community service in payback as I did.

Ralph Shapiro
Silver Spring, MD
May 26, 2012

A co-worker's view of the author.

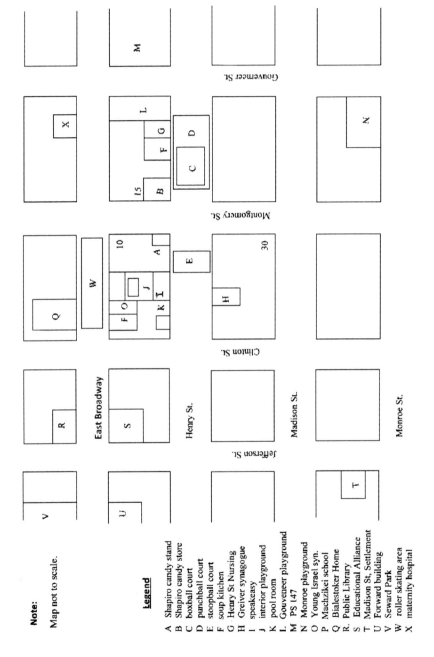

Note:

Map not to scale.

Legend

A Shapiro candy stand
B Shapiro candy store
C boxball court
D punchball court
E stoopball court
F soup kitchen
G Henry St Nursing
H Greiver synagogue
I speakeasy
J interior playground
K pool room
L Gouveneer playground
M PS 147
N Monroe playground
O Young Israel syn.
P Machzikei school
Q Bialestoker Home
R. Public Library
S Educational Alliance
T Madison St, Settlement
U Forward building
V Seward Park
W roller skating area
X maternity hospital

NYC Lower East Side Area of Book Interest.

Birthday wishes in the context of my NASA role from the perspective of my ten-year-old granddaughter.

Nimbus satellite flying over Planet Earth.

Chapter 1

Humble Background

For twenty-four years I worked for the National Aeronautics and Space Administration (NASA) as a highly technical satellite operations manager and program technical manager, yet I grew up on the Lower East Side of New York City, where higher education was not a focus and there was a *web* that confined my cultural perspective to the narrow Lower East Side perspective. In addition, I was raised by humble, hardworking parents who were not in position to expand my horizons. This is hardly the background that is likely to spawn the NASA position I ultimately held.

In this chapter I provide details of my early personal development, a happy young kid who learned good work habits and proper business ethics from his parents and grew up absorbing the social and political messages that living on the Lower East Side provided. In weaving my personal story, I tried to show the distinctive nature of life on the Lower East Side in the 1930s and the related valuable social behavioral lessons learned through the many sports activities I indulged in. I also described many cultural aspects of our country I observed through my efforts to escape from that *web*, which constrained my cultural advancement during my youth. It skips over my work years covered in subsequent chapters and describes my senior-year activity that is a reflection of what I learned in my youth.

Family Background

My parents were representative of the large number of Jewish immigrants from Eastern Europe that came to the United States between 1880 and 1924, after which such entry was limited by the Johnson Act. They were essentially poor immigrants with just a basic education obtained in hometown European Jewish schools and no knowledge of English before arriving in the United States. They worked hard to raise their families on small or modest incomes, lived in crowded quarters, and had little recreational activity, but they had dreams and goals for their children to have a better life.

My father, Louis Shapiro, at the age of twenty-five, boldly immigrated to the United States in 1906 with no family here to help him get started and no knowledge of English. In addition, he was responsible for his sixteen-year-old kid brother Nathan (forever called Nat), who came with him on the ship *Francesca* by way of Trieste, Italy; my grandfather could only afford the travel fare for two. It required a several-week train journey from their home in the Ukraine to the port in Italy and a couple-week cross-Atlantic trip, during which time they ate meagerly to save the little money my father had saved for the trip, which was about $300. My uncle explained that he joined my father rather than either of his other two older single brothers because "I was the only one with the nerve to go to America." He also told me about the burden he was to my father as an irresponsible kid with this example. He saw bananas in New York for the first time in his life; bananas were unknown in his area of Europe. They were being sold by a street vendor. The entrepreneur that he was, he took $10 from my father's savings and bought a large bunch of ripe yellow bananas with the intention of being a banana street vendor the next day. Little did he know that they would overripen fast in the summer heat without being cooled. They ripened and spoiled, so all that the future successful businessman earned was a severe reprimand from his brother for taking the money without asking. Six months prior to coming to the United States, my father had finished serving in the Russian army for two years, which was during the Russo-Japanese War. That experience toughened him up for coming to the States on his own. The brief tailoring experience he obtained in Warsaw, Poland, after he got out of the army enabled him to quickly get a job in a downtown NYC garment factory, which was the source of work for most Jewish immigrants in NYC during that period. He came from the Russian-controlled Ukrainian city of Vladimir Volynsk. This city is located on the Bug River, which separates the Ukraine from Poland. The Jewish residents called it simply "Ludmir," which was the Yiddish equivalent of Vladimir. The city was founded in about the year 1000 by Prince Vladimir, known for converting Russia to Christianity. The Jewish community developed in the early thirteenth century. That general area suffered through the changing political tides that ruled the area (Russian, Tartars, Ukrainian, Polish, and Turkish), and there were genocidal pogroms against the Jews associated with several of these changing political events. The most severe pogrom was during the Cossack revolution against the area's Polish rulers, led by the infamous Cossack leader Bogdan Chmielnicki in 1648, when about half of the city's Jewish population was killed. It again became rich in Jewish culture going back to the late 1600s, when German Jews migrated east to escape Central Europe's terror against Jews and became a largely Jewish city; it was 75 percent Jewish for many centuries. Ludmir was a major Jewish religious center for that part of Europe, with a large synagogue and many small ones, a large yeshiva, and many famous rabbis since its foundation. In the 1900s it was the industrial area for that part of the Ukraine, and the Jews were the major craftsmen, making a comfortable living. However, in the late 1930s there was an anti-Semitic-inspired social action in Poland to buy from Polish merchants rather than from Jewish merchants that resulted in hard economic times for the Jews in Poland. This movement also affected Ludmir, which was located in the area of the Ukraine that was under Polish sovereignty since World War I. As a result of these actions, my father's family living in Ludmir went into poverty. My father and his two brothers and sister living in New York City started sending clothes and some money to their Ludmir Shapiro family. The Russians who had taken control of that area under their 1939 pact with Hitler examined all incoming mail and confiscated the money. When we learned there was no money in the mail they received, we tried sending money hidden in the clothes. My father accumulated the clothes, and I was the packager and mailman, carrying the clothing packages to the nearby post office. In the summer of 1941, that area of the Ukraine was quickly overrun by the Nazi army when they attacked the Soviet Union. Ludmir was turned into a barbed-wire-enclosed dual ghetto. One was a "death ghetto," where the residents were underfed and left to die of malnutrition and subsequent disease. The other was a "work ghetto," where they worked the poorly fed inhabitants to death. The ghetto of twenty-eight thousand Ludmir Jews was enlarged by Jews herded in from neighboring small towns. With no railroads connecting the city of Vladimir Volynsk to the railroads in Poland that then connected to the Polish concentration camps, the Nazis implemented their "final solution of the Jewish people" in Ludmir with the help of Ukrainian police by periodically holding pogroms that slaughtered the Jews right in the ghettos. A survivor described how they periodically shot thousands at a time in the ghetto. Another survivor explained that very few tried to escape from the ghetto because the Germans took harsh revenge on the ghetto members whenever they discovered someone had escaped. Near the end, after all the slaughter that had occurred, some men recognized that staying in the camp was futile, with their impending death in the ghetto unless they escaped, and they tried to escape. One such escapee told how in December 1943, a band of about forty who made it out marched through the city in the middle of the night with their shoes off in the cold of winter to be quiet. They later sang Polish songs while marching through towns to avoid being recognized as Jews, only to die fighting the Germans in the nearby woods with a partisan group; he was the one Jewish survivor. At war's end, there were only 130 Ludmir ghetto survivors. Not one of my father's thirty-eight relatives who were living in Ludmir in 1939 survived.

My mother, nee Beckie Teitelbaum, came to New York City in 1898 at age ten with her father, mother and two younger siblings on the ship *Amsterdam* by way of Rotterdam, Holland. They came from a small town in Galicia, southern Poland. My grandfather, with no skills, had a very small income, first as a street peddler and later working as a helper in his cousin's wood-turning factory in Brooklyn that made wooden spools for the garment industry. He frequently brought me these spools as toys; they were the forerunner of my tinker toy game, which was my favorite childhood game. They lived on Grand Street in lower Manhattan. To get to work he walked to the Grand St. Ferry (long gone and replaced by the Williamsburg Bridge), took the ferry across the East River to Williamsburg, and walked about a mile to the factory located near the Brooklyn Navy Yard. Since he lived by Jewish Orthodoxy rules, he didn't work on Saturday and generally worked half day on Friday to get home early enough for the start of the Sabbath. My mother had to help support the family, which had added two other siblings, so at age thirteen, she gave up her English daytime schooling (she took night classes later) and took on a job in a sweatshop garment factory located at downtown Wooster and Broome streets starting at 5¢ per hour ($2 a week; she didn't work on Saturdays like most garment workers did) and walked a mile to work to save the nickel carfare. At the turn of the century, the New York City garment-manufacturing center was still located downtown and employed mostly Jews, predominately women, living on the Lower East Side. It is where the tragically famous Triangle Shirtwaist Company fire occurred in 1911 in which 147 women and 21 men were killed and over 200 burned and maimed. This incident provided an awakening to the sweatshop problems. In 1906, her younger brother got an appendicitis attack. At that time the medical profession was slow at recognizing appendicitis and was not too well equipped to treat it effectively; he succumbed to the ailment. It remained a troublesome ailment for many years. Two young neighborhood teenagers in my early youth time frame also succumbed to appendicitis attacks.

My parents, meeting through an introduction, got married in 1910 and quickly started raising a family—son Morris, born in 1911, and daughter Irene, born in 1913. My father then wanted to increase his income to support his growing family, so in 1915 he went into business operating a candy stand, a six-by-fifteen-foot shack attached to the outside of an old small building dating back to the Civil War days. The picture, taken in about 1932, shows my father approaching the stand, my longtime friend Tom Connerty behind him, neighbor Mrs. Silver standing guard over her little boy on the left, as she always did, and another neighbor's child, Seymour Levy, left alone by his parents. This was considered safe by most parents in this neighborhood. Jewish immigrants operating this type of outdoor candy stand was very common in Manhattan during that period; there were two other candy stands within one block in two directions from my father's candy stand. Popular cigarettes like Camels, Lucky Strikes, and Chesterfields sold for 13¢ for a pack of twenty, secondary brands like Domino sold for 10¢ a pack. Cigarettes were also sold loose, a penny a piece. A good cigar cost 5¢. It was too hot in the summer to handle perishables like chocolate candy bars, which had to be stored in the building's cool basement. As an example of how hot it was, while my sister and I watched, Mr. Levy, the father of the Levy boy in the picture, fried an egg on the street by putting

a raw egg on a hot stone on the sidewalk and used a large magnifying glass to shine the sun's rays on to the egg to fry it. Another example is what can be gleamed by what happened in our apartment one summer night. My father woke up in the middle of the night, shouting in panic that my mother was gone. To escape from the hot bedroom, she had quietly slipped out of the next bedroom window onto the fire escape, where we found her sleeping. Winters in New York City were much colder then, before all the heat generated by all the skyscrapers built later in Manhattan. The snow, which became ice packed in the street, would hardly melt all winter, much to the kids' delight. Sled riding in the streets was a common sight almost all winter. As a small youngster I frequently made a skating pond on the street by making a ten-foot long snow enclosure near the sidewalk that I filled with water from my father's candy stand. It generally stayed frozen for days and served as a small ice skating rink for myself and a couple of friends who were adventurous to start ice skating with starter skates.

My parents' family kept growing; sister May was born in 1917, Frances in 1921, and me in 1924. I was named Raphael after my deceased grandfather, Raful (Yiddish name) Shapiro. Somehow my name changed to Ralph early on before entering kindergarten. I vaguely remember my oldest sister, Irene, enjoyed calling me Dooly when she took care of me as a youngster. I don't know why she liked calling me by that name other than Dooly was the name of a popular comedian at that time. I asked her that the last time I saw her before she passed away, but she could not remember. I legally changed my name to Ralph when I entered the business world working for the General Electric Company at age twenty-one; it seemed appropriate for professional activity, like getting passports. I was called Rafiyal (Spanish version of Raphael) as a tease by several co-workers during my working career because of my love of Latin dancing.

My father worked sixteen to twenty hours a day except for the major Jewish holidays, when the store was closed. My mother helped my father operate the business, relieving him to give him a two-to-three-hour afternoon rest break in his older years and operating the business when my father went to pick up evening newspapers that were sold in the business. My grandmother served as the initial babysitter, enabling my mother to help my father in the business when the oldest children were still infants. Later my brother and older sisters acted as baby watchers for their younger siblings to enable my mother to provide her candy stand operations support. They escorted their younger siblings to PS 147, the public school one block away, to relieve my mother of this chore; everyone walked to school in those days. As they grew older, all the children helped run the candy stand. My father liked to tell the story about my middle sister, May, who looked older for her age. While operating the candy stand by herself at age twelve, she was able to persuade the health inspector that came along that she was fourteen years old, which met the minimum work age requirement at that time period. I can recall as a little eight-year-old kid getting pleasure out of helping to make the homemade lemon ices by stirring the big barrel in the salted ice-water tub and selling ice-cream cones, mellow roll ice-cream sandwiches, and Dixie cups from the outside ice-cream stand that operated only in the summer. At that age I also daily accompanied my father in picking up the nightly newspapers. We went to Delancey Street, about eight streets away, where the newspaper truck brought the evening newspapers. All the newspaper vendors rushed back to their stores to be the first to have the newspaper available for sale. My early contribution was to take a small bundle of newspapers and rush home faster than the other older competitors could, enabling my father to follow back at a slower pace. Saturday night was the special treat. It required my father taking a bus across town to the Brooklyn Bridge Manhattan-side terminal, where the papers were available early and returning home with heavy bundles of the *Sunday Daily News*. I accompanied him in doing this for several years, and he would make me a progressively heavier bundle to carry on my shoulder as I got older and prouder. Each trip was generally followed by a trip to the neighborhood dairy restaurant where my father had his late dinner and I had my helper-reward dessert treat.

In 1927 my brother Morris, the oldest in the family, contracted rheumatic feverwhich damaged his heart, presumably after going under the water gushing out of an open hydrant onto the street to cool off a gang of kids on a hot summer day, a very common summer practice in New York City in those days. There was no cure for that ailment at that time. The doctor told my mother that he had about a year to live, and indeed he died the next June. His death provided my earliest childhood memory at age four that I retained until today. I was standing at the base of the apartment house stairway with my next older sister, Frances, age seven, watching as they carried the casket down from the second-floor apartment, followed by my parents and two older sisters; burial preparation in the home was a common practice. My sister Frances, who was my caretaker for the day, and I walked behind the funeral procession of family led by my wailing mother and grieving friends from the house to the nearby family Griever Synagogue, where the hearse's rear door was opened during prayers offered by the rabbi, another custom in those days. We were too young to be part of the formal funeral activity. It was a painful loss to all the family. My brother was a delightful son, wonderful helper to the family, and a great student even through his last year in school. For the last four months before he died, he tried keeping up with his high school work at home while being confined to bed, which his teachers cooperatively supported. My mother accepted his death as a touch of fate and never lost her Judaic religious feelings.

The most popular newspaper sold at the candy stand was the *NY Daily News*, followed by the *Daily Mirror*. The other newspapers sold included the *New York Times*, the *Herald Tribune*, and the *NY Journal American*. There were four Jewish newspapers sold at the candy stand, the progressive, socialist *Forward*, conservative *Day*, nonpolitical *Morning Journal*, and the communist-leaning *Freiheit*. The *Forward* and *Day* publishing facilities were actually four streets away (the rolling presses in the building basements were fascinating to watch), and it became my chore to pick up the Saturday-evening editions at these facilities. Most of these daily newspapers were sold early in the morning, when the men came out of the morning minyan (a quorum of ten males required to conduct the Jewish group religious services) in the many small synagogues in the area; women didn't go to daily services. These newspapers were the favorites of the predominately Russian Jews living on the Lower East Side. There were a few German Jews living in the area; some of these customers preferred reading the German American newspaper *Staats-Zeitung*, which my father also sold. The German Jewish refugees who started trickling into NYC after Hitler started to implement his anti-Jewish laws mostly moved to the Washington Heights section in upper Manhattan, where the NYC German Jewish community was concentrated.

In 1936, my father was encouraged by his two nephews, Morris and Irving Shapiro, who operated a very successful cigar and soda fountain store in the furrier district of midtown Manhattan, to step up and occupy the vacant store across from where he had his candy stand and open a soda fountain/candy/cigar/newspaper store with a sit-down counter and tables. The vacant store was previously the local drugstore. The egg-cream soda was the new popular chocolate soda that my father and his family helpers had to learn to make to keep up with my cousin's strategy for making it a successful business. My father and his family helpers quickly learned how to operate this more intensive type of business that required much more family member support. I for one additionally helped by continuing to do the evening newspaper pickup eight streets away, which was discussed earlier, until my mother decided years later that her seventeen-year-old college-student son shouldn't be busy as a newsboy picking up newspapers at 10:00 p.m. and stopped selling evening newspapers. The candy store is behind my mother and father in the picture, which shows a group of people that frequently hung around their store and a view of Henry Street devoid of traffic and parked automobiles. Opening the store was a very fortuitous move that also avoided a family disaster. In the winter after the move, the building the candy stand was attached to was devastated by a heavy rain, and the front wall of that very old building collapsed onto the candy stand that my father had vacated, demolishing it. I later found some rare coins under the exposed floorboard that included an 1830 silver dollar and miscellaneous other old coins which became the start of my coin collection.

Growing Up on NYC's Lower East Side

Growing up in my particular NYC Lower East Side neighborhood in the 1924-40 time period was unusual in so many respects. It was a fully integrated business community with all types of businesses available to support living requirements within a four-block area. There were an unusually large number of kids concentrated in the densely populated neighborhood playing a wide variety of sport games, some probably no longer played anywhere. We played Depression-era city games such as Ringolevio, kick the can and hide, and Johnny on the Pony. We conducted patriotic

activities and conducted community-wide entertainment activity. We were
also privileged to have the Educational Alliance in our neighborhood,
which effectively served as a local community center offering a different
class of educational and entertainment activities. Street sled riding in the
winter was common and summer swimming at Coney Island was most
popular; swimming in the East River also had an appeal to some. How this
community suffered and coped with the Great Depression that occurred
during the 1930s time period left a lasting impression on me.

My growing-up area was basically a four-block area centered at the
intersection of Montgomery and Henry streets within the lower Manhattan
east side area (street map illustrated in the introduction above). My father's
two candy store businesses were located at that intersection and we lived
there as well. My family lived at 30, 15 and lastly 10 Montgomery Street
over a thirty-five-year period, advancing ever so slightly with improved
apartment living accommodations in the three tenement buildings we
lived in. The building at 30 Montgomery Street was the oldest of the three;
it had remnants of the gas lighting system that preceded electrical home
lighting. The first two family homes were in apartment buildings typical
of majority of the buildings in the area. They were generally old five-story
cold-water tenement *railroad* apartments, with one room facing the street
with a window and the other rooms connected serially with no windows
except the last one, so there was essentially no air circulation in the hot
summer. The apartments were heated by coal stove, gas stove, or kerosene
heater. Toilets were in the hall, shared by the floor tenants. Laundry was
hung out of the front window or on the front fire escapes, or out the rear
window if there was one. Iceboxes were standard, refrigerators were only
starting to be used in the late 1930s, and home air conditioners were not
yet invented. There were coal shoots leading from the sidewalk in front of
each building to the basement, where coal for each apartment was stored
in assigned bins; building steam heat wasn't available in the older buildings
until apartment central heat was mandated by New York City regulations
in 1935. The last apartment at 10 Montgomery was welcomed by the
entire family despite my three sisters having to go back to sleeping head
to toe in one double bed. It had a nice bathroom with our own private
toilet right in the apartment and generally brighter rooms compared to
the previous apartment. I slept on a cot in my parents' bedroom until I
was twenty without complaint. There were already a couple of prestigious
seven-story apartment buildings with elevators in the nearby area. This last

apartment we lived in was made available only through the coincidence that the man vacating this apartment to move to the new Amalgamated Cooperative was the vendor of the carbon dioxide gas used to make the carbonated water in my father's candy store and tipped off my father about this impending attractive vacancy. The only new buildings erected in the area during my youth were the new eleven-story Bialystoker Retirement and Nursing Home on East Broadway, and the Amalgamated Cooperative on Grand St., a full block of semi-condo apartments sponsored by the Amalgamated Clothing Workers Union.

Family Living Style. Because my father's business operated seven days a week and practically all hours of the day, we could not have family dinners attended by the entire family except for the religious holidays. My mother accepted the burden of her having to work Saturdays for many years but insisted on her not working on Friday nights when she lighted the Shabbat candles and had a Shabbat dinner attended by my most of the children but not by my father, who worked at the store. My father and one of the girls who helped in the store that night ate separately, fitting in their eating time between store chores.

In step with my sisters, who helped my parents in both raising the family and operating the family business, as a youngster I tried to also be helpful at home. As a very young kid living in the coal-stove-heated apartment at 15 Montgomery Street, I was my mother's heating system helper, carrying up the coal buckets from the basement and emptying the ashes out of the coal furnace. I also helped my father squeeze grapes to make wine and prepare pickles to make homemade sour pickles, an annual activity of his. As a young teenager I helped my mother with Friday cooking chores. For me it was a treat to help make real gefilte (stuffed) fish. She taught me how to scoop out the fish meat behind the large carp fish gills, chop it, add some type of flour (matza meal) to make it dense, and stuff it back into the fish's cavity. Rolling *luckshin* (noodle) dough for the noodles she cooked and the dough for the *rugallachs* (popular small Jewish pastry of rolled dough filled with raisins and cinnamon) she baked were other pleasures. Grilling chicken livers by placing it in newspapers held in a cooking clamp and then igniting the paper with a match was a big treat—and getting to eat it later was the bigger treat. It was a dish made especially for me. As I got older, being able to scrape the large raw radish used to make our own horseradish was another proud achievement. I creatively did the scraping while holding the large radish outside the kitchen window with the window down so the radish fumes didn't get to me.

In the process of helping my mother with household chores, helping my father with the candy store's mechanical maintenance chores (that I described later), and becoming an aggressive sports player, overcoming my short height handicap, I evidently developed an inherent aggressive work attitude, a willingness to take on new work area challenges, overcome obstacles, and to be helpful to the community. As described later, these characteristics continued throughout both my professional career and private life.

Integrated Community. The Lower East Side area where I grew up was predominately Jewish, with a small representation of Polish, Irish, Italian, and black families. My closest friends included two Poles, the two Stan Mikulsky cousins; one Irish kid, Tom Connerty; and one Italian, Tony Peulio. There was one slightly older black guy, Chester Brown, who was involved in all the sports played in the neighborhood, but he elected to stay aloof socially. As we grew up, Chester, who excelled in baseball and basketball, quit playing with the neighborhood boys to play with more-advanced, higher-age groups outside of the neighborhood. We missed his exciting participation in our sports. My Irish and Italian friends attended the St. Mary's Church on nearby Grand and Attorney streets. My Polish friends attended the St. Teresa's Church on nearby Henry and Rutgers streets. Two small and two large traditional Orthodox synagogues, a modern Orthodox Young Israel Synagogue, a previous three-story yeshiva turned into small synagogues in each room (at 13 Montgomery Street, next door to where I lived), and several *shtiebels* (small prayer room) synagogues were in the immediate four-block area servicing the larger Jewish community's religious needs. Nearby was the historic Bialystoker Synagogue founded in 1905 by immigrants from the Polish city Bialystok, which took over a former Methodist Episcopal church that had been built nearly a century earlier and converted it to a beautiful synagogue. My grandparents' first home was on Willett Street near this synagogue, and they attended religious services there for a few years. I went to the Bialystoker Synagogue almost fifty years later when I was staying at my mother's house during the week of mourning for my father. My uncle Nathan Shapiro, who my father brought to this country when Uncle Nat was sixteen, came in from California to attend his brother's funeral and joined me for the daily services. As a reflection of the bond he had with my father, he took my father's tefillin (phylacteries), which he wore until his death; they were returned to me by his daughter Elayne. Two of my Orthodox friends attended the Rabbi Jacob Joseph Yeshiva further down Henry Street. It was named after the respected European Rabbi Jacob Joseph, who was brought to New York City in 1886 to serve as the chief rabbi of the city, European style, but the concept failed, and he never got the appointment. It was mired in controversy due to factionalism among the rabbinical groups in the city.

On Henry Street, within this four-block area, was the local Engine 15 Firehouse with a motorized pressure pumper as well as a relic steam pumper retained for parades, the Henry Street Settlement main office and visiting nurses facility, and a narrow block-long playground extending to East Broadway that was my earliest sports play area. Nearby were the nonsectarian Henry Street and Madison Street Settlement Houses, and the Jewish Educational Alliance Settlement House that provided well-utilized indoor recreational facilities for the larger community. A little further away were the University Settlement House and the Grand Street Settlement House for athletic activities, and the Grand Street Playhouse for theatrical activities. Outdoor recreational facilities included Seward Park with swings and slides, Jackson Park with football and baseball fields, and the Monroe Street playground for softball. After 1935, the East River Drive Park with tennis courts and the Forsyth Street Park with winter ice skating became available thanks to the WPA jobs. All of the public schools that we neighborhood children attended were nearby. PS 147 Elementary School, which all of my family attended, was on the next street. Corlear Girls Junior High School, where my sisters attended, was three streets away. The new impressive Seward Park High School, which we all attended, was six blocks away; my oldest sister, Irene, was in the first graduating class in 1930.

There were four Jewish retirement facilities in the area. One was the large old Hebrew Home for the Aged on Rutgers Street, which was later replaced by their newer facilities throughout the city. Another large retirement facility was the new Bialystoker Retirement and Nursing Home on East Broadway. These two facilities, which I describe later on, indirectly had a profound impact on me. The other two were smaller retirement facilities for religious Jews. One was The House of Sages on East Broadway for retired rabbis to continue their studies. The other was The Home of the Sages of Israel on Willett Street, a nursing home for non-rabbinical but religious-learned people. This street is now named Bialystoker Place to honor the famous Bialystoker Synagogue located on the street.

Commercial Retail Businesses Available. Remarkably, almost every type of commercial retail business was located in this four-block area. That included two candy stands, one candy store, three grocery stores, two drugstores, a kosher and non-kosher butcher shop, a kosher delicatessen, a fish store, barbershop, combined furrier and tailor shop, shoemaker, cleaning store, Chinese laundry, and a dairy restaurant. A new A&P supermarket had opened three streets away in about 1932, but it didn't catch on with the residents of my immediate community; the supermarket was a new concept during that time period. An important service in that period was the iceman who sold ice to all apartment dwellers that only had iceboxes for keeping food cold and delivered blocks of ice to businesses like my father's. Moishe, the iceman, repeatedly carrying a large block of ice on his back up five flights of stairs was always an impressive sight.

A few streets away were several famous business places, such as Orchard Street with its price-competitive street shopping carts and garment stores, the Hester Street food market with delicacies, the Delancey Street restaurants like Ratner's dairy restaurant and Gluckstern's Kosher Dinner restaurant, Jewish delicatessens like Isaac Gellis on Essex Street and Katz's non-kosher *Jewish* delicatessen on Houston Street, and the famous Gus pickles on Essex Street that is still in business on the Internet. The famous Streit's matzo factory and Shapiro's winery were on nearby Rivington Street.

Then there were the ubiquitous street vendors by horse and wagon and by pushcarts that sold cold watermelon, hot corn on the cob, fruits in the summer, and hot dogs and hot sweet potato in the winter. Adventurous roller-skating boys loved to hang on to the back of the wagons as they sped away.

Three popular movie houses were in the commercial districts a few blocks away. A fourth, the Cannon Theater, was in a decaying business district nearby. To encourage attendance it charged two-for-a-dime admission; the other movie theatre admission prices were 10¢ per person. The famous Bowery Street with its adult type of entertainment and booze joints and the Jewish Second Avenue theatre district were just a little further away. There was also the neighborhood Clinton Street Yiddish Theatre, predecessor to the nearby Second Avenue Jewish theatres, until it closed in the early 1930s.

Right in my immediate neighborhood were two general-physician doctor offices located in the small private homes that the doctors also lived in, squeezed in-between apartment buildings. Five streets away was the city Gouverneur Hospital, and on the next street, East Broadway, was a relatively new small private maternity hospital where I and my next oldest sister were born. All the other children in the family were born at home through midwife support, which was the common practice up to that time.

Trucks with kiddy-sized Coney Island-type entertainment, such as merry-go-rounds, Ferris wheels, and carts going around a big circle frequently came to the neighborhood. Hand-led, handheld pony rides also kept the little ones happy.

The area even had *extraordinary* personal telephone services. Very few of the families in the neighborhood owned their own telephone. Those without phones would tell their families or whoever was to call them to call the number of the telephone booth inside the Henry Street corner Meneker drugstore, and kids hanging around would be glad to run to the family being called to tell them, "Phone call, Mr. X" or "Phone call, Mrs. Y," for the small tip they received. When they got that verbal call, everyone knew where to go to answer the phone. When no kids were around, the druggist took a message to be delivered by the next available kid eager for the opportunity to earn a tip. My father's new candy store phone system in the former drugstore took over that service.

Factories and Commercial Businesses. When I was a young boy the Lower East Side area still had active large and small factories and commercial businesses that supported the area economically. The massive former R. Hoe & Company printing-press manufacturer building, which occupied the entire city block on Grand and Sheriff Streets, was active until torn down in 1932 and replaced by the Amalgamated Cooperative sponsored by the Amalgamated Workers Clothing Union. This R. Hoe building got notoriety in 1902 when a very large funeral procession (estimated as many as fifty thousand) for Rabbi Jacob Joseph, weaving its way from synagogue to synagogue on the Lower East Side, passed by the R. Hoe factory building to get to the ferry at the foot of Grand Street and was pelted with rocks, metal, large wooden boards, and other scrap material, and was showered with a water hose, all coming from the factory. Some of the mourners went into the building to retaliate. Three hundred Jews were injured by this incident. There was an investigation, but no formal charges were made against anyone in the R. Hoe building. Rabbi Jacob Joseph, having been rejected for the chief rabbi position that he came to this country for, was without a source of income and was forced to move his family to a squalid Lower East Side tenement flat. He was disillusioned with the Jewish community leadership over the treatment he received when he suffered a stroke at the age of fifty-four and passed away. The lay community evidently respected Rabbi Joseph's good works while he was a community chief rabbi in Europe and attended his funeral en masse to show their respect for him.

A secondary R. Hoe building on Sheriff and Broome streets was still used for incidental manufacturing before the company went out of business and it was torn down in 1942 to make a park in conjunction with the building of the second Amalgamated Cooperative known as the Hillman Houses, which was completed in 1945 on the block of Grand and Columbia streets. My parents moved there after they retired.

There was a large warehouse on Jackson Street for storing the very large paper rolls (about five feet in diameter, six feet wide) used to print various newspapers published in NYC. It suffered a massive, spectacular, lengthy fire in 1932, which was witnessed by large crowds. The dense burning paper rolls smoldered for days; the internal fire could not be extinguished by the firefighters' water, which was all they had to fight the fire with. The warehouse never reopened, ending its commercial operation.

Area horse and wagon commerce was still supported by two neighborhood large stables, one on Monroe Street and the other on Water Street. I joined a large crowd that witnessed a tragic fire at the Monroe Street stable that practically burned the facility down. Many horses were burned to death because they resisted being led past the fire while it was still at the street level where it started. The crying noise of the suffering horses was painful to hear. Two stable attendants unfortunately also perished by staying with the horses and trying to get them to leave and then being caught up in the fire with no escape possible.

Electric trolley cars were still the standard mode of transportation on some streets up to the early 1930s, when they were replaced by buses. There was a trolley barn at the foot of Grand Street to service these trolley cars. For about a year after trolleys ceased to operate, the barn with some old trolleys was unofficially available as a playground for kids.

Unlawful Businesses. The immediate area had all the unlawful services you can imagine, including prostitution. I had not been aware of the prostitution availability and wrote as such, but my sister Frances corrected my draft. She remembered mention of some women on Monroe Street near and Rutgers Street, who were known to be neighborhood prostitutes. The famous rundown Bowery section was not very far away. The neighborhood had an old reputation for racketeering mobsters getting protection money from businesses in the neighborhood, but there was no such incident reported, and my father and the other small businesses in my immediate area were never approached.

As is still customary, despite the poverty, people liked to gamble and played the daily numbers game. The numbers man stood near the Montgomery-Henry street corner pole and openly took numbers—you can be sure he paid off the police. His boss was seen meeting the Clinton Street Police Department sergeant on Grand and Clinton streets once a week, Friday afternoon at the same time, and handing him an envelope as they left.

The billiards parlor (known as the pool room in those days) was located in the basement of a small private building in the middle of Henry Street between Montgomery and Clinton Streets. It was a popular place for more reasons than shooting pool. It had a paper ticker tape to keep up with the scores of all the college and professional baseball, basketball, and football games. It was there primarily to support the owner's sports betting arrangement that he ran in the pool room; young kids like myself fought for the honor of posting scores on the wall chalkboard. A pool table frequently served as the table for blackjack or craps. Periodically, the local police captain would come with an assistant to "inspect the facility." When they entered, someone in the crowd would yell "raid," and everyone would rush to leave through the open basement windows in order to give the owner and the police privacy.

The availability of bootleg liquor that could be purchased was known to all in the neighborhood. The wife of Moishe, the iceman, was the one who sold bootleg whiskey in small kerosene-type cans during Prohibition and kept it up for several years after Prohibition ended. It was almost pure alcohol. My father developed a taste for strong liquor while serving in the Russian army (Russians liked strong vodka and drank a lot of it), and he was a customer. I remember seeing the Polish caretaker of the large synagogue complex across from our home come to our apartment with his hydrometer to measure when the liquor was diluted to 110-120 proof; he received a share of the diluted liquor as payment for his services. My poor brother-in-laws had to cope with this coarse hard stuff at family holiday dinners when they joined my father in the holiday toast.

There was another source of bootleg whiskey in the area available during the country's Prohibition period. In a run-down old apartment building was what looked like a closed store with a dirty storefront. The storefront is shown in the 1931 picture of me and my playmate sister, Frances; a hallway is behind us. When you went through the store door you would find in the back room a speakeasy bar. As a young kid I went through that the building's hallway next to the speakeasy door many times to get to the courtyard behind the building, where I played either with friends or my caretaker sister and never had a hint that there was a business going on in the supposed closed store in the building. One Passover holiday afternoon, when synagogue services ended, my father stepped into the speakeasy to  talk to the owner, Mr. Golden my father's business acquaintance. Since I was with my father during synagogue services that morning, he took me into the speakeasy with him, exposing me to what went on there. When Prohibition ended, the speakeasy business dried up, and Mr. Golden opened up a Jewish delicatessen in a vacant corner store on the corner of Henry and Montgomery streets diagonally opposite my father's candy stand. It became more popular and thriving than the speakeasy.

There was an unusual history associated with the courtyard I just mentioned. It led to the entrance of a small, very run-down two-story apartment house, which was occupied only by two recluse men. It was sandwiched between the large apartment house on Henry Street in front of it and the small apartment house on East Broadway behind it. We learned that it was called a yard house, an obvious name, and it dated back to the early 1800s, probably the last of its kind in the city. I vaguely recollect how antiquated everything looked in the one apartment we were occasionally invited into by the occupants who occasionally ventured out to talk to us.

Of course it was difficult to know what went on in closed doors and beyond the immediate neighborhood, but to my knowledge there was no routine narcotics indulgence either in the immediate neighborhood or in the schools. However, some of the older boys in my large group of friends did occasionally make a sporting trip involving marijuana. They occasionally went to Van Cortlandt Park in the far upper end of Manhattan ostensibly to play softball, but they were there primarily to watch the reaction of the one fellow in the group of friends who occasionally smoked marijuana cigarettes called reefers, which he got from his older brother who was involved in the acting profession where it was prevalent. This "sporting" activity was of no interest to me. Neither was the smoking of marijuana or indulgence in narcotics when it got popular in the 1960s. I frowned on it for my personal and family use.

Through some customers of my father, we were aware of local community members (whose names we did not know nor care to know) involvement in the extortion, prostitution, gambling, and narcotics trade that went on within the broader Lower East Side and in the city in general. Extortion money was known to buy safety from hoodlums and police protection. In 1935, then popular NYC mayor Fiorello LaGuardia pushed to end the widespread racketeering and commercial extortion as well as the remaining Tammany Hall corruption going on in the city. Tammany Hall was an influential Democratic Party organization that earlier ran the city corruptly for many years until LaGuardia took over as mayor. My personal experience with such hoodlums was limited to one occasion. One evening when I was doing my routine chore of picking up newspapers on Delancey and Broome streets, shots were heard and a man was found lying on the ground on Broome Street just below Delancey Street. A few minutes later, I went over to see what had happened. Someone in the crowd, staring at the dead man, said he was the famous gangster Legs Diamond. The newspaper story identified the dead man as another less-known gangster.

Density of the Population. By 1930 and until after the war ended, when returning veterans started getting married and raising families, almost all area residents were mature families;  the small maternity hospital on East Broadway shut down for lack of business. There were lots of children in each cluster of city blocks. The area had mostly five—to six-story apartment buildings with two to four apartments per floor. A picture of me at age three with the Henry Street scene behind me is illustrated. It shows the densely packed-together tenement houses, with the sparsity of cars on the street. The street pole behind me is a cast-iron post, a remnant of a street gas lamp, the only one I recall seeing in lower Manhattan. Street gas lamps were common south of Grand Street until replaced by electric street lamps. The picture of this street corner on page 29, taken ten years later, shows the useless pole removed. The view behind me is the street where the sports activities I describe later on were played. The corner Meneker drug store with the ex-lax sign (ex-lax laxative was very popular and commonly used in that time period) is the drugstore where the extraordinary phone service described earlier was conducted and where my father opened his candy store. Barely seen in the center of the picture is the one street tree in the entire extended neighborhood, planted by the Henry Street Settlement nursing facility in front of their building.

It seemed like most families in my neighborhood had three to five children and lived in three-bedroom apartments. The largest family I knew had eight children. Multiple children sleeping in double beds and the use of cots was the norm. I remember my three sisters sleeping in a double bed until one got married. Starting with the teenagers, most four-block complexes had their own group of boys and girls in four-year age spans (there seemed to be more boy groups than girl groups). The boys in each area generally set up clubs to compete with each other. I was a younger member of a new, age thirteen to seventeen boys club known as the Henmonts; we mostly lived in the four-block area centered on Henry and Montgomery streets, which gave the club its name. My oldest sister, Irene, belonged to the mixed, older-age, singles New Era Social Club, named to reflect the hope of better times ahead.

Street Sport Activities. Sport activity was a major local community activity. Although I was one of the younger and smaller of the boys in the local neighborhood group, I participated in all the sports described below. I was considered a superior player in handball, boxball, and association football; along with roller-skating, they were my favorite sports. Playing sports had a major impact on me that lasted throughout my lifetime. It taught me to overcome my short height obstacle, to help others improve their ability just as I was helped when I started playing with mostly older boys. It taught me to be competitive but play by the rules, and to play fairly—good adages for everyone to apply in their societal behavior.

The sport activities were mostly played on Henry Street between Montgomery and Gouveneer Streets and in the Gouveneer Street playground at the end of the Henry Street block. This street is right behind me in my picture on the front cover. This street play was feasible because practically no one owned a car on this street (or most of the East Side for that matter), so there were no cars parked on the street and only occasional cars passing through to interrupt the game. For the boys there were plenty of sports to pick from—punchball, boxball, stoopball, stickball, handball, association football, two-hand touch football, basketball, and roller-skate hockey. The girls played jacks and hopscotch, and jumped rope in large groups. As a kid, I helped my sister by being a rope twirler in their double Dutch, two-rope jumping. Girls and boys indulged in bike riding together, forming long trains of bicycles riding through the streets. They were rented bicycles; people in the area were generally too poor to own their own bicycles or have places to keep them. Seeing boys and girls roller-skating together down the neighborhood streets was not uncommon.

My roller-skating activity contributed to my only street brawl. While skating on Henry Street, the area's roughneck kid, age about fourteen, kept on bumping into me. When he wouldn't stop I started wresting with him, and we wound up fighting on the ground until someone separated us. He was a petty thief who frequently bragged about sneaking over the transom of a neighborhood Chinese restaurant to steal cigarettes that he sold on the street. He was warned by friends to stop doing it but wouldn't listen. The owner finally got wise and planted a private detective in the store at night. One night when the roughneck kid climbed into the restaurant and started putting boxes of cigarettes in a bag, the detective told him to stop and stay there. Instead, he tried to run out of the store, and the detective shot him; he died in the hospital the next day.

Punchball was played like baseball in the street, from sewer manhole cover to sewer manhole cover, one cover representing the home plate and the other second base. Every street had these eighteen-inch diameter sewer manhole covers in the center of the street spaced about twenty-five yards apart. First base was marked on one side of the street halfway between the sewer covers and third base marked on the opposite side of the street. Balls hit to sidewalks beyond second base were considered fair ball. Infield, pitcher, and outfield defenders were positioned like in baseball. Standing at the home plate manhole cover, the batter would throw up a small rubber ball up with his fist and punch the ball. It was a challenge to develop the right stride to enable punching the ball further. This was a most popular adult game and frequently played competitively against teams from other city areas. In the 1920s, street punchball was a citywide competitive sport with awards sponsored by the *Brooklyn Daily Eagle* newspaper.

Boxball was played like a baseball game. The field was a rectangular box chalked on the street with the home plate in one corner of the box, and the box's narrow side chalked the width of the street, with first base marked inside the box along the opposite sidewalk. The other side of the box was approximately forty feet away, with the inside far corners marked second and third base. The pitcher, positioned diagonally between home plate and second base, would underhandedly throw a soft rubber ball with one bounce to cover the home plate strike zone. The batter would slap the ball down the box in any direction; the objective was to slap the ball past a fielder, like baseball. It was competitive between the strong slapper and the clever slapper as to who got more safe hits. I was in the clever-slapper group. Games on weekends drew large crowds, especially when the older boys played and when they were competitive games with other neighborhood teams. The way the teams were set up for the fun games was a good example of social justice. Team leaders, who were the better players, were selected for that day. They alternatively picked a player from the older boys' group of nominally better players and then picked a player from the younger boys' group of nominally poorer players. It was an integrated arrangement with the most capable and least capable getting an equal opportunity to share the same competiveness goal on an equal footing, with no one left out.

Stoopball was also played and scored somewhat like a baseball game. The playing field consisted of an eight to ten foot wide channel playing field chalked up across the street from the sidewalk with the high stoop to the opposite sidewalk. The playing field channel was divided into three box sections designated as first, second, and third. A ball bouncing on the opposite sidewalk represented a home run. The playing field was defended by three to four players. The objective was to bounce the small rubber ball off the step to get it to bounce on the field before being caught by a defender. The box the ball bounced in represented the type of hit scored; balls caught were out. Hitting the sharp corner of the step would likely get the ball flying directly across the street for a home run, unless caught. This game was played by the younger group of boys and when there were not enough boys around to play the other games.

Playing stickball, which was not as popular as punchball, was confined to the playground to avoid breaking windows since the same rubber ball was hit harder and further in stickball than in punchball. Handball also was not popular but it was a favorite of mine. I developed a good skill at this sport, where size is not a significant factor in being able to play it well. It was played against the wall in the Gouveneer playground with a soft rubber ball. I didn't get to play indoor black ball handball until I got to college.

The ball used in all these types of ball games was a smooth rubber ball slightly smaller than the size of a tennis ball; the Spalding brand was considered the best. On occasion, during one of these street ball games, a home window would be broken; on rare occasion the boys would chip in to pay for the broken window.

Roller-skating was popular among all ages of boys and girls. It was done in the streets and in the parks. A train of roller skaters going down the steep street hills in the area was a common sight. We only used clamp-on skates; the lucky ones had the superior Chicago brand. A few like me enjoyed playing roller-skate hockey in the streets, using manhole covers as goal posts.

Small team association football played on Henry Street was popular in the fall and spring; the streets were seldom clear of snow in the winter to enable playing any sports. This form of football was one of my better sports, both at quarterback passing and at receiving passes. As described later in my college experience section, this capability served me well during college.

Golf and skiing were unknown sports in my community. Tennis started to become popular after the depression-era Public Works Administration built the nearby East River Drive at the lower end of Manhattan with the parks alongside that included tennis courts. It still represented a high-class sport to my group of friends so we didn't start playing tennis.

Facility Sports. Basketball played in the fall through spring in either the Henry Street or Madison Street settlement houses was popular as a broad community competitive sport. I was too short for this sport and hardly participated.

Softball was popular and was played seriously with occasional area team competition played in the Monroe Street playground and played casually in the Henry Street playground. Some pitchers acquired a high level of pitching skills, with risers and curveballs. It was quite a challenge being their catcher; which I accepted often. Otherwise, I was generally a second baseman.

My softball activity resulted in an embarrassing incident, but it could have been worse with a major injury involved. One afternoon during a summer break from high school, I cooked up a softball game played in the Monroe Street playground. A ball was hit over the high protective left field fence and it broke into a second-floor window of the school that was adjacent to the ball field. In all the years I played and watched games in this park, this never happened before. Since it was my baseball, I went to retrieve it. It turned out that the ball had broken into a classroom full of ten-to—thirteen-year-old kids suffering from heart disease, who were being taught by a psychologist teacher on how to contend with their ailment. The ball and the shattered glass frightened them, but fortunately no one was hurt. While I was apologizing and pleading for the return of my baseball, two policemen entered the room; the teacher had immediately called the police when the ball crashed into the room. They wrote up a juvenile delinquency report (I was fifteen years old) and kept my baseball. It required my very embarrassed mother to take me to the juvenile delinquency office in the neighborhood Clinton Street Police Station for an official reprimand for endangering the children.

Summer and Winter Fun. Most boys and girls who could travel by themselves, including me at about twelve, frequently went in groups to the Coney Island beach for summer ocean swimming. Spending money was scarce, so the majority went bum bathing (wearing clothes over their bathing suit on the way to the beach, undressing on the beach, and later dressing on the beach). Some rented changing lockers available at a dressing facility on Twenty-Third Street and Stillwell Avenue, which was close to the area of the beach where the neighborhood swimmers congregated at. Others went to the Washington Baths located in the same area for the convenience of changing there and swimming in its large pool; my oldest sister occasionally offered me this treat. We all went to Coney Island by a nickel hour-long subway ride; a few confessed to periodically sneaking into the subway.

In the early 1930s some adventurous older guys swam in the East River, in the confine of an unused wharf at the southeastern tip of Manhattan Island; the river itself was unsafe for swimming because of the swift current. The East River was still the most sewer-contaminated river in the country, so they swam the *East River crawl* to keep pollutants away from their mouths. This swimming facility also featured daredevil diving off the set of loading platforms located at different levels going up to about thirty-five feet on the side of a closed flour mill/warehouse alongside the wharf. This diving was similar to the diving exhibitions in Acapulco, Mexico. These were special weekend events that drew large crowds who gave the best diver(s) small tips. When I went there to watch this event I always made sure I had a nickel or a dime with me to throw into the diver's pot. Unfortunately this activity ended in a tragedy. A high-dive swimmer went down too deep into the river, and his head got jammed into the opening of a large metal milk container on the riverbed, and he drowned. The city declared the place unsafe to swim at and posted a No Swimming Allowed sign that was strictly enforced.

I personally was neither a good swimmer or adventurous enough to swim in the East River. I settled for occasionally shallow wading among the rubble at the East River waterfront that was left from the Grand Street Ferry Terminal after it was torn down. The river tide was still felt there mildly, so I considered it too dangerous for me to do that alone. I did this adventure with my good friend Jules Shatske, who had the same swimming limitations and shared my respect for the river current.

In 1936 the community benefited from New Deal funding of a nearby large outdoor public swimming facility. This Hamilton Fish pool facility was located on Pitt Street between Stanton and Houston Streets. It consisted of a large adult pool, a smaller kiddy pool, and miscellaneous playground equipment. Being only a ten-minute walk away from my community, new, and free, it gave Coney Island competition.

The community winter sport activity was sled riding, with some minor participation in ice-skating. Sled ownership was scarce, so sleds were shared by friends. It was the same situation regarding ice skates; very few young kids owned them and there was no local ice rink. I inherited my oldest sister's speed skates and looked funny skating with them at a crawl on the small artificial skating pond we made on the street in the winter after big snows and freezing weather.

Depression-Era Games. We played several Depression-era games that were common citywide games at that time, e.g., ringolevio, kick the can and hide, hide-and-seek, and Johnny on the Pony.

In our version of ringolevio, one small group of kids closed their eyes for thirty seconds while the other group hid in the buildings, cellars, and backyards. The first group searched for the hiding players to bring each one back to stay in a big circle drawn on the center of the street. The hiding group of players attempted to sneak into the circle untouched and shout "ringolevio" to free their teammates. The sides would then switch roles if all were captured or if time ran out.

Two versions of kick the can and hide were played. In one version, one player would kick a medium-sized vegetable can as far as he could, and another would go after the can while the kicker hid somewhere. Then the searcher had fifteen minutes to find the hider. This version of kick the can and hide surfaced in the fall of 2010 when an old-time senator quoted this game as the game the Senate was playing with their tax plan—*"kicking the tax policy out on the floor of Congress and hiding from the consequences."* In the other version, after the can was kicked, a group of up to five players would hide, and the number of hiders found within thirty minutes would be counted. They took turns. The group that found the most hiders was the winner.

Johnny on the Pony was a rougher game played. Each player in a group of four to six players would bend down to be a pony and make a pony train on the street, starting from a sidewalk edge, where one guy would stand to hold the bent head of the front pony. Then one by one, players from the other team would get a running start from the opposite sidewalk and leapfrog as far as they could onto the pony train. The objective was to crush (collapse) the train by their weight. With me as the smallest, weakest guy, you could be sure I was a favorite target to land on to break the train.

Patriotic Activities. Independence Day and Election Day patriotism stimulated local community actions that carried on this country's tradition of celebrating these two days.

Fourth of July fireworks were set off in the streets; there was no restriction on selling or using fireworks. Parents set off sparklers and streamers for their kids. The boys had competition as to who could send higher either a small tin can or a half rubber ball after a bomb was detonated inside the open can or under the half ball. Dropping lighted bombs or rattlers behind unsuspecting people was a sport. The evening was capped by a large sky fireworks display from Jackson Park along the East River.

Many cities and New York City in particular, had a long history of celebrating Election Day with bonfires. The Lower East Side carried on this tradition; several local area groups of guys in the fifteen to twenty-five age ranges had their own Election Day bonfire. As a young kid, I remember going from bonfire to bonfire to see which one was more spectacular. The intense fires left their mark on the streets; this condition later became the reason why the city outlawed these bonfires. Most of the fire material was doors and other large woodwork torn out of vacant apartment buildings and frequently thrown out of the windows in spectacular form to get the material to the street; another reason for spectator applause. Old wagons/carts were other fire materials; the local stable managers learned to leave some junk wagons outside of their buildings to avoid having new ones stolen for the fires. This type of celebration ended when the guys started going into the service.

As I recollect, I counted about twenty-six boys from the immediate neighborhood that went into the service, all into the army; two neighborhood guys were killed in the war while fighting in Europe. This picture of two of my close friends, Stan Mikulski on the left and Jules Shatske on the right, was taken in Quezon City, Philippines, in October 1945. They met there by chance. Another close friend made it into the army air force. He was Saul Levy, brother of the boy in the candy stand picture, who so much wanted to get to England where both of his parents came from and thought being in the air force increased his chances. Afraid his somewhat marginal eyesight would disqualify him from the air force, he went on a high-carrot diet for about three months—it seemed to work; he got in. He served as an aircraft bomber gun turret operator flying out of England and got to see his parents' hometown and his British relatives there.

Halloween. Halloween was not a fun day in my immediate neighborhood while growing up as a youngster. We were living in an area between two rival Italian gangs, the Gille gang (a name I can't forget), living near Goereck Street on the east of our neighborhood, and the other gang (whose name I can't remember), living to the west of our neighborhood near Mott Street, which is still an Italian neighborhood. The Gille gang would march through our in-between neighborhood swinging long ladies heavy stockings filled with a ball of rice tied on the end, trying to hit any boy they could who would normally be on the street with a group playing a game. After a few years, my neighborhood learned to have a lookout. When he saw them, he shouted, "The Gille gang is coming," and everyone would run to hide. As we grew older and tougher, we collected small corn-on-the-cob husks before Halloween and were ready to fight back by throwing the corncobs at them as they marched by swinging their stockings. After few of these battles, they stopped coming to our area. Living in this predominately Jewish community, I never saw or knew about the trick-or-treat aspect of Halloween.

Community-wide Entertainment. My community enjoyed two special entertainment opportunities, one unique to the community and the other also offered elsewhere in the city.

After the trolley tracks were removed from East Broadway and the street was paved, the city management gave the community a special treat. For six months, the East Broadway block between Clinton and Montgomery Streets was closed off from automobile traffic every Sunday so that it could be a roller-skating rink for the entire East Side community. From afternoon until late evening, it was swarmed with roller skaters. Of particular excitement was the long line of roller skaters that would be whipped around to be flying in all directions at high speed after the line broke.

After this roller-skating treat ended, the city government offered another entertainment treat. For several years in the fall and spring, once a month on Sunday night, a band sitting on a wagon would play for musical entertainment and social dancing in the street. A block on Henry Street was closed off for this activity. The band played at different city locations the rest of the month.

Educational Alliance Activities. Several wealthy Jews sponsored the building of the Educational Alliance located on East Broadway and Jefferson Street, which opened in 1893. They were committed to advancing the education and lifestyle of the new wave of Jewish immigrants from Eastern Europe, who were economically poor and poorly educated. It provided a host of social and entertainment services that included lectures, a library, gymnasium, workshops, and, most importantly in that early period, night courses in English that enabled the new immigrants to continue working while they advanced their English education. In my time frame it served as a nonsectarian place to enjoy lectures, indoor sports such as basketball and volleyball in the gymnasium, or playing ping pong, checkers, or many other board games on the enclosed roof. My playmate sister, Frances, and I went there frequently in my early youth, learning how to get skilled in these activities.

Coping with the Great Depression. The 1930s Depression had a severe impact on the area. Family wage owners in the manual labor work categories, such as local stevedores and truck drivers, suffered the highest unemployment rates. Workers in the garment industry with short tenure with the company also were vulnerable. The young people through high school age conducted their social activities described earlier in a manner that cost little money. They were impacted harder once they graduated and had to find a job, which was scarce. The boys found it more difficult to find jobs than the girls, who seemed to have more opportunities as secretaries. Some work opportunities for federal WPA and PWA projects run by the city opened up slowly; two older boys in the neighborhood went to work at a CCC camp in Montana.

One of these WPA jobs contributed to an unusual community and personal experience. One fellow with a WPA summer job was working as an athletic counselor at a new playground in Queens together with a black guy from Harlem. They thought it would be nice to have an interracial softball game and arranged to have it held in Harlem on a Sunday afternoon. Someone came up with the crazy idea to make it a picnic-type day and to go up to Harlem by horse and wagon. So we left in the morning to give us plenty of time necessary for the eight-mile trip riding on this rented long, narrow wagon that had benches on each side of the wagon for the team to sit on for the long ride. I sat alongside the driver to give directions. The progress was so slow that when they saw the Houston Street subway station sign they decided to take the subway to get to Harlem. They jumped out at a street intersection stop, including the driver, and I was left to drive the wagon back to the stable, a surprising and exciting experience for a fourteen-year-old who never drove a horse-drawn wagon before. The game had unintended consequences. After the game, which my team won, a few guys went into a nearby candy store to get a soda drink. On the way out they were assaulted by a gang of rough black guys who bruised a few and took all their baseball paraphernalia.

For many years some financial assistance was provided to local residents by the Hebrew Free Loan Society located at Clinton Street near Grand Street. It offered free loans to those who wanted to start a small business or to operate a street-vending operation. During these trying times they also offered free loans to prevent house evictions and to pay for medical expenses.

The city did offer aid to those impacted through the City Home Relief program with modest payment covering rent and food cost; nevertheless, evicted family possessions sorrowfully appeared periodically in the neighborhood streets. The most vivid indicator of the Depression was the daily long lines of unemployed people coming from the entire East Side waiting to get a free hot lunch of soup and a meat dish, served at the Soup Kitchen set up in the very large basement of a large private type house on 259 Henry Street; the long line lasted for hours. The longer line of men went toward Montgomery Street and generally extended around the block almost to East Broadway. The shorter line of women went in the other direction, halfway down the block. The lunch room was set up with several rows of long wooden tables and wooden benches on both sides, separate tables for men and women. The soup kitchen was run by the Henry Street

Settlement under the leadership of Helen Hall, successor to founder Lillian Wald, who played a significant role in city and national efforts to cope with the Depression. As a kid, after school I delivered the *New York Times* to her office down the street from my father's candy stand; she always greeted me with a famous Henry Street Settlement nursing cookie.

The older teenagers made many a Friday night a cheap social evening. A group of boys and girls would congregate on the lighted street corner, where there was a delicatessen that was closed for the evening to sing the latest songs that they had been hearing on the radio. One guy was elected the previous week to go to Delancey Street earlier that evening to buy the weekly song sheets that contained the words to the latest songs they would be singing that night. There were also occasional trips to the Paramount Theater on Times Square to listen to the swing bands of the 1930s era and all their new vocalists singing the same tunes we sang on the street corner. The popular bands were Benny Goodman, Glenn Miller, Harry James, Artie Shaw, and Tommy Dorsey. Watching bobby-soxers dancing in the aisles, especially to Frank Sinatra's crooning, was an extra treat.

Another popular Friday night activity for the boys at that street corner was listening on the portable radio to all the heavyweight boxing title matches of that time period. I can remember listening to the Baer-Schmeling fight, the Baer-Braddock fight, and the two Schmeling-Louis fights. We had heard Hitler ranting on the radio many times, so the Schmeling-Louis rematch with Joe Louis being victorious was the most exciting one, particularly because we all thought Schmeling was a Nazi supporter. However, recent stories about Max Schmeling indicated that his open support of Nazi propaganda statements did not represent his true feelings and also revealed that, in 1938, he saved the lives of two Jewish children, risking his own life.

Religious Education

My Hebrew religious education started at age seven. I went to the Machzikei Talmud Torah on East Broadway and Clinton Street, one block from home, so I walked there by myself. Classes were held for an hour and a half, two nights a week, and on Sunday morning. It was very structured schooling. Initial teaching covered primarily Hebrew reading, writing, vocabulary, and, secondarily, Yiddish vocabulary and writing. Third-year classes in addition covered Jewish history, religious prayer structure, and understanding the prophets. The school provided my Haftorah training (which is reading a section from a biblical book of the Prophets) in preparation for my bar mitzvah held in May 1937 at my father's synagogue, the Griever Congregation on Henry Street. Because my mother was in mourning due to her father's death in January, we weren't going to have a party. However, my cousins who had a business in the new midtown Furrier District convinced my parents to have a dinner for about forty relatives in a large restaurant in their business neighborhood that they had a special relationship with. They even offered to bring in a singer they knew from that neighborhood. My mother consulted a rabbi who OK'd a singer as long as there was no musical accompaniment. The singer was Richard Tucker, the opera singer. He was just a part-time cantor then; he didn't make the Metropolitan Opera until 1944. He stood up in the corner of the room and sang popular songs and famous Yiddish songs without any musical accompaniment; of course everyone was thrilled with his beautiful singing but had no idea he would become famous.

I enjoyed going to Hebrew school and was a good student. I received two books as proficiency awards in Hebrew studies. One book, *Stranger Than Fiction*, by Lewis Brown, had a profound, lifetime impact on me. I essentially learned that the survival and longevity of the Jewish people as a Jewish nation after the kingdoms of David and Solomon was indeed stranger than fiction. The northern kingdom of Israel ended; its Jewish people vanished. Worshiping of idols was frequently commonly practiced by the surviving kingdom of Judah, led by the high priests and some kings. The Torah code of behavior was not followed. Most of the kings were generally viscous toward the people, and many set poor moral standards. The first Jerusalem temple was destroyed, and the kingdom of Judah ceased to exist for about fifty years, with most of its people exiled to Babylonia. What is truly remarkable about the Jews' survival is the entire Jewish population, including those exiled to Babylonia and remained there, those that returned to Judah from the Babylonian exile, and the Jews living in Egypt (Jews had returned to Egypt during the earlier periods of upheaval in Judah), is estimated to be only between 125,000 and 150,000. Furthermore, it was also remarkable that the Jews were later exiled from their homeland for almost two thousand years and still retained a nationhood type of identity and a religion based on the Jewish understanding and values of the Bible. This history book, published in 1933, ended with an optimistic view about the ultimate impact of the large number of Zionist pioneers with the inspiring spirit of the prophets that were coming to Palestine to rehabilitate the Jewish homeland and make it the new Land of Israel; perhaps only a hopeful vision that turned out to be prophetic.

My insight to Jewish history was expanded when I took an adult education course offered by my synagogue that introduced me to Dr. Abraham Sachar's version of Jewish history, *A History of the Jews*, published in 1974. It expanded on the information in the *Stranger Than Fiction* book and also covered the history of the new State of Israel. These two books provided me a good foundation of Jewish history, which I applied when I undertook to write my own book on Jewish history published in 2002, *Jewish History: 4,000 Years of Accomplishment, Agony, and Survival*. The section on the history of the Jewish people in the United States provides an insight as to how the Jews integrated into the United States, the opportunities this country offered to the Jewish people, and the many contributions to American development made by American Jews. It parallels the message of the National Museum of American Jewish History, which in a way prompted me to write this book. My book basically stresses three themes:live by the Bible's moral and ethical guidelines sharply focused on the Ten Commandments, remember the Holocaust, and support the State of Israel. These themes are reflected in my book cover illustration, with the statue of Moses holding the Ten Commandments tablets, the doorpost mezuzah (decorative container with the Hebrew Shema prayer in it), a tombstone for the six million Jews killed in the Holocaust, and the official emblem of the State of Israel. The title summarizes the four thousand years of Jewish history—many accomplishments throughout the ages of Jewish history; many agonizing periods of persecution of the Jews in their homeland and later in the Diaspora for almost two thousand years. With these many challenges to survival, how remarkable, if not supernatural, it is that the Jewish people have survived for the last four thousand years. No other group of people that had been expelled from their homeland for hundreds of years has returned to reoccupy their homeland as the Jewish people have after they were expelled from their homeland twice for long periods.

The second book I was awarded was *In Those Days* by Jehudah Steinberg. It is about an old man telling his son tales of his youth and beyond. Little did I know that 75 years after I read the book I would be emulating the book by telling tales of my youth and beyond to my son in this book.

Reflections on Religion My early upbringing of being exposed to my mother's Orthodox Judaic religious feelings and my Hebrew School education established a life-long bond with the Jewish religion. My mother tried to honor the Sabbath, prefering not to work or ride on Saturday, kept a kosher home all her life, believed in God, in heaven, and in the hereafter. As a youngster, I accompanied my mother on her monthly Saturday afternoon walk across the Wiliamsburg Bridge to see her sister Elsie Katz, a couple of miles walk each way. When I escorted her on an hour-long street car ride, and later driving her to the cemetery annually before the Jewish New Year religious holiday period, I heard her plead to her dead mother to intercede and help eliminate family problems that existed at the time of the visit. Although we ritually filled Elijah's cup of wine and opened the door to let him in at my own family Passover Seders, the coming of the messiah was not a family expectation.

As a Conservative Jew I have no problem driving on Saturday, but following my mother's pattern, I try to avoid physical type of work on Saturday. My wife and I have kept a kosher home since we've been married but we had no restrictions eating out. However, for the last several years when I eat out I have given up eating seafood, pork products, and meat and dairy combined meals. My family is surprised at my new attitude, but adhering more closely tothe Conservative Judaism eating rules makes me more comfortable in view of my current religious practices. I try to go to synagogue every Saturday morning, giving honor to God and praying to God to keep the world community from doing nasty things, for national leaders to do the right thing, and to help cure family/friend illnesses. From the results, God isn't paying attention to me. Unfortunately, the one God over all people created good people, innocent people, and bad people in ancient history and evidently forever; bad people still have too much influence over society.

I assume there is a God who created living beings with all their physical and mental complexities. However, although I would love to see my parents again, I have my doubts about the existence of the hereafter. It sounds too complex, even for God, to arrange who goes to be with which ancestor,I with my father and his family, or I with my mother and her family.

The four thousand-year-old Ten Commandments still serves as my good behavioral guide. My religious feelings are summed up in my devotion to the Shema prayer, "Hear O Israel, the Lord is our God, the Lord is One", which reinforces my devotion to God and my good behavioral objectives.

This prayer that comes from the Bible taught the world monotheism. Hearing a dying man utter this prayer in my youth, and years later, seeing my father take his last breath after I said the prayer for him had a lasting impact on me. It is my most solemn prayer.

Bianca Loren Alamango Shapiro

This is my book called Jewish history by: Ralph Shapiro

Early Taste for Mechanics

When I become an engineer, my family used to brag that I always knew I wanted to be an engineer, because as a kid of seven to ten years old, I was always fixing mechanical things like clocks and toys. The truth of the matter is I used to take the big alarm clocks apart and put them back together, but they never worked. I did have an inquisitive mind as to how mechanical devices worked, early on learning how to use tools to help my father repair the soda-making machines in his candy stand and candy store. In my senior year in elementary school, this experience helped me build a variety of devices in the shop class, including a radio crystal set.

Whiz Kid at Elementary School

My parents were too busy working at their candy stand business to give me much attention, so I latched on to my sisters while they were doing their homework, and I picked up a lot of educational information well in advance of when I would normally learn it in school. Math, history, and geography were my favorite subjects. I could add and do some multiplication at the kindergarten level. This advanced capability evidently enabled me to accomplish my rapid public school education. I skipped five times—1b, 2b, 5b, 7a, and 8a—graduating at eleven and a half years old, the youngest to graduate in my class. I was offered my choice between two graduation prizes; I chose the history prize. My last teacher told my mother, "Your son has all the answers but he never volunteers them." I was shy and modest in school and at the family gatherings my parents occasionally held.

With all my class skipping, I was the smallest and youngest in each class. By the time I was in eighth grade, I was in class with boys that towered over me, and some were five years older than me due to the number of poor students who were kept back several times earlier. My neighborhood sports activity that required me to play with older boys prepared me to get along with older boys in my public school classes, which in the seventh and eighth grades were only for boys. It was a pattern I had to do during the rest of my schooling. I integrated well socially, playing ball with them during lunchtime, going to summer baseball outings with them, and inviting them to play sports with my neighborhood friends. I even helped two older, backward guys with their schoolwork to help them graduate.

I had learned to accept emotional pain at a young age, initially at four when my older brother died and, later, when my grandparents died. I learned how to accept physical pain during my early school years. I was about ten years old when, during lunch period, I joined a stickball game played in the playground across the street from the school. Being one of the youngest and less capable of the boys on my side, I was given the catcher position, considered not important defensively. During the game the batter either rotated too far back in his swing approach or I leaned forward, I wound up getting hit on my jaw. It was bruised badly. The school called the local hospital to come and look at my mushy jaw and I was taken to the hospital for a detailed examination. I was lucky it didn't break the jaw or hit my eyes. I learned my lesson. Never again play catcher position without a face mask; catcher later turned out to be my favorite softball game position.

Interest in Professional Sports

As described earlier, sports activities were very popular in my neighborhood, and I was an active participant in many sports. This area sports activity naturally expanded to an interest in professional sports, and I was caught up with this at an early age. As part of its summer recreation program, my public school offered occasional free trips to see New York Yankees and New York Giants baseball games. The Yankees, with stars like Babe Ruth, Lou Gehrig, and Bill Dickey, won out over the Giants, with Mel Ott and Bill Terry. I became a near-lifetime Yankees fan. The news of Lou Gehrig's ailment and early retirement after being called the Iron Horse and having played 2,130 consecutive games had a strong impact on me. I went by myself to attend the Lou Gehrig Day tribute on July 4, 1939, and can still remember standing up in the Yankee Stadium bleachers tearfully listening to his farewell address with words like, "I consider myself to be the luckiest man on the earth to . . ."

The New York Giants being the better NY football team at that time was the football team I rooted for along with the rest of the neighborhood boys. My favorite game recollection was going to a NY Giants-Chicago Bears game to see Sid Luckman play as quarterback with his T-formation passing game, which he had recently introduced, making the game more interesting. He put on quite a passing show. I also got to see the legendary Bronko Nagurski play that day for Chicago.

Professional ice-skating also captivated some of my friends' interest, me included. We were fans of the New York Rangers; the brothers Muzz and Lynn Patrick were our favorite players. For several years in my teens I joined several friends to see a Rangers hockey game played on New Year's Eve in Madison Square Garden and continued on to nearby Times Square to participate in the massive, festive New Year's Eve celebration that is a famous event held there every year.

Listening to all categories of sporting events on the portable radio that became available in the late 1930s was the thing to do. In the winter it was usually on a Sunday afternoon listening to a Giants football game while playing cards to make it more interesting. There were two standout experiences. On Sunday afternoon, December 8, 1940, we listened to the NFL championship game and heard the Chicago Bears trounce the Washington Redskins a record setting 73-0. What made the result more surprising was that the Redskins had the remarkable passer Sammy Baugh and the Bears came into the game as the underdog. The next year, on Sunday afternoon, December 7, 1941, while listening to the Giants play the Brooklyn Dodgers for the NFL championship game, we heard the breaking announcement that Pearl Harbor was bombed. I rushed into my father's store to tell the shocking news to a group of older guys I knew were in there that would be the most immediately affected with the United States undoubtedly entering the war.

High School Experience

My first year in high school was at the old Henry Street freshman-year annex of Seward Park High School. It was for boys only. Girls in New York City went to their respective neighborhood junior high, which went through the equivalent of the freshman year in high school. Being exposed to that school environment was quite an experience. Besides the Lower East Side Public School graduates, students with poor academic backgrounds from elsewhere in Manhattan and even from the Bronx attended it. It was a rough environment, with students being constantly disruptive and requiring reprimands. In the middle of the first school term, one student in my class was so disruptive he got a teacher reprimand and a two-day suspension. The day he came back, his older brother entered the classroom, shouted words I can't exactly remember but to the effect "*Don't do that to my brother again,*" punched the teacher on the jaw, and ran. The student was expelled. With the news of the expulsion, all the classes quieted down somewhat thereafter.

For the next three years I attended Seward Park High School at its relatively new building, where student behavior was very orderly. Academically, I did very well, getting mostly A grades in most classes, with English and some German classes being poorest. All my state Regents Exam scores were also extremely high; one or two received a perfect score, so I had no problem getting into the City College of New York (CCNY). I did have a problem in my high school singing class that I was required to take. My music teacher rated my monotone voice too flat and had me change classes to a musical instrument class, where I learned to play the baritone. I never followed through; music was not my thing.

I did keep up with national politics and international events, reading newspapers and participating in discussions of these subjects that were held in my father's candy store; sometimes my father would get so involved in the discussion, he ignored his customer. The rise of Hitler with his harsh treatment of German Jews was a concern to me early on, and German devastation of the European countries that were at war with Germany heightened that concern. The history classes I took in my high school junior and senior years devoted a day per week to current events, which gave me an opportunity to express my views. History was one of my most interesting and better subjects.

In the general course I took in high school we were required to take a major foreign language for three years and a minor language for two years. Thinking my knowledge of Yiddish would be beneficial because it is mainly derived from German, I took German as the major language. It turned out to be a detriment; I frequently used the Yiddish expression erroneously for the German one. Spanish was my second language. I did well with Spanish and retained many expressions that are handy today.

I had very little social life in high school, choosing to keep my neighborhood friends for my after-school social activities. Between doing homework while listening to radio programs, such as *The Lone Ranger, The Green Hornet,* and *Sergeant Preston of the Yukon,* and doing the evening newspaper pickups with my father, I had little spare time for social activities.

College Experience

I started attending the uptown main branch of CCNY located at 138th Street and Convent Avenue in February 1940 at age fifteen and a half. I had no advance preparation as to what to expect at college. I made no preliminary visit there, and I knew no one attending or who had attended there to get advice from. I had no friends starting college with me; the only friend starting college that year attended the downtown CCNY Business College. The free tuition made it possible for me to attend college; my parents probably could not have afforded to pay for a private college. It never had to be discussed. I had no interest in attending private colleges. College and living expenses were very low—there was a small registration fee, book costs, and the nickel subway carfare. I even took a box lunch from home for most of my college days.

I attended the School of Engineering, pursuing a mechanical engineering degree. I had no trouble deciding on this career, choosing it early in high school. Besides, the basic mechanical drawing courses, the theoretical mechanical engineering courses were structured toward power plant design, which was of no value during my engineering career. The electrical engineering courses given to mechanical engineering students were focused on electrical power systems; electronics was relatively new, and electronic courses were not available to mechanical engineering students. Math and physics represented the pre-engineering preparation courses. The uptown city campus was not available to girls except for the Engineering School, which recently started to accept them. Other city colleges were available, tuition free, to women, with Hunter College being an all-women's school.

Registration was done alphabetically by the student's last name, so by the time I was ready to pick my freshman classes many freshman-level classes were not available. I was forced to take a public-speaking course normally taken by seniors. That started my college career on a sour note. I was a young shy boy, not very comfortable with public speaking and competing with juniors and seniors in that class. I got the only D grade of my school career in that class. However, I did enjoy one public-speaking class event that I never forgot. A student made a half-hour presentation on his techniques for successfully picking winners at the racetrack. Using the *Racing Form* newspaper, he went through an analysis of the racetrack conditions, the duration of the race versus the horse's past win race durations, the jockey history, and many other factors. He then explained that using his analysis techniques, he picked the winners in most of the races that day. In the Q&A he was asked how much he won that day. His answer: "I don't bet."

Another incident etched in my brain was this sight on 145th Street on my way to City College. A Chinese chef wearing a chef's hat and apron, and with a raised hand holding a large hatchet, was chasing after his dog and calling repeatedly, "Pork Chop, come back. Pork Chop, come back."

The school offered a constructive environment for me to mature socially. My capability to play association football acquired in my youth and my owning a football were contributory factors. In the evenings between afternoon regular academic classes and night laboratory classes, I started playing association football with my engineering classmates on Convent Avenue in front of the school, which had no car traffic. They soon took me into their relatively new Alpha Mu Epsilon (AME) mechanical engineering fraternity. I made good friends in the fraternity and enjoyed many social events. The impending social activities forced me to learn how to dance. My sister Frances came to my rescue with dance lessons. She initially taught me how to dance to the rumba with "Side together forward, side together back, side together forward, side together back." I also explored the Hillel option at the school. It was only a small store on Amsterdam Avenue across from the school that offered Jewish-interest reading material but no social activity.

The CCNY main building was a large Gothic structure with a similar-style large auditorium. The basement had its famous alcoves (open roomettes with large wooden tables), where political propagandizing and national and international issue debates were carried on in the late afternoon, after school hours. The primary participants included every imaginable leftist, Communist, and Trotskyite organization. The debate themes were generally anti-US government and pro-Soviet Union. This character of the debates was earlier encouraged by the large number of Communist teachers at the school; over fifty teachers and staff were discharged after the famous 1940 NY State Rapp-Coudert hearings exposed this situation. This leftist mood came to a climax in the fall of 1941 with a parade down Convent Avenue by mostly the leftist social science students who carried signs and shouted, "The Yanks are not coming." It was in reaction to President Roosevelt's actions to help Great Britain in its war with Germany. Members of the smaller engineering school's student body, including myself, held a smaller counter parade in support of Roosevelt's goals, urging the defeat of Nazism.

My closest fraternity friend was Harry Dornbrand. Being three years older than me, he was my older-brother mentor regarding many activities. After Pearl Harbor day, we had to pick our choice of service after graduating from college; all engineering students had school deferments until graduation. Harry convinced me that it was cleaner to fight on a ship than in the trenches, so he chose the navy and I followed suit. Because of my 20-600 eyesight the navy rejected me. Harry joined the navy after graduation. He was assigned to work for the National Advisory Committee for Aeronautics (NACA) at Moffett Field, California, and learned much about aircraft design. After that navy duty, he subsequently became the vice president of Republic Aviation and then vice president of the Fairchild Space and Electronics Company.

During my first two years at college I was still helping my father with the candy store newspaper pickup at night. When that stopped, I worked each year during the winter break at a different job to get varied work environment experience. I did mail sorting in the post office one year, and loading and unloading freight cars, and unloading ship barges the next two years. These types of jobs were popular with college students and were made available through the school employment office. The latter job was particularly physical and a dangerous challenge, carrying down the barge ramp a handcart behind your back loaded with three bags of seeds each weighing about two hundred pounds. The trick was to keep in step with the pace of the handcart that was essentially being self-propelled down the ramp by its seed bag heavy weight momentum and then to run in a circle inside the warehouse to avoid hitting anything and as you slowed down the handcart.

With the war going on, engineering opportunities opened up with industrial companies that previously had restrictive employment hiring practices. The General Electric Company, which previously only hired Jews with demonstrated successful research credentials, started to recruit at CCNY for their career start-up test engineering program without any ethnic restrictions. With my very good grades that met their standards, they offered me a job in that program, which I accepted. Working for this prestigious company sounded like an honor and a good employment opportunity.

Family Development

My personal family development in a sense mirrored my humble background. I met my wife Ecille Pierce, native of Cleveland, Ohio, at the Green Mansions singles resort in the Adirondacks, NY, in early July of 1954. We were both spending a week's vacation there but didn't actually get to know each other until Thursday of that week. She had spent an evening with each of my two bunkmates and thought poorly of them for their crude behavior. That Thursday, she learned that I was driving to town to buy some refreshments for a mock marriage party to be held in my bunk that evening before the formal entertainment and convinced me to take her along so she could buy some particular delicacies she was determined to have; I did not know her before that. On the drive I discovered she had the same humble family background and had a common interest in Jewish activities. She explained how she got the one-of-a-kind name *Ecille*. Her mother wanted to name her Lucille but felt obligated to name her after her grandfather, whose name started with an *E*, so she combined the two thoughts and out came the one-of-a-kind *Ecille*. She prefers to be addressed informally as *Ceil*. Ecille worked as the secretary of the Young Adult Division of the Cleveland Jewish Community Center, and through its social activities she actually knew two of my former college schoolmates working at the NACA Lewis Research Center in Cleveland. We spent Thursday night through Saturday getting to know each other more intensely, including our common taste for dancing and how well we danced together; we danced all night those three nights. Our favorite dance number was the rumba *Sway with Me*, made famous that year by Dean Martin. We always ask for it to be played at dancing opportunities, although not too many bands know this tune. For our recent fifty-sixth anniversary, because of my wife's deteriorating health, we just went to the local Normandy Farms restaurant for a nice meal instead of a cruise that had become customary for us for many years. The restaurant had a three-piece dance combo, but we weren't even certain if my wife was up to dancing. Unbelievably, we walked in to the restaurant with the band playing our heritage tune, *Sway with Me,* and we started dancing before even sitting down in the restaurant. We closed the place as the last couple on the floor, dancing to our special request, *Sway with Me*. The music rejuvenated my wife.

That Sunday morning after our vacation week ended, I took Ecille to Albany to catch the train ride home to Cleveland without giving her encouragement about pursuing a relationship; all she told her mother was that she finally found the kind of person she could be interested in. When I got back to Ellenville, NY, where I lived, I told my sister about who I had met; based on how I spoke she suspected I was in love. Two weeks later, at my next already-scheduled vacation at the Tamiment singles resort in

Pennsylvania, I realized I was not interested in meeting girls and recognized I was in love with Ecille. We started corresponding more frequently. Each letter contained a different caricature (sample at beginning of the book) of me drawn by a co-worker that showed me in a different situation but always smoking a cigar. That had her worried. She always said she could never like a guy who smoked cigars. I was just an occasional cigar smoker, and I promised to give it up for her sake. She flew into New York City during Labor Day weekend on her planned annual visit to her sister Tessie living on Long Island but later came to Ellenville to visit me. We started her stay in New York with a visit to the Tavern on the Green Restaurant in Central Park, where we rekindled our feelings for each other. I broke Ecille into enjoying a Brandy Alexander, popular in those days and shown in the picture. I told Ecille to look Ellenville over while I was at work. She said it took her all of five minutes; Ellenville was and still is a small town. On the way back to the NY airport, she met my family. For our next get-together I drove to Cleveland for the Rosh Hashanah holiday to meet Ecille's parents, and we unofficially got engaged to get married; eleven-hour drives to Cleveland with family to spend the Passover and Rosh Hashanah holidays with her parents became the standard as long as her mother was alive. Our engagement became formal when I gave her an engagement ring during her return trip to NY in October, and we planned on a wedding in Cleveland on November 20, 1954. It was a super short courtship that worked; we have been very happily married for fifty-eight years.

Our marriage was a typical Cleveland Jewish wedding at the Park Synagogue, with our small families and every (lots) Cleveland friend of Ecille attending. Her youngest brother, Harold, was particularly happy to attend, both because he was so close to Ecille growing up and because he had missed his brother's (Captain Manuel Pierce) wedding to Pauline Locks and his sister's (Lady Marine Sergeant Tessie Pierce) wedding to Private Morris Garber. They came out of the service after World War II ended, and he went into the army and was stationed in the Philippines when both weddings occurred. The New York City *web* still prevailed to curtail some of my family's attendance. Only my parents and two sisters and their spouses attended, coming by train. My former playmate and mentor, sister Frances, was eight months pregnant and couldn't travel. Our rabbi was Rabbi Armand Cohen, a legendary rabbi serving the same Cleveland synagogue for seventy-two years (a record) until his death at ninety-seven years old. He was the proverbial fiery pulpit preacher. In that style he gave me some stern advice in his pre-wedding-day private talk, including, "Don't let your wife go to work," which I didn't quite appreciate. I broke the house down at the wedding ceremony with my unplanned adlib as I repeated Rabbi Cohen's words, "I promise to love and honor my wife forever"—pause—"*and ever.*" It was prophetic, I kept my promise. Our picture under the wedding canopy is shown below. Ecille keeps marveling at how lucky she was to be able to buy this beautiful dress from a dress salesman friend for about $100; it was a sample dress.

The place and how my in-laws, the Garbers, met almost paralleled my own experience. They met accidently at a facility for social meeting, except it was not a resort but the old Jewish Community Center (JCC) on Sixteenth and Q St. in Washington DC. During World War II, the JCC incorporated a USO lounge for Jewish and non-Jewish veterans. In 1943, my sister-in law Tessie Pierce was determined to serve in the military and volunteered for the United States Marine Corps Women's Reserve (USMCWR) to take over a noncombatant military job so that men could be released for combat duty. She was determined to enlist on her twentieth birthday, requiring her parents' consent. She was so eager to join she put up with the DuBarry Success diet—"guaranteed to lose 10 lbs. in 10 days"—in order to meet the weight requirement. On that plan you were allowed to only eat oranges for the first five days of the diet. The day before her

birthday, she pleaded all day with her mother for her consent. She lost the ten pounds, got her mother to sign the consent form, and was enrolled in the Marine Corps on her birthday. My brother-in-law Morris Garber had his left leg amputated below the knee as a result of being hit by a German shell during the last days of the North African campaign in March 1943; he was a forward observer for an army artillery unit. In 1945, Morris had already had a prosthesis applied, was walking pretty well, and was training for a job in Washington DC with the Disabled American Veterans (DAV) organization. They both independently went to the USO lounge one Sunday afternoon. Morris, playing ping-pong struck Tessie with the ping-pong ball. Tessie returned the ball to him, started a conversation, and the wonderful relationship began and continued until his death in 2011.

The next day after our wedding, on our way to our honeymoon at the Laurel in the Pines resort in Lakewood, NJ, I became aware of how badly I misjudged the impact of Ecille leaving Cleveland. I thought her mother in particular would accept it easily because her sister and brother did that many years earlier. Ecille cried for several hours, knowing that her mother would feel alone and feel pained that her close daughter left home. What a way to start a marriage.

Our honeymoon got us started on the right marital path. One night while dancing, we wondered to each other if we would be dancing like the old couple on the floor was when we were their age; they looked to us to be in their sixties. We continued to enjoy American and Latin dancing till today, in our eighties. We danced at a Catskill resort on our summer vacations, lastly at Kutshers before it closed; many times at the end of the show we were the last couple on the dance floor and had a private band playing our choice of dance numbers. We took many cruises, with dancing being a specialty treat for us on these vacations. My wife and I lament over the closing of all the restaurants in the Washington DC area that had our type of dancing—we went to them all. Until recently we did some dancing at Leisure World where we live, a dance group sponsored a dance monthly. My wife's health deteriorated this year to the point that her ability/willingness to dance is touch and go. My wife and I continued our family heritage of devotion to family in raising our own children, David and Debbie. We watched our children's public school and high school grades to see if some talking to was required and supported their social needs for them to keep in tune with their friends. Besides the usual chauffeuring, it involved my being an assistant Little League coach, breaking David into being a good tennis player, and taking him to local ski resorts as a starter to his becoming a great skier. My daughter got her ballet and tap lessons, and we naturally enjoyed her recitals. We gave them a basic Jewish education at our Shaare Tefila Synagogue Hebrew School, culminating in the customary bar and bat mitzvah religious services with the nice parties attended by their friends and most of our extended families; my wife did the Hebrew school carpooling. We took them with us when we attended the High

Holiday religious services and occasionally to Sabbath services to instill the connection to the Hebrew religion that their parents have. We wrestled with the occasional problems kids give their parents.

Our daughter, Debbie, followed the more conventional path as she grew up. She got a BS degree at the University of Maryland, met Darryl Trupp, got married, and is raising two children, Austin, nineteen, and Jenna, fifteen. Before the kids came along, she served as the office manager of an office rental facility. Their son, Austin, seems to idolize me and tries to follow my scholastic, athletic, social, and societal support pattern. He attended Richard Montgomery High School's International Baccalaureate (IB) magnet program in Rockville, MD, rated in the top 5 percent of the high schools nationally, and was a National Merit Scholar finalist. He was on the school varsity basketball and tennis teams and even served as the assistant coach for the basketball team. Austin helped create the new B'Nai Brith Lantos AZA chapter and served as its first president. During high school summers, he did volunteer work at the Children's Hospital Brainy Camp, a summer camp for children with diseases such as epilepsy, autism, Down syndrome, and sickle-cell anemia, getting compliments from the kids for his services as best counselor of the year. He became so passionate in working at these camps that he devoted this entire summer to working at the camp as a full-time employee for Children's Hospital. He is currently attending the University of Maryland at College Park. Jenna attends the Wooton High School in Gaithersburg, MD. She has an affinity for learning and speaking Spanish and history. Her talent is swimming. She is a member of the school swim team and the area swim team, swimming well in statewide competitions. This sport is especially challenging, with almost daily swim practices from six to eight in the morning before school starts, again after school, and with weekend swim meets. Her mother is her chauffeur and is very active in the parent swim team support group for both swim teams. I don't know how they both can keep the pace required.

David had a more checkered life pattern. He dropped out of the University of Maryland, lived in Southern California, came back to Maryland University, dropped out again, lived in Aspen, Colorado for five winters, and finally back to Southern California, where he settled down and received a marketing degree from Pepperdine University. He put his parents to the test many times; he says we never failed him. In 1993, he met a relatively recent immigrant from Great Britain, Alexandra Alamango. They got married in 1996 and had triplets in 1999 with grandmother-to-be

Ecille in the delivery room. Grandma was just thrilled to watch the triplets come out one minute apart and hearing them cry. There had been an earlier concern about how the three were laying in the womb and some brief consideration of a reduction. Three years later, we got an unexpected shock. David's wife asked for a divorce. They got over the acrimonious divorce proceedings and now collaborate on raising their children. David has his thirteen-year-old triplets—Bianca, Grayson, Leila—every other weekend and two days during the week. He continues to be a very interactive father. David's children will be achieving Bar and Bat Mitzvah under the auspices of Cantor Steven Puzarne's Vision of Wholeness ministry. As part of their Mitzvah project, they will be working with Cantor Puzarne to establish the Denise Wertheim Fund For Spirituality and Special Needs. This will enable Vision of Wholeness to expand vital spiritual support for special needs children and their families, while at the same time honoring the memory of David's dear friend Denise, who adored David's children and who recently died of esophagus cancer.

The many business trips I had to California starting in 1962 gave me plenty of welcomed opportunities to see David and my other California relatives, namely my uncle Nat who my father brought to this country back in 1906 and his daughter and granddaughters. I had a close relationship with daughter Elayne in New York while we were in our late teens and early twenties. Her body never fully recovered from infantile paralysis when she was eleven, and it handicapped her socially. She followed her father's adventurous footsteps and went to live in California alone, with no family or contacts there. Elayne married a teacher, Abe Protes. They were raising their two small children when he abandoned his family. To help his daughter under these circumstances, my uncle moved to California and served as the stand-in father rather than the customary grandfather role of getting the pleasures without the burdens. I enjoyed my many visits with him there, learning much about my father's early years and lessons from this successful businessman.

I made this important observation based on my uncle's life experience in California. As long as you have a responsibility and feel needed, the mind will stay crisp and the body stays relatively healthy. This was my uncle's pattern into his ninety-first year—he lived alone and was sharp as a whistle. This incentive to keep going ended when his two granddaughters became teenagers. He rapidly deteriorated mentally and physically and died within one year. I also saw this rapid mental but slow physical deterioration happen to my ninety-one-year-old brother-in-law living in Dallas, Texas, when his girlfriend passed away and he didn't need to be mentally alert and ready to talk to her when she called him every morning and evening from Beaumont, Texas. My sister May essentially followed this pattern of deteriorating mentally shortly after her home-keeping responsibilities ended. She had virtually no logical thinking capacity or family recognition except for her daughter when she passed away at age ninety-two.

Because of the relationship I developed with her two daughters, seeing them on most visits, with treats at the soda fountain, my cousin Elayne honored me by twice having me march down the wedding aisle with her as the stand-in father, giving the girls away in marriage to two guys who were wonderful to my cousin after the long dormant infantile paralysis virus reactivated in her body and she needed practically daily dialysis and other care.

We brought David and kids east for our grandson Austin's Bar Mitzvah celebration and for just a summer family get-together two years later, showing them the highlights of Washington DC. We see our local family frequently and tried to see David's family twice yearly; however, my wife's health has deteriorated to the point where travel is a challenge but we are preparing to go there as I am completing this book.

The extended Shapiro/Pierce families reflect the current society's mores—divorces, mixed-religion marriages, mixed-racial marriages, and open gays.

Here is another adage for the young readers to reflect on. *Grandparents never stop worrying about their children and grandchildren; their children's and grandchildren's concerns are their concerns.*

Special Personal Experiences

There were two experiences in my youth that had a lasting effect on me, one having to do with my political orientation and the other with my religious perspective. They both coincidentally indirectly involved retirement homes.

Experience Impacting My Political Perspective. As the 1930s started, the part of the Lower East Side where I lived started to become very politically focused. The Depression hit the area as it did the rest of the country.

Unemployment was very high, high school students found it difficult to find jobs, some people had to take advantage of the city's home relief program for their food and lodging support, and the sight of a long soup kitchen line visually highlighted the economic problems. President Roosevelt had instituted the New Deal in his first term and wanted to extend this concept. Fiorrelo LaGuardia had become the Republican mayor of New York City, supporting Roosevelt's policies and pushing to continue ending vice and political corruption in New York City ; his Sunday-night radio broadcasts were stimulating. Herbert Lehman had become the first Jewish governor of New York State with an agenda for state-funded improvements of New York City facilities to provide work for the unemployed. All of these subjects were of direct interest to my impacted community. Although barely in my early teens, I was exposed to these political considerations in my seventh—and eighth-grade elementary school classes and had taken a keen interest in this subject. My extensive knowledge of past and current American history contributed to my winning the history prize when I graduated from public school at eleven and a half.

Political rallies were held on Sundays in the summer and fall before each Election Day. The New York City newspapers and even the Jewish newspapers provided stimulating coverage. Political rallies were held in two locations, in front of the old Hebrew Home for the Aged on Rutgers Street and in the local Seward Park. The Hebrew home was a charming old facility, a large white building with a high porch set back from the street and with a large courtyard in front of it that could accommodate a large crowd listening to the guest speakers over the loudspeaker. It served as the popular place for the Democratic and Republican parties to conduct their political rallies. Seward Park was the alternate place for smaller rallies. I attended several rallies with my older sister Frances and occasionally by myself. Scheduled events were held rain or shine; I remember attending some rallies and seeing a sea of umbrellas.

The strong community interest in elections was demonstrated by the unusual election-night facility available in the neighborhood. Every election night the *Forward* newspaper publisher set up a twenty-by-ten-foot screen outside their facility and projected election results as they came in, watched by a large group of people standing in Seward Park across the street from the screen.

The 1936 election was of major importance. President Roosevelt was running for a second term and NY governor Lehman was running for his third term. They both were promoting the extension of the New Deal policies. By then my community saw the benefit of these policies with neighbors employed by the WPA, PWA, and the CCC and some private job growth. The Democratic Party held a major rally at the Hebrew Home that featured Eleanor Roosevelt and Governor Lehman. With these two speakers, the attendance was tremendous; the street in front of the home was closed off for the rally. Eleanor Roosevelt, with her squeaky voice, gave a lengthy, persuasive presentation supporting the New Deal extension plans that was essentially complemented by Governor Lehman's talk that followed. Their economic agenda and community-supportive strategy made quite an impression on twelve-year-old me; already having seen the benefits of these policies enjoyed by the community strengthened my reaction to what I heard. It set me up to be a lifelong Democratic Party candidate supporter, with just a few exceptions when the candidate had extremely isolationist foreign policies or restrictive economic policies. My concern about American isolationism increased in the 1939-41 period, when isolationists in Congress opposed Roosevelt's attempts to aid Great Britain in their resistance to the German onslaught.

Experience Impacting My Religious Perspective. One Sunday morning in 1936, on my way to Hebrew school, I noticed a group of people looking at a man lying on the ground in front of the Bialystoker Retirement and Nursing Home on East Broadway across from my Hebrew school. Out of curiosity I went over to see what was happening. He was an elderly man, lying there slightly quivering. Suddenly I heard him feebly say in Hebrew the Shema prayer—"Hear O Israel, the Lord is our God, the Lord is One"—and then lay still again. I waited a while and left before the medical aide came in order to get to my Hebrew class on time. I later found out that the ailing man was a resident of the Bialystoker Nursing Home and that he died there on the street. I mentioned the incident to my Hebrew schoolteacher. She explained that it is the goal of religious Jews to have their last utterance be the Shema prayer. This is based on the stories about several Jewish martyrs shouting this prayer before being executed for not giving up their Hebrew faith, the illustrious Rabbi Akiba being one such martyr in the year 135 CE, when the Romans ended the Bar Kochba rebellion against Roman rule and executed Rabbi Akiba and the young warrior Bar Kochba.

This experience had a strong impact on me at age twelve, and I remembered it. I had occasion to apply this lesson twenty years later. I was working in Ellenville, NY, when I got a call from my sister Frances that my father was at home close to death. I knew he was dying of the cancer that he had for many years. I immediately took the two-and-a-half-hour car trip to my mother's house on Grand Street on the Lower East Side. By the time I got there, my father was so close to death that the neighborhood doctor examining my father had already written my father's death certificate. I found my father lying in bed, breathing feebly. I told him how much he meant to me and the family and how much I loved him. Then after saying this to him and remembering the earlier Shema incident of twenty years ago, I said the Shema prayer for him. He expired just a few minutes later. To this day, often when I say the Shema prayer during Sabbath religious services, it evokes a special feeling about the prayer.

My father and I had a very strong bond, starting in my youth. Initially, during Passover afternoons, which were his only free time, he took me wherever I wanted to go. Early on it was the Barnum & Bailey Circus yearly. As I grew older, it was to zoos throughout the city and then the NY Museum of Natural History and the NY Metropolitan Museum of Art. As I explained earlier, he involved me in conducting his candy store business, which taught me how necessary it is to address all problems/tasks associated with your work. He helped me develop a taste for mechanical work that was a precursor to my profession. I learned to show respect to my elders through his lecture to me when, during a political discussion in my father's store, he heard me address a senior neighbor by his commonly used nickname, "Ike." He immediately told me to show respect to seniors and always address our neighbor as "Mr. Abramowitz." My father demonstrated to me the avoidance of racial prejudice by continually offering credit to two black families until the $30 limit (a lot of money those days) was reached even though it was very likely they would not pay their debt to him; he explained he had been offering credit to white customers with the same prospect. I learned of the personal satisfaction one obtains from volunteerism from seeing him continue to volunteer even under difficult personal health conditions. Three years before he died, we spent a wonderful week together in my Ellenville apartment catching up on his lifetime experiences and just enjoying being together.

Religious Affiliations

As a youngster I grew up under the influence of grandparents who adhered strictly to the Jewish Orthodox religious practices; going to Sabbath services was their norm. My mother would have preferred to also observe the Sabbath, but she accepted the need to work on the Sabbath to have sufficient income to raise her large family. I later learned to appreciate how my parents applied behavioral Torah guidelines in their business interactions with their customers who occasionally couldn't pay their charge debts. They also treated all kinds of customers equally. I escorted my mother on her annual visits to her parents' graves and heard her connection to the Jewish faith expressed in prayers there. After my bar mitzvah, I went to my parents' synagogue almost every Saturday morning as a proxy for my mother, that pleased her very much; I kept this up for about three years. My parents and grandparents kept an affiliation with the synagogues they each attended. With this background, I joined the Conservative Congregation in Ellenville before my son was born and retained my membership until I left Ellenville. I started going to Saturday services after my father passed away in 1957. My little son and Rabbi Herman Eisner's son had fun climbing up the bimah (platform where prayers are conducted) and running around the synagogue together like they owned it. Rabbi Eisner was much admired and respected by the Ellenville community. He survived several concentration camps, including Auschwitz, before he came to this country. The street in front of the synagogue was named Rabbi Eisner Square in his honor after his death. He taught me how to read the haphtorah (reading of the prophets) at Saturday-morning services on the anniversary of my father's death to honor my father.

While we lived in Ellenville we drove to Cleveland every Passover and Rosh Hashanah to be with my wife's parents. I accompanied my in-laws to the holiday services at the Park Synagogue Conservative Congregation, where we were married. They had been members of Park Synagogue at its previous location under its original name, the Cleveland Jewish Center, since about 1933.

There was no synagogue in the Silver Spring, MD, area that we moved to in 1960. My mother-in-law passed away in the spring of 1962, so we didn't go to Cleveland for the fall Rosh Hashanah holiday. Instead we attended holiday services at the Shaare Tefila Conservative Congregation in North Central Washington DC that several of our neighbors belonged to. We joined that congregation in 1963 after they made plans to build a new synagogue facility in the White Oak section of Silver Spring, MD, nearby where we lived, which had a large and growing Jewish population and was very close to where we lived. Our two children went to the Shaare Tefila Hebrew School through the confirmation class and had their bar and bat mitzvahs at the synagogue. The demographics of the Silver Spring area where the synagogue was located changed so the membership decided to sell the facility and build a new synagogue facility in Olney, MD. It was completed in September 2011. We have retained our membership in the Shaare Tefila Congregation despite the awkwardness of attending services at public schools, the Olney Theatre, and other varied facilities these last four years. Credit has to be given to Rabbi Jonah Layman, Cantor Wendi Fried, and the lay leaders who have continued to keep the synagogue activity vibrant in spite of facility problems and the decreased membership resulting from the relocation plans.

I made an effort to support my Shaare Tefila Congregation Synagogue in its formative stage after it started operations in the White Oak facility. My early volunteer work is described on page 80. I initially served as corresponding vice president, moved on to being a member of the board of directors for about ten years, then served as assistant adult education chairman, and, lastly, served on the budget committee. Unofficially, I was Mr. Tuesday, supporting the Tuesday daily morning minyan for about twenty years and on call for other mornings when the required attendance of ten males was short a male.

I got involved in two major congregational issues. Rabbi Martin Halpern, with almost fifty years of service to the congregation, was ready to retire and asked for a final two-year contract. Two factions emerged, one for the contract and the other opposed to any contract extension. I sided with the group that respected the rabbi's services and wanted to give him a two-year final contract. However, I didn't like the bitterness in the discussions with the other faction, which was leading to animosity between the groups and tending to tear the congregation apart. I undertook a maverick approach to resolving the issue, sending out a letter to all congregation members encouraging civil discussions and showing Rabbi Martin Halpern appreciation for the many years of constructive services to the congregation with at least a compromise one-year contract. Both groups then became annoyed with me. After many member presentations at the congregation meeting to address the contract issue, the members were asked to select between no contract, a one-year contract, and a two-year contract. A one-year contract was approved. Unfortunately, Rabbi Halpern did not get to enjoy his retirement. Shortly after his one-year term was completed, which was still tainted with some carryover bitterness between the rabbi and the congregation leadership, he was diagnosed with melanoma and passed away within a year.

The other congregational issue had to do with our cantor's contract, which was up for renewal. The leaders of the synagogue were only going to offer our much-respected cantor Gershon Levin a part-time contract, claiming we couldn't afford a full-time salary. I joined others in opposing the part-time offer. We felt his services were needed on most days, morning, noon, and evening, deserving a full-time contract; and the suggested opportunities for his outside half-time work were slim and degrading. I analyzed the congregation budget presented at the congregation's contract-approval meeting and identified two budget items that had unnecessary reserve funds that could cover the full-time contract cost. With that revelation, the membership passed a full-time contract. The budget committee chairman liked my financial acuity and asked me to serve on his budget committee, so I wound up being rewarded with several more years of congregation work.

Our current rabbi, Jonah Layman, occasionally encourages members to present Dvar Torahs (a talk relating to the section of the Bible that was read that Saturday or a subject of current interest relating to the Torah section). I got up the courage to present two Dvar Torahs.

The first Dvar Torah offered my perspective on the power of the Passover Seder and the Haggadah that appeals to religious Jews and to many secular Jews with no religious affiliation. It is a message of hope that all people deserve to be free and the hopeless can ultimately be free. It exhibits a cry for justice, for all in the way the four sons of differing capabilities received equal treatment in the Haggadah. In the way that non-Hebrew oppressed were allowed to join the Hebrew exodus from Egypt, it is a message that freedom for everyone is desirable and possible with extraordinary effort. We learn that freedom does not come easy; it takes patience, determination, and persistence.

In conjunction with this Dvar Torah, I set up a display of samples of my large Haggadah collection and discussed them briefly in my talks. My still-growing thirty-two Haggadah collection includes:

1. Haggadahs received over a twenty-five-year period from the Diskin Orphan Home of Israel in response to my annual donation that are replicas of beautifully illustrated Haggadah masterpieces printed in the seventeenth to nineteenth centuries in different European countries with respective language interpretations.

2. Modern versions from different sociological perspectives, such as the New Model Seder (1971) with a simplified Seder story of supplemental readings including the Matzah of Hope dedicated to freedom of Russian Jews, Dr. Martin Luther King's Freedom Speech, and a benediction composed at Bergen-Belsen because Torah-prescribed matzah wasn't available.

3. Several traditional American versions, such as the Hebrew Publishing Company's Haggadah (1942). In conjunction with this Haggadah I presented highlights of the commentary by former chancellor of the Jewish Theological Seminary, Rabbi Louis Finkelstein. His definition of a Jew: "A Jew is someone always trying to be a better Jew." His synopsis of the Seder is that the Seder is concerned with redemption; the ceremony ignores human inequality; everyone must participate equally in the celebration. His conclusion: "Freedom gave birth to the Passover, and the Passover gives birth to freedom."

4. The Pierce family Haggadah, created by my Cleveland niece Amy Pierce, which contains the Hebrew prayers/four questions with transliterations to help those youngsters who don't read Hebrew well and the Seder process in English broken down into small sections. In addition, it presents brief Passover lessons about the Afikomen, the start of the Passover tradition, the Elijah connection to the Seder, and more. The structure and instructions embedded in the Haggadah makes it so easy for everyone at the Seder to participate. The leader offers a short reading for each Seder process step followed by a brief response either by all the assembled or by individual participants. It ends with the English version of the Passover song "Echad Mee Yodaya" ("One Who Knows"), which compactly tells the biblical messages and some Jewish custom highlights progressively in thirteen verses. We now use this fourteen-page Haggadah regularly in our family Seders.

The second Dvar Torah that I presented addressed Deuteronomy section *Eikev* (meaning "because"). This Torah section has been cited by rabbinic scholars to support their opinion that the current version of Deuteronomy, the fifth book of the Bible, was written during the Judean kingdom of Josiah. The basis of this theory is the story in the biblical book of Kings that King Josiah, who ascended the Judean throne in 640 BCE at age eight, decided when he was twenty-five years old to conduct a religious reformation and restore the Holy Temple to practices in conformance to the biblical commandments. In my Dvar Torah, I presented my rationale for agreeing with this theory about Deuteronomy's Josiah-era authorship. It is fundamentally based on the strategic use of the section title, the word "because." Josiah's grandfather, King Manasseh, earlier had a major negative impact on the religious practices by the Jews in the kingdom, allowing widespread idol worship that he himself conducted. He also implemented widespread societal degrading actions that deviated from Torah principles. Josiah's Bible writers realized that the people needed a strong tonic to disband the long-standing idol worship practices and their disregard of Torah principles in their lifestyle. For example, the section starts with "*Because* you listen to the earlier commandments and keep them and do them, God will keep his covenant with you which He swore to your fathers." That "because" warns that the Jewish people will not have God's favor unless they obey the Bible's commandments. Another example is how the Ten Commandments in *Eikev* uses a stronger active verb rather than the passive verb in the earlier Exodus version, such as the active "Observe the Sabbath" in Deuteronomy as opposed to the passive "Remember the Sabbath" in Exodus. "As the Lord thy God commanded thee" was added in *Eikev* to add some strength as to why one should observe the Sabbath is another example. Deuteronomy also warns of the consequences of not adhering to Torah principles with this statement, "*Because* you would not listen to God, you will perish as a nation just like the nations you conquered that honored other gods."

We moved to the Silver Spring, MD, Leisure World Retirement Community in June 2000. It has a large, organized Jewish community, the Jewish Residents of Leisure World. They sponsor many social and Jewish cultural activities and conduct monthly Conservative and Reform Jewish services. We maintain a membership in this organization and attend some of their religious and social functions.

Interest in Zionism

My lifelong interest in Zionism developed in conjunction with my strong interest in US and world history as a young boy in elementary school. An understanding that Palestine was the homeland of the Jewish people before they were expelled by the Romans was taught early in my Hebrew school. It was made much clearer in the *Stranger than Fiction* history book I was awarded in Hebrew school at age eleven. I read with interest many US newspaper articles pertaining to Zionism; however, Zionism was not my family interest or of strong interest to my neighborhood Jewish community. My interest in Zionism was prompted by two friends of mine, brothers, who attended the Rabbi Jacob Joseph Yeshiva where they learned the importance of Palestine and Jerusalem in particular to the Jewish people. After their two older brothers made aliyah (Hebrew, meaning "ascent") to Palestine in 1935 through the Mizrachi religious Zionist movement, they convinced a few of their friends, including myself, to attend Saturday-afternoon Mizrachi youth meetings. I learned more about the organization's goals and achievements but developed no interest in becoming a member and dropped out after several meetings.

After the Holocaust ended, I, of course, watched all the news relating to Jews trying to get to Palestine surreptitiously, the ship *Exodus* being the most famous one. There was nothing more thrilling than hearing the United Nations pass the resolution dividing Palestine into a Jewish state and a Palestinian state, capped shortly later by Ben-Gurion's declaration of the State of Israel and the rapid recognition by President Truman. Reading about the Israeli army victories over the much larger Arab armies fighting them during the War of Independence was stirring. There was a critical Israeli military situation after the initial Egyptian success during the surprise Yom Kippur War started by Egypt. It prompted many local synagogues to conduct a rally at the US capital, encouraging US government support of Israel by resupplying the Israeli airplanes and other military weapons devastated by the surprise Egyptian attack; I joined my synagogue in participating in the rally.

I once considered moving to Israel. It was after a lost my job in 1950. I had just acquired experience as a machine tool designer and thought I could contribute to the State of Israel's manufacturing growth. The country's early growth was fantastic, but their economy needed to expand more to accommodate the anticipated large immigration. I stopped exploring this consideration after I consulted with my sisters, who convinced me that going there would devastate my mother. She never fully got over losing her other son at a young age and would get depressed about me being so far away in the turbulent Israel and the possibility of not seeing me again.

My interest and concern about Israel hasn't waned from my youth's feelings and interest. The Jewish history book I published in 2002 made a strong case for all Jews to support the State of Israel. I frequently send inputs to the Letters to the Editor section of the *Washington Post, The Wall Street Journal*, the *Washington Jewish Week*, and *The Jewish Daily Forward* in response to their news articles about Israel that I feel do not present an appropriate position regarding the State of Israel. My criticism has occasionally been directed at the State of Israel as well. Years ago it was at their behavior during the Lebanese War. More recently it related to the continuation of Israeli house construction on the West Bank which was interfering with the peace process with the Palestinians getting started, officialdom's failure to treat Conservative and Reform Judaism on an equal footing with Orthodox Judaism, including the denial of Conservative and Reform Judaism conversions and marriages, and the lack of equal treatment for women praying at the Western Wall. Although I am a dues-paying member of the Zionist Organization of America, I have occasionally criticized as unrealistic some ZOA proposals for suitable peace terms between the Israelis and the Palestinians, and some ZOA proposals for Israeli actions to help restart the peace process.

I have purchased State of Israel bonds since their inception and routinely buy them for myself, my children, or grandchildren in response to my synagogue's annual Israeli bond drives. I view the purchase of Israeli bonds as providing both fiscal and psychological support to Israel. I feel these family purchases help to instill in my children and grandchildren the understanding of the importance for all Jews to support the State of Israel.

Society Payback—Volunteerism

As a small youngster, occasionally on Saturday mornings I would walk to see my grandfather at the synagogue he went to for Saturday services. It was in the building next to where I lived so I could go there by myself. He was always helping set up the after-services snacks they served, so he felt free to give me a cookie or two, my treat for seeing him. Twenty years later after my father retired, but before he got sick, I was told that my father loved to help with the Saturday kiddush (snacks) at his synagogue. I was in town one Saturday and saw him in action. He evidently continued to do that when he sort of recovered from the periodic cancer treatments he received up until he became completely incapacitated. These two volunteerism examples must have made a lasting subconscious impression on me, for during my lifetime I have taken on a variety of societal volunteer tasks, starting at a relatively early age. Volunteering to aid societal programs has been personally rewarding.

Such an opportunity came up in Ellenville, NY, in 1958 while I was doing yearlong memorial services for my father. The communitywide Ellenville Hebrew School was undergoing a traumatic curriculum modernization change in conjunction with the new, modern teaching staff that had been hired. The changes were affecting and disturbing the old principal and the students and their parents. Rabbi Eisner of the synagogue that I was attending for memorial services asked if I would volunteer to represent the synagogue and work with the Hebrew school management in addressing the curriculum-change challenges, which I accepted. It took almost six months of step-by-step changes to resolve and incorporate the curriculum changes proposed, to incorporate the teaching style changes offered by the new teachers, handle teacher reaction issues, and contend with the principal's reluctance to accept changes; but the student/parent issues were a continuing proposition. After those issues calmed down, I also supported the school's journal fundraising effort. After I moved from Ellenville I received a nice plaque acknowledging my leadership, guidance, and sincere devotion to the school.

This affinity to synagogue volunteerism that I apparently had surfaced again when the Shaare Tefila Synagogue, which I recently joined, opened up its new facility in White Oak, MD, in 1965. The synagogue finances were poor, requiring many members to step up to conduct a variety of administrative and maintenance services to save money. Although my NASA job required periodic weekly out-of-the-area travel and, later, emergency evening support, for two years I made it my business to find one evening every two weeks that I could devote to running an addressograph machine to address over two hundred news flyers to be mailed to the synagogue members. I also sorted the incoming bills for payment, helped set up and break down the chairs in the auditorium for holiday services, and helped the administrative vice president with other facility maintenance chores. About ten years later I stepped up to assist the new adult education chairman reactivate the adult education program. I attended two of the courses. One was a presentation of a personal Holocaust experience told by Shaare Tefila schoolteacher Harriet Steinhorn, who previously withheld talking about her painful Holocaust experience to anyone, including her own children, for about thirty years. Her vivid description of the torture she went through, starting with how as a young girl she missed her mother so much that she sneaked into the initial concentration camp her mother was put into, was painful to hear. The other course was a study of medieval Jewish history by synagogue member Dr. Arthur Bressler. This insightful history lesson was helpful to me when I wrote my own book on Jewish history. Years later, for one year I conducted a remedial reading class for students in our Hebrew school who had difficulty reading Hebrew. Currently, my Shaare Tefila volunteering consists of on-call evening minion support and occasionally conducting weekday-evening religious services.

While I was working at NASA/GSFC, the Washington United Jewish Appeal (UJA) asked me to take a turn soliciting annual contributions from Jewish employees, which I did for several cycles; and later I was asked to support a super-Sunday UJA telephone campaign. Later, stimulated by this experience, for a couple of years I volunteered to spend two weeks of my use-or-lose accumulated annual leave assisting the UJA office staff. I had a wonderful experience supporting Mr. Herman Taube, who was then managing the UJA synagogue solicitations. Mr. Taube, a holocaust survivor who later became a famous Jewish poet and author of several books covering Holocaust themes, charmed me with his stories between my volunteer work duties.

In 1991, I started a six-year long Meals on Wheels volunteer effort that ended when I suffered a pericarditis attack. This activity was rewarding in two respects, the deliverance of the food to those that needed it and the wonderful relationships I developed with several recipients. This program was a nonsectarian service by the Jewish Social Service Agency (JSSA), which provided kosher meals free to those in need and for a fee to those who were incapable of making their own meals and wanted the prepared meals and could afford to pay. It essentially was a once-a-week whole-afternoon effort. All of the recipients lived alone and appreciated having someone to talk to; I accommodated them. They each essentially had a different need. For example, Mr. Schnapper, a retired economist with several publications, living almost as a recluse in an old large house full of books, longed to tell old business stories and those of his professional accomplishments. His favorite story, told to me a couple times over the years I serviced him, was how the *New York Journal American* newspaper that he worked for as the newspaper liaison representative with the NY Jewish community wouldn't accept his statement that he was not Jewish when he applied for the job. When he was interviewed, he had just left the Jewish Orphan Asylum on Amsterdam Avenue, where he had lived since he was nine years old. He was a German Protestant whose father abandoned him and his brother after their mother died. The Orphan Asylum took them in. Living and growing up in this Jewish facility and being exposed to related Jewish activities taught him enough about the Jewish lifestyle and community interest to qualify for the Jewish community relations job. Mrs. X loved to brag about her economist daughter making another contribution to Utah Senator Orin Hatch's legislature agenda but actually never knew any details. She just liked to talk and also needed someone to eat some of the cakes she loved to bake; I took home lots of delicacies. Mrs. Ottenberg, who lived in the fancy Washington DC Rittenhouse Apartments needed to tell someone about her weekly new little complaints; her doctor son, who happened to be my family's orthopedic physician and her working daughter gave their mother little time. Mrs. Goldstein, a Holocaust survivor widow with no children or secondary family in the Washington area longed for someone to talk to. Mr. Abrams, a lonely veteran, had little to say and needed stimulus to make conversation but seemed to appreciate it.

My professional work practice of paying attention to details and my civil practice of adhering to the rules/laws were instrumental in saving the lives of two of my Meal on Wheels recipients. One Tuesday when I went to Mrs. Goldstein's door I found a Meals on Wheels food bag on the door handle. Knowing that the JSSA delivery rules say not to leave the food bag on the door unless the recipient advised the JSSA office that they were out that day, I suspected something was wrong and went to the apartment building supervisor's office to tell him of the situation. He entered her apartment and found her unconscious on the floor. I visited her in the hospital after she recovered somewhat and found out what happened. On that Sunday afternoon before she was found on the floor, for some reason that she couldn't recall, she took off the medical alert she always wore. Ten minutes later she fell and couldn't get up to get to the telephone or to the medical alert that she had placed on a dresser. I told her how lucky she was to have survived after being without food and water for two days, and at her age as well. Her comeback was, "That was nothing. I had plenty of practice. I went without food and water for three and four days in the concentration camps."

The other recipient involved was Mr. Abrams, a frail old World War II veteran, living by himself in a county-subsidized basement apartment. He always quickly responded to the upstairs lobby doorbell and spoke on the intercom, offering the same expression with a very distinctive voice, particularly his name, something like, "Hello, this is Mr. Abrams, what can I do for you?" I gave him my answer, identifying who I was, and he buzzed the door to let me in. Then he greeted me at his door. That day he answered, but his voice did not sound the same, particularly the slurred sound of his name was different. Because I sensed this difference from his usual response, I went to the office for them to go in with me. He seemed to be in the midst of having a stroke. An ambulance was called to take him to the hospital. He never fully recovered from the stroke he did suffer and was moved to a veteran's facility where he lived for at least a year, which was the last time I checked.

In 1999 I took a few years' break from volunteering until after we settled down in our new home in the Silver Spring Leisure World Community. Then I started a new volunteering effort in 2001. I had earlier spent some time visiting my wife's ailing cousin, Jack Cutler, residing at the Hebrew Home of Greater Washington, which served long-term sick seniors. During these visits I was exposed to a lot of other patients and learned that when they needed to visit an off-site facility or physician for special medical services they required an escort in the vehicle that transported them to the off-site medical services facility. The escort provides services that the incapacitated patient is not equipped to do by themselves, e.g., bring the patient downstairs to the transport vehicle, provide the transport driver the destination information, make sure the doctor's orders are brought along with the patient, escort the patient from the delivery vehicle drop-off to the medical service room, call the transport facility to arrange for the timely return of a vehicle to pick up the patient, escort the patient during the ride back to the home, and return the patient in a wheelchair back to their room. I initially tried a couple of escort service tasks and found them rewarding. The services were important, and I met interesting people who appreciated getting some attention. I signed up for this scheduled support service as well as substituting for other escort volunteers, as required. I provided this service normally once every two weeks.

In 2005 I volunteered to perform an additional service at the Hebrew Home. Every month I devoted about four hours, or more if required, supporting the Hebrew Home nursing training director. I updated the official facility nurse-training database (approximately 450 nurses) with records of the training that each individual nurse received the previous month. The nurses were required to get refresher training in every nursing task every three years; accurate records were required to assure each nurse did not miss a required training session and to avoid any potential malpractice issues in connection with missed training.

On two occasions I performed another volunteer job for the Hebrew Home that was disappointing. The Home annually ran a hole-in-one golf event in conjunction with their annual fund-raising campaign, and I served as a hole-in-one witness at one of the holes—was so disappointed not to have witnessed anyone succeeding to hit a hole in one at my hole. The close calls didn't count.

In 2007, I broke my right hip (upper thigh bone) playing ping pong with the Leisure World Ping-Pong Group at the Silver Spring Leisure World Retirement Community where I live. This group of about twenty men and women senior citizens plays doubles ping pong twice a week for two hours. I play aggressively, chasing after balls ("playing like a young pup," as one player frequently comments), and that day I was too aggressive, slipped, and fell. After the fracture, I gave up the Hebrew Home volunteering efforts. After several months of recuperation I felt well enough to go back to playing ping pong. It was my only routine exercise regimen. However, my general health deteriorated somewhat with periods of dizziness, causing me to interrupt my ping pong playing routine, and I ended all my community volunteering effort for several years.

In November 2010 I received an e-mail from Hedy Peyser, the Washington Hebrew Home volunteer coordinator, asking whether I would be available to support a volunteer program she had just set up. She indicated that, based on what she saw of my past volunteer efforts at the home, she felt that I would serve the program well and also enjoy it. I began serving as a patient service representative for short-term home residents who were using the home rehabilitation facility. I visited patients in their rooms or elsewhere in the building where they might be, and occasionally with their families, chatting with them to learn if there was any problem with any of the services rendered at the home or just offered them conversation. Complaints first needed to be looked at closely to be sure they were realistic or if there were mitigating circumstances causing the problem or service deficiency that was outside of the Home attendant's control. Some types of problems are initially investigated as to whether there were mitigating circumstances causing the deficient services. The follow-up challenge was to diplomatically present the complaint to the respective nurse or attendant for them to provide the requested services or to work with the Home facilities staff to rectify any facility-related issues. Another challenge was to learn from talking with patients who were ready go home whether they were troubled that there was inadequate care at home. This required follow-up with the Home's health-care services department to arrange for the appropriate services. Below is a picture of a group of volunteers on this program honored at a breakfast, with me on the lower right.

Patient Service volunteers Aaron Erez, Lily Groh, Gail Klein, Sydell Rappaport, Dr. Yvette Rubianes, Ralph Shapiro, and George Spectre come from all walks of life, but they share a joint mission: to ensure every rehabilitation patient has a positive experience. They will find an engineer to repair a TV remote, ask the dietitian to stop by, or report a concern to nursing, and their reports to go to top levels of management. "I can't think of anything more rewarding," said one volunteer as the group was honored at a breakfast with CEO Warren Slavin, Pat Carter, Hedy Peyser and Patty Hagen.

Society Support—Charity Giving

The Bible, in Leviticus, mandates giving to the poor. We should all do our best in this regard. Regardless of their wealth, or lack of it, the Lower East Side Jewish people of my youth honored this Torah commandment. I remember charity solicitors coming to the home door and asking for contribution to charities in Palestine; my mother never refused to give. In 1925 my grandmother made a $1 contribution to a charity in Palestine shared with her brother through the efforts of a charity's representative. In that time period and considering her financial circumstances, that was a big donation. She got a formal receipt from the solicitor, shown below, which had been

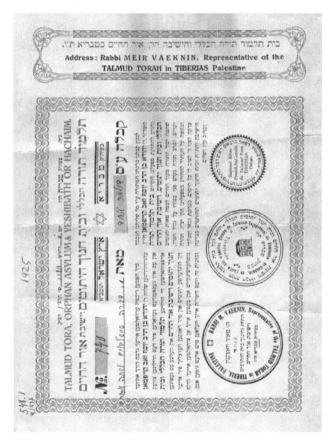

saved as a family treasure until I donated it to the New Museum of American Jewish History in Philadelphia. The museum has displayed this receipt as an indication of the Jewish immigrants' expression of appreciation for what this country offered them.

The Jewish National Fund's blue charity box was the charity-collection device that was very common in homes. My Hebrew school gave one to all students to have in the house and collected them yearly. My father was very helpful, having one on his store counter for customers to contribute—and many did.

Needless to say, I learned to contribute to charities from my grandparents and parents. My comfortable financial situation in retirement enables me to honor the biblical charitable commandment. I remember the downtrodden people I used to see in New York City and have been giving to the NYC Catholic Covenant House, which takes care of youth afflicted by today's societal challenges. How can I resist giving to Boys Town USA after seeing the movie *Boys Town* ages ago; with this contribution, how can I resist giving to the equivalent Boys Town Jerusalem and to Friends of Yad Sarah, which takes care of orphaned girls in Jerusalem. Native Indians still living under depressed conditions get my support. You name a medical research organization, veteran's organization, police/fire organization, children's aid organization, Jewish charity, or a national sectarian charity and you will likely find it on my charity list. The biggest recipient of my charity giving is the United Jewish Appeal of Greater Washington, which supports local Jewish organizations, indigent local people, and noteworthy Israeli civic organizations. My longest recipient is the Diskin Orphan Home in Israel. They reward me with contributions to my large collection of Passover Haggadahs with their annual solicitation.

Caught In the Lower East Side *Web*

At the start of the twentieth century, the Lower East Side became the home of the new wave of immigrants coming to the United States, slowly displacing those who had improved economically and moved to other affluent areas of the city. With the curtailment of immigration in 1924, this population pattern changed. The immigrant population in the area stabilized and was joined by their first-generation American children. With their large growing families and very low to modest incomes, most families couldn't afford travel vacations, which wasn't much in vogue to begin with. With the onset of the depression, the situation deteriorated further. The absence of cars in the area was a telltale of the situation. The big trip was to Coney Island by subway. Most boys depended on the free vacations at a summer camp in upstate New York offered by the Henry Street Settlement and the Educational Alliance. The girls had an opportunity to go to their camps on Long Island. There were no tales told of family trips or camping vacations.

My experience basically fit into the community pattern I described, except for my friends going to summer camp. My mother shielded me from outdoor cold-water exposure because of her suspicion that it was the cause of my brother's sickness, which led to his early death; and she didn't allow me to go to camp with my friends. The restrictive exposure to places outside of New York City was compounded by my parent's inability to have free time for family vacations and their lack of understanding of what the country had to offer me in terms of natural beauty and places of cultural interest. As a very young kid, a ferry ride trip to Staten Island was a big treat. Later, a thirty-mile boat excursion up the Hudson River to Bear Mountain as a birthday treat was adventurous, and at eleven, a car trip with my brother-in-law Sam Moskowitz and oldest sister Irene to the beach at Riis Park on Rockaway Beach across from Brooklyn was a big thrill. I had gotten a small taste of the country outdoors earlier when I was nine and again at eleven years old. My mother took me and my playmate older sister Frances for a week's stay at a small resort called the Shapiro (no relation) Farm Hotel located in Mongaup Valley, near Monticello, NY. My sister Frances led me on a path through the woods to wade in a nearby creak that we were told about. It was also a challenge to try to catch the small fish swimming in the creak with nets the hotel gave us. On our second vacation there I learned more about the outdoors and a little about hunting. On another path leading to the creak we passed a hunter's cabin. The hunter invited us in to show us his hunting rifles and then took me outside to pull the trigger of a rifle he held like I was shooting at a rabbit. It was all very exciting to me; I was too dumb to realize how much danger we were potentially exposed to. We got a reprimand when we got back to the hotel.

In elementary school I was very much interested in US history and geography. They were my favorite subjects and I did well in them. I longed to visit places I learned about, like the Grand Canyon and the Niagara Falls; to see the giant redwood trees grow in California; and to see places of historical interest, such as Valley Forge, Boston, and Williamsburg, VA.

This interest was enhanced by a teacher who told us of her vacation out West. She showed pictures of the Grand Canyon and showed pieces of wood from the Petrified Forest and cups of colorful sand from the Painted Desert that she brought home from her trip that summer.

Yes, until I matured and entered the working world, I was caught within this *web* surrounding the Lower East Side; I did not get far from NYC, and none of my interest in seeing the country was satisfied.

Escaping from the Lower East Side *Web*

I initially got out of this proverbial *web* that previously restricted my exposure to places outside of the Lower East Side when I graduated from college and started working for the General Electric Company in the summer of 1944. The nature of the job was such that I moved approximately every three months to a different city, including Schenectady, NY; Lynn, MA; Erie, PA; Pittsfield, MA; and Bridgeport, CN. I didn't own a car while living in these cities, so my adventures to surrounding cultural and historic areas and sites was very limited.

A major change occurred after I owned my first car in 1948. Initially it enabled me to go with friends to many singles resorts in New York, New Jersey, Pennsylvania, and Connecticut on summer vacations and long weekends, including Green Mansions, where I met my future wife six years later. I still remember two odd experiences that occurred early in these social explorations. At the White Roe resort I learned how to get the right swing to hit tennis balls by swinging the racket to the tune of the then-popular "The Blue Danube" song. Tennis novices should try it; it works. At the Berkshire Country Club I planned on going horseback riding with a group of friends. I was a novice at horseback riding, having been to a dude ranch only once before. The attendant had to boost me up on top of this giant horse they gave me named Walla Walla. He was so big compared to the other horses I was so afraid he would be too fast for me to handle. It turned out I couldn't hit him hard enough to get him to stay at the pace with the others; he barely moved. I turned him around and ended this horseback-riding experience quickly.

My next significant exposure to Americana occurred early in 1950. I had lost my job, and my initial attempts to find a new job were unsuccessful, so I decided to take a vacation in Miami Beach, Florida. It was during a minor recession period, so engineering job opportunities were scarce—a discouraging situation. I planned on staying as long as the budget I set held out. It actually lasted ten weeks. It turned out I had many interesting and exciting experiences in that short period, which would normally take a lifetime to acquire.

I started the trip to Miami accompanied by the younger brother of a friend of mine who wanted to practice his driving after recently receiving his driving license and had funds to cover a short stay in Miami, a new experience for both of us. We went down south through the then-favorite scenic route, which included the Tobacco Road in North Carolina; this was before I-95 was built. It was a most scenic and educational drive. The American history themes represented by the gadgets sold at different tourist souvenir shops along the way were most interesting. The tobacco farms and the shanty towns were also absorbing to see. We next stopped in Charlestown, SC, to see a young girl contact I was given. We were shown around this very interesting city with a heritage going back to the country's founding days by this informative contact. She also showed us the Jewish section of the city and gave us some of its interesting history. Her family had us for dinner, where I heard Yiddish spoken with a Southern accent by her grandmother. We then continued on to St. Augustine, FL, where we spent a good part of the day in its museums, learning about its colorful history in relation to the early Florida explorations.

The stay in Miami Beach was an exposure to lifestyles and activities quite opposite to what I had been previously exposed to while living on the Lower East Side. To stretch out the stay, we stayed at the low-priced Taft Hotel on Washington Avenue in South Miami Beach. We had a contact in Miami, Mrs. Johnson, the mother of a friend at home who thought she was dying and wanted to make her last days pleasant by living in Miami by herself; her husband and family were back home in New York. She supported herself there by being a racing tout, getting 10 percent of her client's winnings. She had developed a large racing clientele and had lots of local contacts. She got us special low rate at the Taft Hotel. Food

expenses were low in South Beach; a T-bone steak platter at a food stand cost $1. At the hotel, I met a recently retired business man from Chicago with a small yacht who took us out fishing. He let us keep the big batch of red snapper we caught, which I traded to the hotel chef for a couple of weeks of free lunches. The picture shows the batch of fish we caught, me holding the fish, the boat owner, and my travel companion, Jack Egelstein.

When I was on my own, I ventured to the uptown beach area and went to the classy Fontainebleau Hotel to see what it was like. I ended up at the pool, where I struck up a friendship with a New Yorker who claimed to be a bookie for a living. One day he pleaded with me to go out on a double date with him that night and accompany his date's girlfriend. He had me meet him that night at a bar with the two girls he brought. We had a couple of drinks and talked. The next thing I know, he and his girl got up and left, sticking me to pay the entire check. Needless to say, he avoided me afterward; I never saw him again and learned a lesson not to be so gullible and watch out for Florida hucksters.

Early in our stay Mrs. Johnson had taken us to see dog races in South Beach and then to jai alai games and the Hialeah racetrack with their pretty flamingos, both located north of Miami proper. I met a girl at the Taft Hotel who wanted the experience of seeing horse racing. Knowing where the Hialeah racetrack was located, I took her there. I tried using the technique of picking the winners that I learned in my college public-speaking course that I described on page 60. I lost my $2 bets on all the races. She only wanted to bet on one horse race, on a horse whose name sounded like her father's company name. It was the winning technique; her horse came in first.

Mrs. Johnson stayed at a low-rent old rooming house on the eastern end of the Tamiami Trail that cuts across Florida, which is Southwest Eighth Street in Miami. I was well acquainted with that place because every time we got together I drove there to pick up Mrs. Johnson since she didn't have a car. I became friendly with a senior Jewish man from Brooklyn staying there, a widower of a couple of years, who was melancholy with little interest in anything. This disposition changed when a couple of women who were nurses back home in the Midwest showed up. They initially convinced him to sponsor Friday-evening parties for the facility; he had me help with some arrangements. It was good medicine for him; it rejuvenated him from his lethargic state. Then they persuaded him to invest in a new small nursing facility near Miami that they would set up and operate for him. He started to search for a facility when another guest at the rooming house looked at a newspaper from the home city where the women came from and learned that these two women had been in prison for drugging a man they were in business with and embezzling his money, and were just released. That exposure ended his relationship with the two women and convinced me it was time to go back home to New York.

I had two nice experiences on the trip home. I planned on taking highway US 1 all the way north to New York. It was a prime road north before Route I-95 was built. Not long after I got going, I picked up a hitchhiker dressed as a collegian with a large duffle bag, so I felt comfortable picking him up. He told me his whole story. He had taken a break from college in Vancouver, Canada, to be a ship hand on a very large yacht sailing in the Caribbean. He saved enough money and was ready to go back to school. I suggested we stop for lunch, and he showed me what he had learned. He pulled four Hershey candy bars out of the small bag he carried and explained that he learned that candy bars were a cheap way of having a nutritious lunch. Since I didn't have much money left, I went along and had two of his candy bars for lunch and learned a lesson I applied the rest of the way home. He left me somewhere near Jacksonville at Route 10, which went west. The next day I picked up a young sailor with a duffle bag. He explained that he was declining to reenlist in the navy after hearing this song, very popular at that time, "Enjoy yourself, its later than you think. Enjoy yourself while you're still in the pink." He was heading to his parents' home in Pennsylvania for his last leave before being discharged. My desire to see the Western United States that I learned about and was exposed to indirectly in elementary school was initially fulfilled with a cross-country trip in 1966. We drove to Dallas, TX, to attend a family wedding, and then we continued west on Route 66 to New Mexico, Arizona, Colorado, and back home via the northern route through Nebraska, Illinois, Indiana, Ohio, and home to Maryland. The highlight to me was the visit to the Grand Canyon, which was most spectacular, and the drive through the Petrified Forest and Painted Desert that I visualized since my elementary-school days. On the other hand, my two kids, ages eight and ten, had no interest in the last two areas and practically slept in the car while I excitedly described what I saw as I was driving. Carlsbad Cavern, Pueblo Indian houses on top of a mountain plateau, an active Indian village, a drive up Pikes Peak, and an exciting drive across Colorado that ended up a mountain in Western Colorado and seeing snow on the ground in July were other highlights.

My sister Frances was my activity leader in my youth. The roles reversed when my wife and I and Frances and spouse Murray Schenker went on summer vacations together for over fifteen years. The vacations consisted of a three-to-five-day sightseeing trip followed by a week's vacation at a large resort in the NY's Catskill Mountain Borsht Belt (hotels and bungalow colonies that initially sprung up in the early 1900s for Jews from the Lower East Side to get away from the hot city in the summer.) Every year I picked a different scenic historic area for us to drive to. The trip to Newport Rhode Island with its historic Touro Synagogue, followed by a stay in Boston and seeing its local area sights and enjoying many nice meals, and then hearing President Nixon resign while driving west to our resort stop was the most memorable trip. Other trips were to Niagara Falls, Montreal, with visits to Expo '67 World's Fair grounds and famous Moishe's Steak House, to Detroit with a visit to the Ford assembly line in Dearborn, and to northern Vermont and New Hampshire, where we saw the Man on the Mountain. I bought some Civil War—period books at a small-town bookstore, including one from the *Battles and Leaders of the Civil War* series, dated 1884 and priced at 50¢. It had an article by General Pope, who was brought in to lead the Union troops at the impending *Second Battle of Bull Run* in Northern Virginia just outside DC. He described how General McCellan, later removed from his command, was more focused on capturing Richmond than defending the capital. His description of President Lincoln's reaction to the war planning-discussions was touching. The generals communicated long distance by telegraph like we communicate by telephone today. We ate at a small family-type restaurant where I acquired a taste for delicious apple-rhubarb pie.

The first Catskill resort we went to, and until it closed about ten years later, was the famous Grossinger's Hotel that gave entertainers like Eddie Fisher their start. Then we went to Browns Country Club, which helped make Jerry Lewis famous; it, too, closed a few years after we started going there. Lastly, we went to the Kutsher's Country Club, famous for the Maurice Stokes Benefit Game, a charity basketball game that initially raised funds for the injured professional basketball player Maurice Stokes and later raised funds for needy former players from the game's earlier days.

The four of us also took two lengthy flight trips in between the driving trips. On the first trip in 1980 we started in San Francisco and drove down the exciting Pacific Coast Highway overlooking the ocean to Los Angeles. We stopped at tourist attractions such as the San Francisco restaurants,

Pismo Beach, Hearst Castle, McClintock's Restaurant, Getty Art Museum, Hollywood and the Universal Studios Hollywood Theme Park, and the Wiesenthal Center. The sightseeing actually started in the Muir National Park just north of San Francisco, where I finally got to see the real giant redwood trees that I longed to see in my youth, and it ended with our first visit to glitzy Las Vegas. That turned out to be an unusual treat for all and set a pattern for my sister Frances that still continues. Caesars Palace treated us to fancy honeymoon suites with raised beds and mirrors on the ceiling and a delightful Barry Manilow show. During the trip before we got to Las Vegas, by 10:00 p.m., my sister Frances couldn't wait to get to bed. That first night in Las Vegas we all went to bed early and left Frances in the casino. She stayed there until 4:00 a.m., playing the slot machines. This Las Vegas gambling experience revitalized the gambling interest that she had as a teenager, playing roller ball poker games in Coney Island to win cigarette prizes that she gave to my father. She started visiting the slot machine places in Atlantic City, where she still continues to go to for some entertainment as a lonely widow.

The other summer trip took in Aspen, Denver, New Orleans, and Atlanta, covering diverse Americana. Aspen, with an Aspen mountain scene shown, was an important stop because our son David, the skier, lived there for two years; and we wanted to see what attracted him there. Based on a recommendation, driving on the way to Aspen from Denver we made a detour to Leadville, Colorado, high up on a mountain, and had an unexpected but delightful treat visiting an exhibit put on by the new museum to be opened there. We hadn't known about Leadville and its claim to fame. They put on little skits that related to the silver mining and gold prospecting and notorious characters that lived there in the previous century and invited exhibit visitors to volunteer to dress in the costumes of that time period and reenact the roles the staff had put on.

We stopped going on summer vacations with my sister and brother-in-law after he developed prostate cancer. My wife and I continued to make an annual summer visit to Kutsher's until 2010, when my wife's physical condition deteriorated. Kutsher's had many special values to us. The last few years we had the nightclub orchestra playing dance music for us alone; after the evening entertainment ended we generally were the only seniors with the energy to remain in the nightclub, and we danced for another half hour to our own dance band and choice of music. After the formal nightclub show the Speedy Garfin trio entertained in the lobby singing delightful humorous songs for an hour. In the mornings after breakfast, Social Director Jack Landsman offered folk and line dancing for the guests, which I enjoyed doing. Generally I was the only male in this dance group. I hadn't done this type of dancing since my single days many years ago. Every summer, Jack always honored me by having me give a ten-minute talk about my Jewish history book during his afternoon current events discussion. After the daily morning dance session, Larry Strickler, Kutsher's athletic director, gave a delightful, invigorating aerobics-type exercise class for half an hour that both my wife and I participated in regularly. We have been exercising to Larry's aerobics CD with the same routines at home for many years. It has helped keep us both in relatively good physical shape. For two Kutsher vacations, former Cantor Hal Jeffrin delighted us with his singing of Yiddish, Israeli, and American popular songs; we have two of his CDs with this variety of songs in our car that we still enjoy listening to.

My wife and I took a most memorable international trip in 1972 to coincide with our son David's stay in Israel. He was on a B'nai B'rith six-week work-travel trip that we gave him as a confirmation gift. He worked two weeks on a Moshav in the Galilee and was toured throughout Israel, visiting most points of interest in that country. Our trip consisted of a twelve-day visit to Israel, followed by three-day visits to Athens, Greece, and to Paris, France. The highlight was our visit to Israel, made more educational and enjoyable by our wonderful guide Abraham; for each site we visited, he gave us the development history and the meaning and importance to the State of Israel and to the Jewish people in general. Praying at the Western Wall in Jerusalem and putting a note with a prayer for the family in a crack in the wall was a very emotional experience; a picture of me praying at the wall is shown below. The visit to the old fortress of Masada was special. We sat among the ruins, hearing the details of how Jewish Zealots held out against the conquering Romans for three years before committing suicide rather than surrender. A picture is shown of our guide standing at what is speculated to be a rabbi's podium in an open synagogue at the top of Masada. One afternoon we stopped at the Dead Sea for a lecture on the historical significance of the Dead Sea and the local area, and my opportunity to casually float on top of the Dead Sea, reading a newspaper with no effort required. Our visit to Yad Vashem was tender, reminding me of my father's family that perished in the Holocaust, and bringing into focus the history of the Holocaust that I was already very familiar with. The visit to Yad Mordechai was enlightening and stirring. It was a piece of Jewish history I was not aware of. Yad Mordechai is a small kibbutz in southern Israel named after <u>Mordechai Anielewicz</u>, the leader of the <u>Warsaw Ghetto Uprising</u>. At the start of the War of Independence the small number of residents of this community almost miraculously held up the Egyptian army that was attacking Tel Aviv, enabling the Israeli army to prepare to stop the Egyptian army advance on the city, which they did accomplish. We also had a sobering tour of the Golan Heights. The battles explained by our guide who was a tank commander in the Golan Heights campaign made the tour particularly interesting.

The lectures that accompanied our visits to Old City Jerusalem, Nazareth, Hebron, the Dome of the Rock, El-Aqsa Mosque, the Church of the Holy Sepulcher in Old Jerusalem, and the town of Bethlehem broadened our knowledge of the area's religious history and of Palestinian Christian and Islamic religious practices. The visit to the Cave of Machpelah, located under a large mosque in Hebron, was an exceptional experience; Israel had full control of the West Bank then, so there was no tension associated with the visit. Seeing the sepulchers representing the tombs of the patriarchs Abraham, Isaac, and Jacob, and of the matriarchs Sara, Rebecah, and Leah was quite stirring, bringing into my imagination's focus the biblical stories we read about them.

The visit to Israel had a personal side. I got to see two distant cousins who were living in Israel. They came to our hotel in Tel Aviv on Saturday, the day after we arrived in Israel. Pepi (shortened from the Yiddish Pepiless) Atlas came with another cousin, Mordechi Ginsburg, and his wife, Sarah. Pepi was a charming woman who personified the spirited, bold-looking, attractive Israeli pioneer. She came to Israel with her husband Yitzchak in the early 1930s as part of the Fifth Aliyah group and helped start Kibbutz Einot in Ramat Gan, near Tel Aviv. She had lost a son in the Sinai battle of 1954 and was later widowed. We kept in touch with her for several years until we learned from one of her children that she died. Moredechi was the other type, a quiet man without the dynamic pioneering spirit, who worked in a Jerusalem supermarket. The following Saturday when I had a rented car, we drove to Afula, a small city located in the northern part of Israel. It was in search of another cousin from Ludmir, who we somehow heard might be living there after surviving the war as a member of the Russian army. The Israeli cousins we met did not know of this possibility. The stores in Afula were closed for the Sabbath, and the few people we met only spoke Rumanian (I was hoping they spoke English or at least Yiddish, which I could manage), so we gave up the fruitless search. Another of the trip's personal reward was the group of Israeli mementos we came home with that still adorn our home thirty-seven years later. One was a replica of the Ten Commandments tablet made of unusual Israeli decorative wood. Another was a hammered copper plate artwork of hands blessing the Sabbath candles, and another was a watercolor of a scene of men praying at the Jerusalem Wall by the well-known Israeli artist David Gilboa. These are illustrated below. We also brought home a set of coasters that are replicas of the famous twelve stained-glass windows in Jerusalem's

Hadassah hospital by artist Marc Chagall, which represent Jacob's blessings to his twelve sons.

I also had a few unusual personal experiences on this visit to Israel. On a free weekend from the tour, I took a solo walk through downtown Jerusalem and wound up on Mount Olives, where I took a camel ride offered by a Palestinian vendor; riding a camel is not comfortable. Later, while driving a rental car through the West Bank up to the Galilee to see our son staying at a Moshav in the Northern Galilee, I saw an elderly Palestinian couple standing on the roadside in the middle of nowhere with their hitchhiking thumbs-up sign. I picked them up with no thought to any danger involved; it just seemed like the right thing to do. I gave them a ride to their destination up the road while struggling to make conversation with their poor English. While my tour group was busy buying tourist souvenir jewelry in Netanya, I drove to a car dealer about thirty minutes away to return my rented car. The tour bus driver offered to take me back, so he followed me with his bus to the car rental return facility. As we left the car dealer to go back to the tour group, he teased me into driving the empty large Israeli Egged bus back to the tour group. I was young and still adventurous (and foolhardy) and accepted his invitation; it was my first and last experience driving a big bus.

The visit to Greece that followed the Israeli visit was somewhat disappointing, especially after having such a wonderful guide in Israel show us the interesting sites. Our Greek guide took us to two antiquity museums, and we were on our own in both museums. The museum display notations were not very informative, so there was little to learn. The visit to the ancient Acropolis in Athens was too quick and also lacked historical explanations. However, the two-hour trip to a small Greek island in the Aegean Sea for a dip in the warm seawater from a tiny beach just below the shear high island rock was a novelty.

The next trip was to Paris, France. Paris had its interesting museums and other historical sites, and the trip to Versailles was rather interesting. However, the guides were not too informative and the Parisians were cold to us as tourists. On the way from the airport to our hotel, we were riding in a car with another couple who were also on our French tour and with our respective guides. One of the other tourists was a French teacher in New York City anxious to use her French, and she asked her tour guide a question in French. His response in English was, "Madame, your French is not very good. Only speak English while you are in France." She was devastated. On the way to Versailles, our bus tour guide only gave this advice in English: "If you don't understand English you are on the wrong bus and please get off." Two German couples on the bus didn't know English and therefore didn't understand his instruction; they went on to Versailles essentially without the benefit of a guide. It turned out the tour guide also spoke German but elected not to ask if anyone on the tour only spoke German; many tourists were German. We went into a photography store to buy film. My wife asked the salesperson in English where there would be a nearby fruit stand. He responded feebly that he didn't understand English. Then when I asked him in English for the film I wanted to buy, he turned to my wife and gave her directions in English to a nearby fruit stand. Another annoying incident occurred on a tour-free night when we independently explored the Paris Montmartre entertainment area. We went there by subway and expected to return the same way. On the return we were surprised that the subway change booth was closed and we didn't have the right change. I went upstairs to a newspaper vendor nearby, and he refused to give us change even when I offered to buy a newspaper, so we wound up sneaking into the subway to get back to our hotel.

When I retired from NASA in May 1985, I left NASA on a Friday and started a new job the next Monday, deferring a retirement celebration. We later found a celebration trip that sounded exciting—a Princess Love Boat cruise over New Year's that went from San Diego to Acapulco. I went to San Diego to accomplish some work for a few days on a task I had been working on previously, went back home, packed my bags at night, and my wife and

I took a plane right back to San Diego the next day to start the cruise; I was young and energetic then. It was our most enjoyable New Year's Eve party. It started at about five in the afternoon and lasted till the early hours of the morning. Princess Lines was generous with a free open bar and the crew participating in the party, a most unusual, nice gesture to the crew. The band performed a musical and played dance music almost nonstop inspired by the show "The Love Boat". There were also musical games and dance contests. Below is a picture of me participating in a pass-the-orange dance contest. No one cared that dinner was a grab-it-when-you-want-to buffet.

We particularly enjoyed two other cruises for the dancing they offered. One was actually called a dance cruise, a Norwegian Line cruise in the Atlantic to nowhere. It featured three well-known bands, with two of the three bands playing every day in separate ballrooms for afternoon and evening dancing. It was one of our most enjoyable cruises; they played our type of dance music, and we met some interesting people, including a couple of single men the ship brought on board to be dance partners to the single women passengers. After that cruise we had enough dancing for a long while. The other cruise was to the southern Caribbean on a small cruise line that catered to both South Americans and North Americans. It also had two dance ballrooms, one band playing dance music for the North Americans and the other playing strictly Latin dance music for the South Americans. After we sampled the ballroom with the Latin dance music, we danced there the rest of the cruise. We blended in so nicely with the South American dancers, especially after we did the *pasodoble* (double step, fast dance) which I hadn't done for over thirty-five years since I learned it back in Ellenville in 1953. A woman watching us dance tried to make conversation and compliment us in Spanish. I tried to tell her in my feeble high school Spanish that I didn't speak Spanish, but she wouldn't accept my answer and kept trying to make conversation almost every night.

In our later years, my wife and I started going on other Princess Line cruises to celebrate our anniversary. We tried to pick cruises that left from Los Angeles to conveniently fit in a visit with our son and grandkids, and my other California relatives. A two-week cruise to the Hawaiian Islands offered the best arrangement—four days just sailing on the ocean, going to and returning from Hawaii, with five days of Hawaiian Island sightseeing. The visit to the USS *Arizona* Memorial Museum (shown on next page) in Pearl Harbor next to the remains of the sunken *Arizona* was very moving and unforgettable; we went there on both of our trips to Hawaii. The first trip had a special, long-lasting value to me. The nutritionist lecturer very thoroughly explained the biological mechanics of how blueberries are effective in preventing the brain cell decay associated with Alzheimer's memory problems. She also provided a less intensive explanation of how the potassium in bananas contributes to better health, including the energy level. She made me a believer; I eat both with my daily breakfast meal. My memory, other than name recall, has held up extremely well. We took two other enjoyable cruises leaving from Los Angeles, one taking in the Mexican Riviera ending in Acapulco and the other going through the Panama Canal. The divers off the high cliff were the Acapulco trip highlight. The Panama Canal trip was mostly of historical interest.

We went on one very interesting Mediterranean sightseeing cruise preceded by a few days' visit to Rome. The ship voyage stopped in Nice, Barcelona, Lisbon, the Azores, and ended in Galveston, Texas. The Rome visit was the highlight—walking through Vatican City including the Sistine Chapel, the ancient Roman ruins including the Coliseum, and walking through Rome's interesting streets and the novelty of throwing coins into the fountain in Rome that was used to film the famous movie *Three Coins in the Fountain*. Our special treat was a personal tour led by a young Jewish guide who we contacted through the local Jewish community website. He took us to the old Jewish quarter (site of the old Rome ghetto) with its impressive large main synagogue. He also described how two hundred Jews were saved in Rome during the Holocaust by being kept for about two years in the large ward room of a Catholic hospital on the island in the Tiber River, which he showed us. The hospital put up a big sign outside the room marked "*Quarantined*", so the Nazi inspectors were reluctant to enter the room. The next stop was to Nice, France, with a tour drive to Cannes, Monaco; I paid my dues at the Grand Casino there. The next ship trip to Barcelona, Spain, was memorable but for the wrong reason. On the way to see the large cathedral that was being built over an unusually long ten-year period, we passed by a woman sitting on the ground with her back to the wall and her hand out with a cup, begging for money. Softhearted me took the wallet out of my pants back pocket and gave her some money and continued on to look at the cathedral. Shortly after, the tour group was marched into a nearby tourist gift shop where a restroom was available. While entering the shop I felt a touch on my backside. I reached into my rear pocket and realized my wallet was gone. I shouted, "My wallet has been stolen," and started to run out the door to see if I could spot the pickpocket. My guide did the same. We spotted two men running away but they got lost.

I went as far as where the beggar woman was seated earlier. She was gone. She apparently fingered me as a good target for her pickpocket cohorts. I went to the policeman at the cathedral to ask where to report the theft. He told me that the police station is where I had to report it, but they only take such reports after 4:00 p.m. (when we are back on the ship). It appears that pickpocketing is one of the better organized and successful businesses in Barcelona. Three other passengers reported equivalent experiences to the ship purser, and their money was lifted from presumably safer places on your body to keep your money. The failure of the tour guide or the cruise ship personnel to alert their clients about this danger was a contributory crime—travelers beware. The visit to Lisbon, Portugal, turned out to be a special treat. While seeing the interesting exhibition of the areas of the world explored by the Middle Ages Portuguese adventurous sailors, I was able to *express my power* by *casting my shadow over the Middle East* as indicated in the illustration with the illusion that I took my own picture.

I also got to see Fairbanks, AK; London and Oxford, Great Britain; Tokyo, Japan; and Munich, Germany in conjunction with my satellite operations manager activity. These trips are described in the related sections that follow.

Yes, after I matured and entered the working world, I escaped from the *web* surrounding the Lower East Side. I got far from New York City, and my interest in seeing the United States was becoming satisfied.

Cultural Exposure in My Senior Years. When I moved to Silver Spring, I was anxious and enthusiastic to be a tour guide for my visiting families, taking them to the museums and interesting governmental buildings in DC and the immediate area. The most profound site was the Lincoln Memorial with a statue of President Lincoln with his eyes looking at you from whatever direction you looked at him and reading the potent Lincoln addresses. The most entertaining site was Washington's home in Mount Vernon. The somber site was the Arlington Cemetery in general and the Kennedy family grave site in particular. It always evoked my story of taking my son David, age seven, down to DC to witness President Kennedy's funeral; it was an event for posterity I wanted him to experience and remember. The fun site for the kids was the Smithsonian Air and Space Museum, with its different space-related movies, while I had a grand time being an unofficial museum guide, explaining about the satellite exhibitions, including a Nimbus model. The chilling site was the Holocaust museum, looking at the Nazi process and tools for killing six million Jews, and reflecting on the Shapiro family victims of the Holocaust.

After retiring for the second time, once from the government and the other from private industry, I took advantage of my free time to make my second round of visiting these national institutions, expanding the visits to cover the close-by national memorial sites. I made these sightseeing ventures generally with my two sisters May and Frances, who shared the same hunger to see national shrines reflecting the country's history, which we learned about in our Lower East Side public schools ages ago.

When we moved to Leisure World, we met several people who told us how much they enjoyed their trips with the Elderhostel educational travel program. We found one trip that was particularly appealing to me for two reasons—the trip's agenda related to the Jewish history book I was writing, and it was given in Los Angeles, which gave us another convenient opportunity to see our family there. The Elderhostel trip, described below, turned out to be most rewarding.

I would not have thought to explore any Confederate museums on my own; I didn't even know of any such museums. However, I had a cousin, Ralph Shapiro, living in Richmond who offered to take me to the Museum of the Confederacy in downtown Richmond, VA, on my next visit to him. I did get to see the museum with my sister May in conjunction with my next visit to see him.

Visits to National Memorial Sites. The first two sites my sisters wanted to see were the Arlington Cemetery and the Lincoln Memorial. On later visits, my two sisters joined my wife and I on two other memorial site trips that were very impressive. A tour guide recording enabled us to take our car through the Gettysburg memorial site at our own slow pace and to hear the historical details regarding each battle site. There was so much to learn about the battle details—the large number of deaths on the Union and Confederate sides, the heroes, and the losers. The physical appearance of the large cemetery was also impressive. The other outstanding trip was the visit to Harpers Ferry followed the next day with a visit to the Antietam National Battlefield, where the largest deaths in a Civil War battle occurred. The combined visit put the Civil War story in context.

Elderhostel Trip. We took a weeklong Elderhostel educational trip in the summer of 2002. The study subjects were Jewish history and biblical themes, appropriately held on the campus of the University of Judaism in Los Angeles. We lived in the dormitory while the school was out for the summer. The agenda included four days of miscellaneous study groups and a visit to the Skirball Cultural Center. I found three presentations particularly meaningful.

A newspaper reporter presented his experience of living in Israel as a background for presenting his view of the conditions to be offered to the Palestinians in the forthcoming peace negotiations to achieve a meaningful peace between the Israelis and Palestinians, and then defined these conditions. He was a young American soldier who helped liberate a concentration camp at the end of World War II after the war ended. He was so impressed by what he learned about the underground Jewish organization Bricha (Hebrew; "flight," "escape"), which smuggled Holocaust-survivor Jews into Palestine while the gates were closed to Jewish immigration to Palestine by the British White Paper rules. He moved to Palestine when he got out of the army. He became an American recruit to Haganah, the Israeli underground army, describing how poorly equipped they were. When he asked for a rifle, his officer told him he will get one from a dead Egyptian soldier. He stayed in Israel for eighteen years, first living in a kibbutz and then as a reporter in Jerusalem. He made a strong case that for lasting peace between the Israelis and the Palestinians, the peace terms have to offer the Palestinians political self-respect and economic self-sufficiency. This message resonated with me when I read about Israeli Prime Minister Netanyahu in 2010, explaining he was taking steps to have the West Bank improve their economy so a peace accord, when it would come, would have a better chance of survival. This message still applies.

Another presenter offered the prospect of Israel and the Arab world being able to live in reasonable harmony based on old historical examples. Under Arab domination of the Mediterranean countries and of the shipping between them, starting in the eighth century, copies of the Babylonian Talmud were distributed to the Diaspora rabbis who were able to communicate back to the Babylonian chief rabbi, a major factor in the spread of Talmudic Judaism. Jews became merchants under Arab rule, later bridging the Arab community on the south side of Europe with the Christian community on the north side. The Golden Age of Jewish life living in Spain under Arab rule and the Moslem world hospitality to Jews after their expulsion from Spain in 1492 were other examples cited.

A Reform rabbi presented his analysis of the Akeda (binding of Isaac) biblical story and its implications. Isaac must have been at least a teenager to be able to carry the altar firewood up the mountain. He couldn't have been very smart if he permitted his father to bind him and put him on the altar. Abraham had already told Isaac there was no lamb for the sacrifice, yet there is no hint of Isaac's resistance in the story. Isaac's mental shallowness is reflected in the lack of any meaningful accomplishments during his lifetime described in the Bible, even being duped by his son Jacob in his dying days. God didn't intend to have Abraham go through with killing Isaac, which would have ended the great Hebrew nation he promised Abraham. Sarah evidently knew what Abraham was considering and never forgave Abraham. The Bible says she died living away from Abraham, and Abraham indicated he was a stranger to the area where she died when he went to mourn her death, so Abraham evidently didn't see her after the Akeda incident. In recent years, when I have been going to Sabbath morning services, I picked up this rabbi's technique of reading between the lines of the Torah when I read the Sabbath Torah portion in English.

The visit to the Skirball Cultural Center located not far from the University of Judaism was educational. Few, if any of the Elderhostel class members, heard of this facility. "Its mission is to explore the connections between four thousand years of Jewish heritage and the vitality of American democratic ideals. It seeks to welcome and inspire people of every ethnic and cultural identity in American life." It had very informative exhibits.

Visit to the Richmond Museum of the Confederacy. My sightseeing sister May hadn't seen our cousin Ralph Shapiro, living in Richmond, VA, for several years; so we made a visit to the Museum of the Confederacy in Richmond, which she had learned about in conjunction with our visit to him. My cousin Ralph Shapiro was a Holocaust survivor from Soviet brutality rather than the German brutality we normally think of. When the Soviet Union took over the eastern part of Poland under their pact with Hitler in 1939, Stalin sent about ten thousand young Jewish men to Soviet slave labor camps in Eastern Siberia because the Russians didn't trust their loyalty to the Soviet Union based on some flimsy political reasoning. My cousin, who was one of them, explained how that happened to him. He was asked by a Russian official if he wanted to be a Polish citizen or a Russian citizen when the war ended. All his life he was a Polish citizen, so he innocently told them he preferred to be a Polish citizen. As a consequence, he spent the next five years in a work camp near Vladivostok on the Pacific Coast. He was down to about ninety pounds when he used his initiative to survive. There was a call for anyone in the camp who was an electrician to help the campmaster's wife fix her house's electrical problem while her husband was away on an extended trip to Moscow near the war's end. He volunteered even though he was not an electrician and barely knew anything about electrical equipment. He satisfied the woman's needs in more ways than one, and he received food from her to rehabilitate himself. At war's end he found his way to his home city, Vladimir Volynsk (a.k.a. Ludmir). A Gentile friend told him that the Ludmir Jews were exterminated en masse and urged him not to stay there. Depressed over the loss of his parents and other family, he found his way to Warsaw, Poland, where a distant relative who was a minor Communist authority told him there was no future for Jews in Poland and advised him to flee Poland. He entered a kibbutz in Poland that was set up before the war by the World Zionist Organization and reactivated for Jewish Holocaust survivors in preparation for moving to Palestine. With the British White Paper again in effect, limiting Jewish immigration to Palestine to a small number, he changed his goal and hoped to go to the United States. He joined many survivors who found their way to a displaced persons camp in France. While there, he put a notice in a New York Jewish paper that helped survivors locate relatives in the United States, asking for Louis Shapiro who had a candy store in Brooklyn to contact him. He had vaguely remembered about his uncle Louis Shapiro who had a candy store in Brooklyn that had mailed boxes of clothing and canned food to his parents before the war when Jewish economic life in Poland deteriorated. I now remember this piece of history too because I helped with those mailings. The problem was my father lived in Manhattan rather than Brooklyn. Fortunately, a Brooklyn friend of my father who read the notice guessed it was a mistake and contacted my father. My father, with the help of his brother Nathan, put a notice in the newspaper to bring Ralph to this country. The two brothers who came together to this country forty years earlier collaborated again, this time to help another Shapiro start a new life in this country. There was a two-year wait for the visa to come through. During that period, Ralph contacted his future wife, Carole, who he had met in the Polish kibbutz were he stayed for a while after fleeing from the Soviet concentration camp, and convinced her to join him. At the start of World War II, Carole and her parents and two brothers had been moved from their home in Poland to a Russian work camp in the cold northern Ural Mountains for two years; and then they were moved again, this time to Bukhara, Uzbekistan, in hot Central Asia. They struggled to survive in that city on their own with little opportunity to work. Undernourished, they all became sick one time or another, with both parents dying from lack of medical attention. She became an orphan there at sixteen. In 1945, she and her brother, who had been living in an orphanage since their parents died, were sent back to Poland. She found her way to a kibbutz that helped desperate, lonely Jews with no home or family in Poland to get to Palestine. Carole had a cousin living there since 1936, and she hoped to join him there. In 1946, while in the kibbutz, my cousin Ralph entered the kibbutz with the same initial goal of getting to Palestine. This common objective helped solidify the friendship that developed. Carole accepted Ralph's invitation to join him in the displaced persons camp in France. During the two-year wait, they got married and had a son, Jack, born before coming to this country and getting established in Richmond, VA, through the help of the Hebrew Immigration Aide Society (HIAS) and his two uncles.

The Museum of the Confederacy had many interesting exhibits about life in Richmond during the Civil War, stories about the Confederate Army major officers I knew something about from school history and stories about the Confederate White House located in Richmond, which was part of the museum. I learned that President Lincoln made a visit to the Confederate White House a couple of days after the war ended in an interest to quickly reunite the country.

Unusual Family Event at Book Completion

The plans I had in place to celebrate my eighty-eighth birthday as the final personal event to be described in this book was replaced by a special, unusual family event. It was the seventy-fifth anniversary of my bar mitzvah on my next birthday, so I arranged for this event to be remembered at my synagogue with an acknowledgement of this during Saturday morning religious services followed by the *kiddish* luncheon that I sponsored. My wife felt healthy enough to try dinner and light dancing that night, to be followed by a birthday dinner out with daughter Debbie and family Sunday night. It all changed with a phone call informing us that my ailing brother-in-law, Manny Pierce, had died the Monday night before that big weekend planned for me, so instead, I had an ironic weekend. We flew down to Dallas, Texas, to attend my brother-in-law's funeral on Friday before my birthday. The funeral service held at Temple Emanuel, where he was a member for many years, was most unusual. In honor of his twenty-five years of singing with the Temple choir, the Temple choir sang several tender religious memorial hymns accompanied by the Temple organ. His daughter, two sons, two grandsons, and sister Tess all gave glowing eulogies extolling his personal virtues, his family values, his personal accomplishments, and his passion about his Judaism. They expressed their indebtedness to him for the values he taught them and for the guidance he gave them. In respect for his military service in World War II as army captain, he had a military burial service complete with honor guard, taps, and flag service.

With my brother-in-law's productive life of ninety-four years, his three children, twelve grandchildren, and eight great grandchildren turned this somber event into pleasant three days of family gathering at his son Greg's house, including a touching *shiva* (memorial) service led by the Temple Rabbi Saturday night. The family gathering was repeated with a luncheon at son Larry's house on Sunday. They converted the sad weekend into pleasant family and friends gatherings, and held a set of birthday parties for me and my darling niece Amy Garber who shares my birthday with songs and birthday cakes—I got a birthday booklet from my great-great-nephew Parker, signed by thirteen different groups of Texas relatives. My wife and I took advantage of this rare opportunity of being together with our Texas relatives and with my wife's sister and brother and their families who also came for the funeral, enjoying their company as usual, and getting to know the Texas little ones.

Chapter 2

Professional Experience

My professional experience described below includes working for General Electric, the General of the Army, and General Motors. I quipped to all my grandkids that their grandfather has the distinction of having worked for the three biggest generals in the country. My *smart* grandson Austin Trupp came back with, "What about General Mills"

This chapter covers my experience, which was a prelude to my work at NASA as the Nimbus spacecraft operations manager and the professional work that followed as a retiree. My spacecraft operations manager professional experience, a major focus of this book, is described in Chapter 3.

General Electric Company Employment

Schenectady, NY. I was pretty excited about starting my job with the General Electric Company in Schenectady, NY, even though it presented a whole set of personal challenges to me. I had lived a pretty sheltered life living at home through college, and there was so much to learn about regarding everyday living—where do I stay, where to eat, who does the laundry, what do I do with my spare time, you name it. I hadn't even taken a train ride out of town before. With no previous similar challenges presented to my older sisters to learn from, my family was of no help other than knowing my father took a bolder move traveling four thousand miles to come to the United States on his own without speaking English or a job—that was a tremendous challenge. So I brought a big trunk, stuffed it with practically all the clothes I owned, said good-bye to my parents that Saturday morning, took the subway to the Grand Central Station on Forty-Second Street, and boarded the NY Central Railroad to Schenectady.

The GE employment office had provided some alternative places to consider staying at, but with a salary of 90¢ per hour the YMCA was an easy choice. This Y worked with GE to accommodate the large staff of GE test engineers with low salaries, so many rooms were equipped with upper and lower bunk beds to lower the individual's room rent. I met my roommate when I checked in, also a new test engineer from Newark, NJ. I offered to take the upper, and he didn't argue with me; it looked like a nice challenge and I thought I could handle it better because I was more agile than he was, being a few years younger and smaller. Besides, I slept on a cot most of my life starting at age seven and never fell out once.

The GE test engineering program was a way of enabling new GE engineers to pick a field within the company for their career by serving as test engineers on a variety of company products produced at different facilities around the country. My first stop was Schenectady, the headquarters and largest facility, where all new test engineers generally started. My assignment was testing large electrical motors for US Navy ships of all sizes. It was not a creative job. We followed testing procedures developed by the design engineers and just needed to check that the step by step test results were within an acceptable range. There was one exciting incident that I still remember. To load down the motor being tested, a similar type motor was connected to it but used as an electric generator to load down the motor. This particular motor to be tested was wired to the terminals opposite to the previous model, but this wasn't caught by the engineer that provided the test wiring instructions. So after the motor was running and the switch to the alternator was closed to load down the motor, sparks flew everywhere. I was in the middle of all this, watching the meters and instruments, and got showered with sparks but wasn't hurt. The stay in Schenectady was not particularly exciting. Having to eat out two meals daily and buying a box lunch, just learning how to expand my narrow food taste from my mother's kosher cooking, was a primary challenge—and to do this on a small salary. The social opportunities in Schenectady were not fulfilling, so for excitement my roommate and I explored the neighboring cities together on several weekends; traveling by bus was inconvenient.

I was there six weeks when I responded to a call for volunteers to go to Lynn, MA, to work on steam turbines; it was a six-day-per-week job, which helped make it attractive. A CCNY classmate who had joined GE also considered accepting the offer. We concluded being there together should be appealing and accepted the offer.

Lynn, MA. The stay in Lynn, MA, started off with quite an experience for me. After riding the old Boston and Maine railroad we checked into a hotel right in the center of downtown Boston. For sailors, Saturday night in the summer in a navy town during the war was a hotbed of sexual activity in the open—an unusual sight to see. My travelling buddy was more mature than me and went into the hotel bar where he met two sisters who convinced him to be a roomer in their house. They were a French Canadian family living near Lynn, and the family supplemented their income by taking in GE workers as borders. My friend may have thought he was getting more than a bed to sleep in, so he accepted the offer and convinced me to join him. We moved in on Sunday; my stay lasted one day. I was not very comfortable sleeping under a big cross with the figure of Jesus Christ on it hanging on the wall over my head; they were a very religious Catholic family with religious artifacts throughout the house. My friend stayed on until he left Lynn.

The company personnel office put me in touch with a Mrs. Clancy, who took in borders for a living. I interviewed with her and liked her arrangements. It was $26 a week for room and board, including two meals and a box lunch six days a week and two meals on Sunday, including laundry—couldn't beat that deal anywhere. She was a sweet old widow with no family who tried to be very accommodating; her borders were her family. She adjusted her cooking style to avoid serving me pork products and seafood, which I didn't eat then. She even taught me that you eat the hole in the donuts. She loved to bake dessert for the borders, including donuts and the donut hole balls. She was a delight to talk to. It was my first Jewish holidays away from home. I didn't work those days and filled in the days talking to her; I learned about her history and she learned about Jewish customs. She is shown with two children belonging to her previous border.

Her life story offered a lesson on how bigoted some people can be. She was from a Dutch Protestant family living near Hyde Park, NY, when at sixteen she was smitten by a local traveling insurance salesman. He was an Irish Catholic ten years her senior. When she decided to marry him, her parents disowned her for marrying a Catholic. Before the turn of the nineteenth century, anti-Catholicism was particularly prevalent in that part of the New York State and elsewhere in the country. She converted to Catholicism and became a regular churchgoer. They had moved to Lynn, MA, and her husband made a comfortable living, owning a home. During the start of the long Depression they helped an unemployed church member's family earn some money by doing their landscaping, gardening, and maintenance and housekeeping chores. Ten years later the situation reversed. Mr. Clancy had died and Mrs. Clancy had to rent the house now owned by the woman she had helped during the Depression; her husband got a defense job to afford buying Mrs. Clancy's house. About two months after I moved in, Mrs. Clancy took in another GE employee as a border. The woman threatened to evict Mrs. Clancy because she took in a Cuban foreigner on top of taking in a Jew for a border. It didn't matter to the woman that the foreigner happened to be Catholic and a professional engineer. In a few weeks, his family came to join him and he moved to his own apartment and the fracas ended.

The work involved testing steam turbines used on naval warships. It was an end-to-end test arrangement. We had to arrange for the specific mechanics, such as a steam fitter, pipe fitter, mechanic, or electrician (tightly unionized by narrow labor category) to do each step of the turbine equipment transmission and load generator assembly, and the installation into the facility steam source. Each setup and test took about two weeks. The work environment was awful, very hot from the steam (if I remember correctly 120-130°F), required wearing head sweatbands and taking salt tablets; drinking lots of water was a necessity. I also worked midnight shift, so I was out of sync with most social activities during the week.

Sunday was my day off and entertainment day. My school buddy who came to Lynn with me didn't like the work and left GE to take on a design job, so I was on my own. I was just breaking out of that Lower East Side *web*, so I went to every place of historical interest a bus would take me within twenty-five miles of Lynn. I explored Revere Beach, the Boston area, Swampscott, and places in-between.

My early visit to Revere Beach offered the first of a few distinctive characteristics of the area. They took liberties with the term "kosher." One food stand on the boardwalk had on its signboard above their counter, "Kosher minced ham sandwich." The Sunday Blue Law was handled loosely too. No drinking at the bar allowed on Sunday, so on Sunday they set up small, low tables and benches in front of the bar, which was allowed because no one was standing at the bar. Politicians' records were also looked at liberally. James Curley, a previous three-term mayor of Boston, with a reputation for corruption, was popular, running for reelection for Congress while he was under federal indictment and already had served in jail for an earlier corruption charge; Boston was a largely "Irish City" and Irishman Curley couldn't lose no matter what he did wrong. He did win the election, was convicted, and did go to jail before being pardoned by President Truman.

There was one family incident that started out disturbing but wound up being pleasant news. As I occasionally did, I called my parents' store phone one Saturday to see how they were. After calling repeatedly with no answer, I worried that one of them was ill, causing them to close the store; there was no precedent in all the years they were in business to close their business if it wasn't a religious holiday. My folks had no home phone, so I got through to one of my sisters who explained that they decided to close the candy store on Saturdays. Although it was their busiest day of the week, they chose to close on Saturday because my mother never liked working on the Sabbath; she was reverting back to her parents' practices. It was also a comforting, healthy move for them. For sixty-year-olds, the seven-day-week work pace was too severe.

After working in Lynne for three months I had to rotate to another location and picked Erie, PA, to transfer to. I was ashamed of my behavior the last night at work. Public transportation from where I lived to the GE plant was not convenient, so I paid one of the GE technicians working my shift to take me to work. He and a buddy also working that shift used to stop at a bar for a drink before picking me up. That night they wanted to say good-bye to me in a warm, personal way, and I was picked up before their bar stop to join them for a drink. They were two Irishmen who liked their boilermakers. I never had a beer with a shot chaser before, and my father didn't break me in to handle this dynamite. They had me drink two while they showered me with compliments. Needless to say, I couldn't handle my task that night.

Erie, PA. The stay in Erie, PA, was disappointing professionally but refreshing socially. The GE Erie factory was noted for its electric locomotives, but the important deliverable during the war was a gun turret for the B25 bomber. After the initial month of testing of various electrical components, they had me work on the gun turret testing. It was fundamentally a test of the gun turret system's servomechanisms. This device converts the gunner's steering device's pointing direction to the target aircraft to a set of signals to the gun turret motors to point the gun turret accurately. The procedure was set up so it didn't require a professional engineer to conduct the testing. Some of the testers working alongside of me were trained female technicians; males were scarce for the workforce during the war. The testing was repetitive; it was essentially a production line. After a month of doing this repetitive work I felt that I should be doing more complex work and asked to speak to the home office personnel administration VP for a transfer. I was warned that if he came to Erie before his normal visit to speak to me, which wasn't scheduled until the summer, my work 2-f deferment would be rescinded. Nevertheless, I asked for the personnel VP to come to Erie so I had an opportunity to speak with him. He came and arranged for me to transfer to Pittsfield, MA, in March, where he assured me I would be working on more complex equipment.

In Erie I boarded with an elderly Jewish family, the Silvers, this time with only breakfast and dinner included, so I was treated to Jewish home cooking again. They had Jewish neighbors and other friends through whom I met a couple of Jewish girls that I dated. The one dating event that stands out was a Christmas Eve night out. It was Sunday night and we expected to find some place downtown to dine and dance at, but all places we knew were closed, so we walked a few blocks to the large Catholic Church to see what a Midnight Mass was like. We were impressed with the intensity of the people's prayers, but we didn't feel like kneeling down as everyone else did at various times in the service. Although a few others in the church also did not kneel, we began to feel it was somewhat disrespectful not to be kneeling, so we left.

I had made good friends with another GE test engineer, Walter Bruening, who was older than me and more mature than me. He took me under his wing and broadened my horizons. His car provided the flexibility to do things away from Erie and not be restricted by bus limitations. The major activity I enjoyed through him was going to the Friday-night dances held by the volunteer firemen in a small town about six miles away from downtown Erie. I danced with everyone who wanted to dance with me. There was one six-foot-tall girl who couldn't find anyone to dance with, so we frequently danced and were the most comical couple on the floor, her head towering over me. A few months of this dancing helped me become a better dancer. Walter occasionally took me to a private social club where I did a little card gambling and he did that and some hard drinking; private clubs seemed to be in every Pennsylvania City. Seeing a priest with his collar off, gambling, was a revelation; I had to be told he was a priest. We drove one weekend to Cleveland to see his alma mater, The Case Institute of Technology. When I first met my wife, who is from Cleveland, and I told her I went to Case Institute, she was impressed; it took her a while to figure out it was just for a couple of days.

Erie provided a memorable winter experience, one I could have done without. One Sunday night I left downtown Erie at about 8:00 p.m. after an afternoon of bowling and the weather was clear. After breakfast I tried to leave the house and couldn't open the front door. The landlady explained that the snow drift on the porch blocked the door, and I should climb out the window to get out to the porch. I then found out why she had asked me when I first moved in if I owned arctics (high rubber boots), which I didn't. Because of the heavy snow, I struggled to walk the five blocks to the bus stop. The snow, still coming down, was already up to my crotch in places where the drift was high. Of course no bus came and I needed to struggle home. Erie had a record snowfall that day, thirty inches in twenty-four hours. There was no bus traffic for three days. Erie had about thirteen feet of snow that winter, more than the eastern snow capital Buffalo, NY, that year, requiring army helicopters to drop food to locked-in small communities.

Pittsfield, MA. The GE VP kept both his words. Two weeks after I moved to Pittsfield to start more interesting work I got my notice to report to the draft board in Springfield, MA. With the war seemingly winding down, they tightened the physical requirements rather than relaxing them. Since my eyesight hadn't improved, I was rejected again.

A primary output of the Pittsfield GE plant was very high-voltage transformers, which is what I started working on. The testing task involved understanding the test article's composition and application to develop the right test process, which made it interesting. Working with very high voltages, e.g., 100,000 volts, was risky and made it more challenging.

About a month later, we were advised that transformer testing was put on hold, and we were to start testing electronic cubicles on an expedited, overtime basis. They were ten-foot trailer box rooms filled with different transformers, instruments, and distribution panels. We were never told what the application was. After the atomic bomb news announcement, we realized it was for the Manhattan Project supporting the atomic bomb development. This work lasted about a month and then we went back to testing high-voltage transformers.

The stay in Pittsfield was very pleasant in a lot of respects, and it gave me some new experiences, a taste of the outdoors, and a romantic experience. There was a large group of test engineers that engaged in group athletic and social activities, such as weekly bowling and softball, and occasional parties. I met a girl whom I liked who I took out every few weeks and to the parties. However, I felt I was in no position to settle down and consider marriage, so I didn't let the relationship heat up.

Large Pontoosic Lake was a short bus ride away, and I spent a lot of free time in the summer at the lake. It was a summer extension of the YMCA in Pittsfield where I had been staying so I had a cabin available when I occasionally stayed overnight at the lake. Pittsfield was in the Berkshire Mountains, so it was generally too cool for swimming. I got friendly with a man who lived at the lake all year-round. When I first met him and asked about the weather, he said, "Pittsfield had two seasons, winter and summer, and if it was cold on July 4th, it only had one season, winter." I learned how to handle a canoe, which was the boat used on that lake, and swam the brief time the water warmed up for swimming. My friend Walter from Erie came to Pittsfield in the summer so I spent time with him. On one trip up to the lake with him he stopped the car on the road, got out, and told me to drive, which I did comfortably—my first driving experience. We drove down to the Tanglewood Music Festival to listen to the Boston Pops Orchestra several times; I did not know about Tanglewood or the Boston Pops when I grew up in New York City.

I stayed at the downtown YMCA, which was very comfortable. I recall being impressed by a group of young business owners and other professionals who spent Wednesday afternoons playing serious volleyball at the Y. Their routine exercise through sports set a good example for me to follow most of my life. My eating was routine in Pittsfield, same restaurant next door to the Y for breakfast and dinner, served by the same friendly waitress, and with "Racing with the Moon" by Vaughn Monroe repeatedly played on the juke-box every day.

There were two special events that occurred while living in Pittsfield. When V-E day was announced, the plant allowed people to take time off to celebrate. I hitched a ride with a guy planning to drive down to New York City to join the Times Square V-E Day party, which was quite a joyous event, and spent the next day with my folks, whom I hadn't seen for almost a year. The other event was painful. I had been hearing pieces of news about the horrible treatment of Jews in the concentration camps. The Pittsfield Synagogue called a special meeting to hear a speaker from one of the mainstream national Jewish organizations who had the latest statistics broken down by concentration camp and presented other details, including some pictures from the camps taken over by the US Army. The information presented was shocking. When I was asked later by the wife of a co-worker I bowled with why I missed that important bowling night and I explained, her comment was something like, "You Jews are something else. You worry about all Jews, not just your relatives"—a very profound remark.

Bridgeport, CT. The work at this plant covered the GE commercial/ household products as opposed to the industrial and military equipment, such as electric motors, fans, and small appliances. The testing process involved testing the devices under different application environments. There was no sophistication to the testing, so it wasn't much of a learning experience. However, it did result in many experiences that got me outside of that Lower East Side *web*.

There were two Americana experiences I was treated to. A co-worker I previously met in Schenectady, Sid Blumenthal, took me to his alma mater, Yale University, in New Haven to attend the famous big football rivalry game at Yale Stadium, the Yale Bulldogs vs. Harvard Crimson. We took the open city trolley used for football games crowded with passengers sitting on rows of benches and standing on the outside floorboard, all shouting loudly the famous Yale cheering songs, Boola Boola, Bulldog Eli Yale, and others. After the exciting game, he showed me around the campus, and then we went to the famous bar outside the campus where the college students do their beer drinking and college-song singing on Friday nights. The other enlightening experience was seeing how Halloween was celebrated in a fun way. Bridgeport had a street parade down the main street with adults and children parading in all sorts of costumes and bands in between the groups of paraders. It seemed to be witnessed by the whole city. It was a dramatic enjoyable change from my youthful Halloween experience.

There was a very violent strike at the General Electric plant in Philadelphia that lasted over two weeks. The unions at the Bridgeport plant went on a sympathy strike so the plant in Bridgeport shut down. The nonunionized workers were asked to work at home, which of course we test engineers couldn't do, so I had a paid vacation. I took advantage of the free time to take my first trip to Washington DC to spend some time with a close friend going back to my youth, Murray (Monis) Handler, who was now working in Washington DC. I boarded a trolley at the railroad station to get to where he lived and was exposed to a nasty Southern racial discrimination practice that we did not have back home; I wasn't prepared for it. I boarded the trolley and made my way to the back where there were lots of empty seats. The trolley operator (or attendant) firmly told me to move up to the front of the trolley because the rear was for blacks only, and I did. During my stay I got to see the major government buildings. The picture shows me and my friend at the Supreme Court building, which we visited. I got my first taste of the Marriott Hot Shoppes restaurant, taking the Sixteenth Street trolley to the end of the line at the Silver Spring city border where it was located.

I almost got to experience a sport that was outside of my Lower East Side sports world, skiing.

I had a co-worker who grew up in Westchester, NY, just above New York City and skied. He had a car and took me along twice to go skiing, once to a ski resort near his home and the other time further north in the Catskills. There was not enough snow on the ground to ski at either place, and that ended my experience as a skier. I did take my son David to ski resorts in Pennsylvania when he was first getting his taste for skiing. He did the skiing—I sat in the chalet. He went on to become a top-notch skier.

I did get the experience of learning how to polka and square dance. There was a dance ballroom located a few miles out of Bridgeport that my local friends took me to. Tuesday night was polka night for the large Polish community in Bridgeport, where they played ethnic Polish polkas. I learned to dance this type of polka, whooping it up as we danced; they were wild and fun dances. I never experienced dancing these polkas in any other location where I danced the polka later on in my life. Thursday night was square dance night, timid in comparison.

In Bridgeport I was involved with the Jewish community more than I was at the previous GE locations. I lived with a Jewish family in East Bridgeport not far from the plant and learned about functions of interest through them. I also had made friends with two brothers I knew from Pittsfield who had just moved to Bridgeport. They had an incentive to get involved in the Jewish community, so we participated together in some Jewish community center social and athletic activities.

Bloomfield, NJ. My next move in the spring of 1946 was to work at the GE Bloomfield, NJ, plant where they made air conditioners. The manufacturing of these products was being resumed after being stopped to take on manufacturing equipment to support the war effort. This was a team effort, about six engineers collaborating to get the parts assembled and tested. The testing was around the clock and for a couple of weeks to feel confident of the quality of the product. A long-term life test of an equivalent unit was conducted, operating the equipment in a thermally controlled, humidity-controlled chamber to simulate the application loads.

The first product tested was a large stand-alone store air conditioner. The first test was a failure; it took excessive power to perform the required cooling. The test results debriefing was a conundrum; all the parts and components were purchased from the original vendors, but the assembly didn't work right. It turned out the coolant liquid (Freon) vendor forgot how to manufacture the Freon properly.

Working in Bloomfield gave me the opportunity to live at home, see my parents and friends, and save some money. The commute took about an hour and a half each way, involving short walks, a cross-town bus ride, a Hudson River subway (tubes) ride, and another bus ride.

Schenectady, NY. I was transferred back to Schenectady for my last test engineering assignment and assigned to work on large electric motors again. The work was essentially a repetition of the testing conducted on my previous assignment and wasn't very stimulating. However, this stay here in Schenectady turned out to be very rewarding for me later on at my work at NASA. I took a six-week course in electronics offered by the community college at night and learned the fundamentals of electronic components and electronic circuit design, which was not taught in my college curriculum for mechanical engineers.

The three-month stay in Schenectady was more interesting socially, interacting with some new co-workers to attend local dances and to explore the surrounding area. A shocking sight was the run-down condition of the shanty-like neighborhood just behind the state capital in Albany. It was much worse than the poorest area on the Lower East Side and resembled the shanty towns I learned about in history and had seen in the movies. Two other trips in the area remained in my mind.

A friend and I decided to go to the Saratoga racetrack to see horse racing for the first time. We went to the highway that was a straight run up to Saratoga Springs to hitch a ride, which was common in that area at that time. A car quickly stopped, and the driver told us to hop in to the backseat. Before we got started, the driver, a fifty-year-old man, took out a pistol and placed it on the seat next to him. He raised some pleasantries to talk about and then started to complain about the mistreatment he had gotten at his job before being laid off and ranted about his former boss. I was so certain he was going to take our money; I carefully took some money out of my wallet and hid it in my pocket to have carfare to get home. I was so wrong. We got to Saratoga, he let us out, we thanked him, he wished us good luck at the track, and said good-bye.

My mother went to Sharon Springs, NY, for a two-week treatment of therapeutic water baths helpful for rheumatism, which Sharon Springs is noted for. I was anxious to see her. At about ten Sunday morning I went to the nearby main road that went directly west to Sharon Springs and started to hitchhike with my thumb up. It didn't take long for a young man in a convertible to stop and give me a ride directly to the outskirts of Sharon Springs. He was on his way to see his girlfriend in Syracuse, further west on that road. After a pleasant visit with my mother, at about five that evening, I went back to the same spot where I was dropped off at in the morning to thumb a ride home. Unbelievably, the same guy in the convertible stopped to give me a ride home. What are the odds for that to happen?

There was another unforgettable experience. A few weeks before I left Schenectady I met a girl at the local social dance whom I took out on a couple of dates. They were just casual, get-to-know-each-other evenings, not terribly romantic. I evidently made too good an impression. When I prepared to leave Schenectady I said good-bye with a clear understanding that we wouldn't be seeing each other again. A couple of weeks after I moved back to New York, she showed up at my father's candy store; from our earlier conversations she figured out where it was located. I took her to her hotel and disappointed her again with another good-bye.

Near the end of the test engineering phase I started to explore opportunities for my next phase of employment with GE as a design engineer. The opportunities offered were not very attractive; neither was living in Schenectady appealing. I responded to a *New York Times* advertisement and accepted a position with the Markwell Manufacturing Company in New York City in 1946.

Markwell Manufacturing Company Employment

The Markwell Manufacturing Company sold stapling machines and other office products. The staplers used a proprietary-shaped staple that they manufactured. The sale of staples was the real moneymaker for the company; owners of their staplers could only use/buy their staples. The goal of the company when they hired me was to expand their line of stapler products, manufacture their stapler product line internally, and expand their staples-production equipment.

I worked for the company for three years and had a very gratifying experience. Management was very helpful, training me in all aspects of the work that was essentially new to me, and the co-workers were very pleasant to work with. They even taught me bridge and chess. My work consisted of new stapler product design and the design of their production-stamping tools and dies, the design of automation equipment to manufacture a line of staples ready for packaging, planning lathe and milling machine operation, and the patent search and patent application processes. The job terminated when the company decided not to go ahead with their plan to establish their own manufacturing facility. The start of a minor recession and an attractive offer from the company fabricating their current product line influenced their decision.

The company was located in a large office building on Hudson and Canal Streets on the west side of downtown Manhattan, NYC, just across town from where my parents lived. It enabled me to live with my parents, which for the first time in my working career enabled me to save some money. I bought my first automobile, a well travelled 1940 Oldsmobile sedan with 100,000 miles from a florist friend of my florist brother-in-law Murray Schenker. I felt comfortable buying this old car from a friend of the family. It served me well for a few years. None of my close friends had a car so it served them well too. During these few years that I worked and lived in NYC we drove to many resorts in New York State, and to cities like Stamford, CN, and Philadelphia, PA, to attend Jewish Community Center socials. I used it to rush my sister Frances to Beth Israel Hospital, with her sitting in the back seat having such severe labor pains that I went through several red lights to get her there quickly. Her son Jeffrey in the womb must have developed an affinity for that car during this drive. When he was 1-2 years old, he just loved to stand on the front seat behind the steering wheel while it was parked on the street outside where he lived. I used the car on my trip to Florida after this job ended and then to Philly for my next job. It was nice not having to rely on public transportation to get around, as was the case when I earlier worked in all those cities for the General Electric Company.

My social life revolved around my old friends. They came back from their army service and started a cellar club with the old name The Henmont Social Club in the large basement of a private house. It had a very large front room that was the social dance area and a smaller back room set up for ping-pong, card playing, or overflow crowd on party night. Open dances were held most Sunday nights for girls to come in and meet the guys. Sunday-night dances became a popular community activity. Couple parties were held for holiday occasions. Two marriages resulted from these relationships in the three years I was involved with this group.

My summer activity involving going to singles resorts with my friends was discussed earlier. While waiting for the next job to start with the Frankford Arsenal in Philadelphia, I did go to a resort by myself to cope with the waiting anxiety. I spent a week at Camp Unity, a low-cost large adult resort located near Wingdale, NY, run by a politically leftist Labor Union. I had gone there with friends previously and found no political environment at the camp. Nevertheless, as we had done previously, I registered under an alias to avoid being tagged as leftist by any government investigators and particularly because I opposed leftist causes and Soviet Union policies. Going there by myself, they placed me in a cabin for four that had a vacancy, and so I spent a week sharing the cabin with three black guys. It was an interesting experience. They chased after white girls at the resort, and the black girls chased after them, ignoring me. The week there was a good distraction from my job hunting anxieties, and the week with my roommates turned out to be very copacetic.

I also took advantage of my free time to go to the famous Roseland Ballroom near Times Square. I was entranced by the dancers gracefully dancing around the long ballroom in a circle. The favorite dance I liked to watch was the Peabody with the long strides mixed with the Manhattan step and the girls doing the swivel step. I had admired my sister Frances doing the Peabody years earlier. It was one dance I never mastered.

New York City had a long tradition of celebrating Armistice Day, now called Veterans Day, with a big parade on Fifth Avenue. I took advantage of being back in New York City to watch this parade annually. A rooftop view and street-level view of the parade is illustrated. The large crowds lining the street to watch the parade can be seen.

Frankford Arsenal Employment

After I returned from my Florida stay, I got serious about finding a job. There were few opportunities advertised in the newspapers, and the

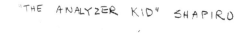

unemployment office offered no leads. In addition, New York City didn't have many industrial companies where my experience would be applicable. A friend of the family, Bill O'Loughlin, who worked for the Federal Trade Commission, advised me that under my circumstances I should consider working for the federal government. I took his advice. I went to the federal government employment center in Hudson Street, NYC, and found an opening with the Fire Control Instrument Group (FCIG) of the Frankford Arsenal Research Laboratory in Philadelphia, PA, that I applied for. It took about six weeks for the appointment to come through, and I started the new job in August 1950.

Frankford Arsenal was an element of the Army Ordnance Department run by an army general that manufactured military equipment. The FCIG component conducted research and development over all aspects of fire control for military weapons. It involved instrument systems as complicated as antiaircraft weapon automatic-fire control systems and as simple as a new material jewel bearings used in military watches and required testing the devices for satisfactory operations in all operational environments. This involved testing in cold chambers down to -65°F to cover polar area operations. A co-worker, Sid Trachtenberg, characterized me in various working and social situations. A sample caricature shows me working on a fire control plotting device; I have twenty-two different caricatures he drew of me. A sketch is also at the beginning of the book. I was involved in working on a wide variety of components, devices, and systems. In addition to the technical experience, I surprisingly found myself being the research report writer for the teams I worked with and also for some other team efforts. This was a surprise to me. I never considered myself a good writer at school and had little writing responsibilities on my previous jobs. This writing skill, which got enhanced with all the writing that I performed there, probably was the most valuable experience I obtained at Frankford Arsenal. I, of course, I didn't foresee that then.

I got my first taste of flying with a trip to the Army at Fort Sill, OK, to demonstrate the fire control plotter system I developed; the trip had some trying moments. It was a flight from Philly to Washington National Airport, a plane change to Oklahoma City, and then a plane to Lawton, OK. Looking out the window I saw the plane come in so low over the Bolling Air Force Base runway I thought it was the ready to land. When I saw the Potomac River under the plane, I was sure it overshot the runway; I didn't know about Bolling Airport then. The ride home was equally scary. There was a severe storm brewing, so they wanted to get the small plane going to

Oklahoma City off the ground quickly before the storm hit. They had me running to the entrance ladder at the rear of the small plane. No sooner did they close the ladder/door than the plane took off. I hadn't even gotten a chance to get to my seat. I was told to rush to sit in the first available seat. The wind was so strong it seemed like the plane took off vertically, blown by the wind.

I rented a room on Warnock Street in the North Philly Broad and Olney area. My landlady, Yetta Greenberg, operated a one-person beauty shop in her house. She had two sweet young daughters, Carole and Roberta, ages nine and eleven, when I moved in. As I got to know and interact with them, I felt like an older brother. I fixed up Yetta with a very good bachelor friend of mine in NY who was her age. They saw each other a few times in NY and Philly, liked each other, but broke it off for practical reasons. She wouldn't move to NY and he wasn't in position to move to Philly. Yetta is shown with Sid on the left, one of my Philly friends. He grew up as an orphan with no family ties and was pretty much a loner until we became friends. He helped me improve my tennis and bridge games, and I helped him improve his social activities.

I became good friends with several married co-workers at the lab, the dearest was Leo Weinreb and his wife, Adelle. They lived in the other part of town, South Philly, but it wasn't an obstacle in my being at their house frequently. Adelle's parents were former chicken farmers living in Freehold, NJ. I visited them one weekend with Leo and Adelle and learned how the Jewish Agricultural Society helped Jewish immigrants take up chicken farming in that area of New Jersey in the early 1900s. Adelle and her sister suffered from Myasthenia Gravis. Adelle was able to bear a healthy son before she died at a relatively young age; her sister died at a very young age. I kept up a friendship with them and last met Leo again when he later worked for RCA in Hightstown, NJ.

Another friend and very interesting co-worker was the lab chief scientist who was the lab electronics specialist. He led the lab effort to convert the antiaircraft fire control systems from mechanical integrators to electronic systems, working with the AT&T Bell Labs in Edison, NJ, that was developing applicable new electronic components and devices. I didn't work in this area, but he took the time to give me some basic lessons on the new devices, expanding my limited knowledge of electronics, which turned out to be very helpful when I started my spacecraft operations manager career at NASA. He was steeped in Judaic religious practices and biblical history from his early Yeshiva education, but as he grew intellectually, his outlook on Judaic practices changed dramatically to frowning on formal religious practices and taking a modern philosophical view of biblical history. Knowing my interest in this subject, he liked to give me lectures on his outlook. In spite of his distaste of Judaic religious practices, he annually held a large Passover Seder to which he invited many Gentiles for stimulating discussions on the messages of freedom he felt the Passover story told and then expanded it to cover current international issues. I went to two of these most unusual Seders.

I had played so many different sports in my youth. Nevertheless, I learned two more sports working at Frankford Arsenal. The lab had a soft-pitch hardball interdivision baseball league, and I played third base on the lab team. I had the distinction of hitting into a triple play with a base hit. Yes, it happened. With the bases loaded, I hit the ball over second base for a base hit. The man on third scored and the man on second got tagged out trying to score. The man on first tried to go to third base on the throw to home, changed his mind, and went back toward second base while I was trying to get to second base. The second basemen managed to tag us both out while we hesitated in this base-running confusion; both of us couldn't be on second base and neither one got there. My friend Sid portrayed my talent in the following caricature. The other sport I learned to play was golf, which I barely mastered. I did get to play golf intermittently during my later working career. I took it up again seven years ago when my grandson Austin at twelve wanted to get a taste for this sport. I played with him occasionally every year since then, and just recently as I finished this book. Even after a year gap, with his natural sports ability he had no problem driving the ball two hundred fifty yards. I struggled to exceed one hundred yards.

I occasionally attended social events held at the large downtown Sephardic synagogue. However, my memorable synagogue event was hearing author Robert St. John on a Saturday night in 1951 at the large synagogue on Roosevelt Circle pitching Israeli bonds for the very first

Israeli bond drive. At that time he was a newspaper foreign correspondent who had lived in Palestine and watched Israel become independent and grow after it became a nation. His vivid descriptions of how desert areas were turned into green pastures, how swamps were drained, and how Israel

met the challenge of absorbing new immigrants who couldn't speak Hebrew or even the second language English and with few applicable skills was stirring, especially coming from a Gentile. Nobody in the audience could resist buying bonds; I bought my first State of Israel bond that night, which I repeated over the years.

There was another experience in Philadelphia that was very important from my family standpoint. After I left home to work in Philly, my parents decided to retire and close their candy store after working hard in the business for almost forty years. After a while my mother started getting gloomy. Within about six months, it turned into depression. It was a new experience; the family didn't know what to do. Out of desperation

I contacted a professor of psychiatry at Temple University for advice. He asked me to describe her family background and her behavioral pattern. He had a clear answer. Jewish and Italian women with her background who helped directly in the family's small business and were involved in its finances, counting the daily business proceeds like she did when my father came home at night, were very prone to suffer depression, which he emphatically said she had, even without seeing her. He advised a set of three brain electric shock treatments, which he indicated had been very successful in treating patients with her background and with hercondition. When I got home the following weekend I discussed what I had learned with my sister Franceswho was essentially my mother's caretaker. She told me that my mother, while listening to her favorite radio station, WEVD, the Yiddish news and social hour with Seymour Rexite who sang popular American songs in Yiddish, heard a Doctor Gordon invite listeners who had mental anxieties to see him. It struck a chord with my mother. She had my sister make a quick appointment. After her examination, the doctor proposed to give her a set of three shock treatments. It sounded ominous to my sister; she had no knowledge of anyone undergoing such treatments. When I told her what I learned from the Temple University doctor, she was comforted and agreed to go along with the doctor's proposed treatment. My mother underwent three shock treatments and was cured. She had no further mental problems for the last ten years of her life.

After working at the lab for almost three years, I started to question the wisdom of staying at Frankford Arsenal. The recent lab work didn't point to meaningful future development challenges, and I questioned the longevity of the facility. Being single gave me more flexibility about a career move. I responded to some *New York Times* job openings and found one with the Channel Master Corporation in Ellenville, NY, that I liked. I took an interview over the weekend and was offered the position. I gave my supervisor, Irving Katz, two weeks' notice on Monday. He didn't ask about my new opportunity or wish me well. I later learned he was angling for a higher-level supervisory position and evidently felt my departure as his key staff member and report writer would hurt his advancement opportunity. About three years later I learned from my friend Leo Weinreb at the lab that Frankford Arsenal was indeed closing.

Channel Masters Employment

Channel Master Inc. was located in the town of Ellenville, Ulster County, NY, in the foothills of the Catskill Mountains of New York. It was started in 1949 by three Resnick brothers, Joseph, Harry, and Louis. Joe Resnick had an arm disability and served as a freight ship radio operator during World War II. Using this communication knowledge, he got involved in the early days of TV that blossomed after the war ended. He was a partner with fifty others in a company that fabricated and sold the simple roof/window antennas that were suitable for New York City TV reception. That size partnership was terribly unwieldy, so he decided to open his own television antenna manufacturing company joined by his two older brothers and named the company Channel Master. They started the business in their father's old empty barn in Ellenville. Their father owned the barn and farmland property from his days as a Jewish farmer. The notion that Jews should become farmers was promoted and supported by the Jewish Agricultural Society at the turn of the century. Channel Master grew quickly from the initial simple drill press operation, and they needed more capital to build the advanced manufacturing and office facilities. The local banks didn't have the right vision. They wouldn't give them the $25,000 loan requested. The company was sold in 1967 to the Avnet Corporation for many, many millions of dollars of Avnet stock. Joseph Resnick had dropped out of the business a couple of years after it was started and later served as a member of the House of Representatives representing Ulster County; he unfortunately died at an early age. Harry was the president and chief operating officer. Lou served quietly as employee relations manager. In much later years, Harry and Lou applied their accumulated wealth to health, education, and other philanthropic causes in the town of Ellenville and in the Ulster County area.

In 1953 Ellenville was a small town with a population of about two thousand in the winter that swelled to about four thousand in the summer from New York City summer vacationers. The only other industry in town was the small General Sportwear Co., Inc., a clothing factory known by the founder's name, the Rosenstock factory. This small-town isolation from a larger community didn't concern me; I felt the access to the nearby resort hotels and the short two-plus-hour drive to New York City would offer sufficient social opportunities.

By the time I started working there in 1953 the company had expanded considerably. The design of the newer, more complicated, larger television antennas used around the country in homes further away from the television signal source incorporated a lot of aluminum tubing so that most of the cost of the large antenna was the aluminum material cost. The company wisely went into the aluminum-tubing manufacturing business, starting from the raw aluminum ingot to the finished tubing. The company initially expanded into lawn recreational equipment and then into imported radio and other consumer electronic equipment.

The mechanical engineering department staff when I joined the company is shown in the picture that follows; there was also an equivalent electrical engineering/design department not shown. Notice all the drawing boards; all mechanical designing was done manually in that time frame. Al Carthey, the chief engineer, is to the left of center with me next to him on the left. The assistant chief engineer, Dick Heller, is to the right of center, with Joe Pluchino on his right. The man at the upper drawing board table on the right is Luiz—a Cuban American who had me, as a bachelor, attend some Tuesday-night socials the local Cuban American community held where I learned to improve my Latin dancing, including the tango and samba, and learned to dance the fast pasodoble.

I initially worked under Al Carthey, designing new antenna products and devices to test their electrical performance. The challenge was to design the progressively larger antennas in a way that they could be fabricated and assembled economically and folded easily for compact shipment packaging and for later reopening for installation. Joe Pluchino went on to become the tool room chief, responsible for all the production equipment design and fabrication. I then worked for him for the majority of my time with Channel Master, doing manufacturing equipment design. Under his tutelage I learned to design progressive stamping tools and dies, plastic injection molding dies, assembly handling fixtures, extrusion press dies, and much more production equipment. This design work required paying meticulous attention to parts dimensioning precision so that the die-machined parts would fit together properly and had proper draft angles required for removing the injection molding part from the die. This experience of learning to apply careful attention to details and accuracy carried over beneficially to my later spacecraft operations manager activities with NASA. I also handled the equipment installation and the tool design for the company's new rivet—and screw-making machine production lines;

this internal company hardware production was another approach to reducing antenna material costs, making Channel Master antenna products more price competitive. When the company president came over to see the first rivet machine operate and heard the machine rhythm beating out rivet after rivet, he kiddingly said in rhythm to the machine beat, "A penny for Harry Resnick, a penny for the employees, a penny for Harry Resnick, a penny for the employees." My proudest accomplishment was the design of the factory-long, automatic-welding, aluminum-tubing manufacturing machine that converted a large roll of aluminum sheet into two-inch-diameter tubing cut to eight to ten foot lengths. It involved designing an overhead *flying sheet-feed system*, incorporating into the basic machine design a roller straightening-bending system to shape the flat sheet into the round tubing, integrating a commercial automatic tube-welding system, designing a press to cut the tubing to the correct length and the design of the automatic tubing handling fixture.

The company recruited engineering and office professional talent who wanted to work on new product design and who also wanted to enjoy working for a small company in a country atmosphere. Both of

these objectives were essentially satisfied. In the summer, Chief Engineer Al Carthey made his home pool available to the engineering and office staff during an extended lunch hour. In the winter several of us would go ice-skating on a local pond that generally froze over for most of the winter. Everyone could conveniently go home for lunch if they wanted to.

My second boss, Joe Pluchino, had lived in the congested Bronx, NY, all his life. After joining Channel Master, to enjoy county living, he bought a house in the small town of Pine Bush, ten miles away from the Channel Master factory, that came with a barn that he converted to a stable and bought a couple of horses. I joined him to go horseback riding many times, including adventurous bareback riding. Before I got married, he and his wife, Rose, had me over for her great Italian dinners loaded with spaghetti, first as an appetizer and then as a dinner vegetable. I could never understand how most Italians I knew, including the Pluchinos, could eat all that pasta and stay slim.

The company was run by fun lovers. In the summer, on Friday afternoons, the large office and professional staff could enjoy a company outdoor appetizer buffet or join the craps or blackjack games held on the front lawn. Clambakes were held frequently all year-round, and parties were held at the nearby Nevele Hotel to celebrate every big sales win the company had.

My first year in Ellenville was nice but not particularly exciting. I did have many very friendly, hospitable co-workers who rotated having me over for dinner periodically. There was no Jewish singles social activity for me, so for entertainment I rotated between going to the Jewish Community Center in Poughkeepsie, which was about an hour's drive away, going to the Grossingers Country Club a half hour away on a weekend evening, and driving to New York City for the weekend to join my old neighborhood friends. After sampling a couple of rooming houses in Ellenville, I was fortunate to find a small furnished apartment with a kitchen that provided many benefits. I made my own meals as a change from previously constantly eating out in the two small restaurants in town, Sam's Restaurant and the Hebrew-National Delicatessen. I then became the host, inviting two new Channel Master engineering employees, Martin Schwartz and Al Balin, to join me for dinner at my apartment almost every evening until their families came to live in Ellenville several months later. They made interesting dinner companions and expanded my Lower East Side-constrained cultural horizon by breaking me in to enjoying delicate wines with dinner. Being able to have my father come stay with me was a big treat, as was my sister May's later visit.

The only problems I had that first year in Ellenville related to car driving. I knew that Ellenville was located in snow country, so I bought snow tires for my car even before I moved there. I felt comfortable driving with these tires going up and down the snowy treacherous Wurtsboro Mountain on Route 17 on my way to New York City for Thanksgiving Day with my parents, watching other cars slide on the snow. I safely got down the mountain into the flat road area near Tuxedo, and the unexpected happened. A large trailer truck jackknifed, spun across the road, and blocked the road in both directions. Other accidents quickly happened, and we couldn't make U-turns to take another road to New York. I was stuck there overnight sitting and sleeping in my car until noon the next day; it was in the park area with no local houses for telephone access and no restroom facilities. Not having heard from me well past my expected arrival time, my parents were frantic. My sister knew enough to call Al Carthey at home, and he was able to reassure them that I wasn't in serious trouble or I would have called or they would have heard from the police. The next day the locals were thoughtful and kind enough to offer the stranded drivers coffee and a sweet until the road got cleared by noon.

The other car problems ended up having serious consequences. I got a wedding gift in the mail from the Motor Vehicle Bureau when I came home from my honeymoon. It was a ninety-day suspension of my driver's license for three traffic violations, and my new wife hadn't yet learned to drive a car. As a result, we did a lot of walking to town. Since Ellenville or the surrounding towns had no furniture stores to accomplish furniture shopping for our new dwelling, we trekked to the midtown New York City furniture stores by bus and then by subway to stay at my mother's apartment downtown on the Lower East Side. On our first trip that way I treated my wife to a 10c New York City egg-cream soda after we came out of the subway; I was a big sport. She still frequently reminds me of that experience. That drink was new to her; she only knew of chocolate phosphates in Cleveland.

I got my first of the three speeding tickets on a Sunday night returning from New York City to Ellenville. I was crawling behind a slow trailer truck going through the long well-known 25-mph speed zone trap on Route 17 in Chester, NY. I found a chance to just go around the truck very quickly and then got back down within the speed limit. After driving a few miles and getting out of the speed zone, a police car stopped me to give me a speeding ticket. I told the officer I was driving within the speed limit and asked why the ticket. He politely explained that three miles back I went too fast when passing the truck. When I later went to pay my fine to the undertaker in Chester, who was also the traffic court judge, I explained the circumstances behind getting the ticket. He said it probably made up for the times when I deserved one and didn't get one and nicely assured me it wouldn't go on my driving record.

I got my next violation also on a Sunday night when driving back to Ellenville with two passengers. One was an older guy who worked in the Kerhonkson Penal Institution who knew most local state troopers. Since he appeared to be sleeping I decided to take him home first so he wouldn't be disturbed by my dropping off the other passenger who lived in Ellenville, He lived in Kerhonkson, which was ten miles past Ellenville. It was a quiet Sunday night with no one else on the road besides me. After I passed through the Ellenville Center and going up the slight hill out of town, I started to speed above the 35 mph a short distance just before the end speed-zone sign. A state trooper caught up with me and gave me a ticket for doing 45 mph. When the trooper left, my *sleeping* passenger popped up with, "I know that guy. I should have said something." I could have kicked him.

The third violation also came on a Sunday night in the small town of Loch Sheldrake on the way home from an evening at the Grossingers Country Club; Channel Master employees had entrance privileges to Grossingers. I was approaching the speed zone that I was very aware of, having driven that road many times, and there was a car behind me with the bright lights on, distracting me. I didn't go into the 35 mph zone very far when I slowed down and waved the car tailgating me to pass me by. As he passed me by, he waved back at me to move over. He was a state trooper who gave me a speeding ticket. I wanted to protest but got advice from a lawyer friend who spoke to the Ellenville chief of police, who spoke to the judge in nearby South Fallsburg involved with handling the violation. The judge's advice was, "No need to protest or come in. Just mail in the traffic fine payment. Don't worry. It won't go on your driving record." Well, all three tickets went on my driving record. With no driving schools in town and me unable to drive, we depended on three of my friends to give my wife her driving lessons. With different teaching styles, it was somewhat confusing to her. Nevertheless, she passed the first time she took the driving test.

The car-related annoyances didn't end there. I called my Lower East Side politician connection to see if he had an MVA connection that could expedite the suspension removal. I called his contact, an MVA manager in Albany, and made an appointment to see him. I nearly froze in the ice-cold morning waiting for the bus to Albany. I met the MVA official and explained what happened. He simply responded there was nothing he could do and I had to wait until the ninety-day suspension expired. I called my New York contact to find out why he sent me on the fruitless trip. He berated me for not paying the MVA official $200 under the table. He said, "Everyone knows that it is how it is done"—that is, everyone except me.

I enjoyed living the next five years in Ellenville as a family man. We moved from my bachelor apartment to a new five-room bungalow with a basement garage at 4 Phyllis Drive. It was in a group of ten homes built on a hill across the road outside the Channel Master factory by the retired Ellenville Lumber Company owner who wanted to help Ellenville grow by supporting Channel Master's new professional employee housing needs; rent was a low $60 per month. I tried painting our unfinished apartment, but when there was more paint on my face than was on the ceiling I was trying to roller paint, I gave up house painting forever. We didn't listen to our marriage rabbi's advice; my wife quickly got a secretarial job with the Ellenville Hardware Company, which kept her comfortably busy during the day while I was working. Furnishing the house through trips to New York by bus was the only somewhat unpleasant aspect of our young married life in Ellenville. My closest friends, Jerry and Fran Schwartz, Marty and Edith Schwartz, and Al and Rhoda Ballin, helped my wife Ecille get settled and integrated into Ellenville life. We had our two children relatively fast, David in one year and Debbie two years later, and she was busy being a mother. The David and Debbie toddler picture is shown below.

Living in Ellenville which was only a couple of hours' drive from New York City enabled us to enjoy our families frequently. My sister Frances and family came to a bungalow colony in the area every summer for many years prior to my moving to Ellenville and had more reason to do so with me living there. The picture below shows a view of a bungalow colony lawn and a typical summer family attendance of Frances and boys, nieces, my son, David, in his mother's arms in the center, and my mother in the back. My wife's sister, Tessie, her husband, Morry, and two kids, Cheryl and Gary, occasionally visited us from their home on Long Island, an hour outside of NYC. We also went to see them in the summer at the veterans' lake, pool, and recreational facility in Ossining, NY. It was established and operated by the 52 Association, a group of restaurant and nightclub businessmen from NYC's Fifty-second Street area to honor and support disabled World War II veterans. They wanted disabled veterans to be able to swim with their families without being self-conscious about their incapacitated physical condition in public. The association bought part of

the large five-and-dime Kress estate outside of Ossining to create this facility and invited veteran families to enjoy weekends at the facility as their guests. It was heartwarming to see double amputees swimming in the lake and crawling up the float on the lake by themselves and looking so happy. The first year we visited there, my brother-in-law had been fitted with his first waterproof artificial leg, which enabled him to swim normally again. My brother-in law sang with his brother's choir at the Nevele Hotel for the Rosh Hashanah Jewish religious holiday; that gave us additional opportunities to see them. My wife's parents and older brother and sister-in-law came to visit us for the Fourth of July weekend. We certainly enjoyed the visit, but it came with an embarrassment for my wife. After having told them many times she couldn't stand a man having a beard or a mustache, they met me sporting a mustache and a goatee. Ellenville was celebrating its centennial as an incorporated village and required its resident males to have a beard and mustache for one month, which I dutifully did wear to my wife's chagrin.

Our first family jolt came just before my son's bris (the circumcision required by Jewish males eight days after birth in accordance with the biblical covenant between God and Abraham). My mother-in-law called to tell us that Ecille's father suffered a massive stroke and they couldn't make it. She actually called me and I had to tell my wife who was still recovering from the childbirth. Otherwise, everything came off as planned. We got the courage to take the normally eleven-hour trip to Cleveland to see her ailing father when our infant was five weeks old; it took two hours to drive the first twenty miles on the icy roads, so it took thirteen hours to get there that day. For the next few years we spent most major Jewish holidays in Cleveland with my wife's family. My father-in law slowly, but never fully, recovered from his stroke. He walked with a hobble, and his memory and speech were poor.

A year later, we learned how important it is to have the right doctor treat your ailment. My father had been suffering from a slow-growing bladder cancer for several years. His surgeon was an old professor of urology at NYU for many years but not up to most recent urinary surgical techniques developed. After his last surgery, the doctor said there was nothing more he could do for my father. The cancer spread to the kidneys and elsewhere. I was disturbed about this prognosis and called the Sloan Kettering Memorial Hospital in New York City, seeking a doctor who might provide my father some help. I randomly chose a Dr. Prout from the list of doctors they gave me. He turned out to be wonderful. After he examined my father, he said my father was too far gone to be saved, and his deteriorated heart could not take the complicated surgery that could have been possible ten years prior when he was younger and stronger. He did offer to perform surgery that would make the last year of my father's life more comfortable by bypassing the bladder with a catheter and urine collection bag. He also offered to fix my father's hernia, which had required him to wear the uncomfortable truss for many years. He even told my sister to think about spending all that money the surgery would cost, knowing in advance his life could not be saved; he sensed the family had modest means. He performed the surgery, and my father thought he was in heaven not having to wear that uncomfortable truss any more, and urination was no longer was painful.

Our Ellenville family physician/obstetrician, Dr. Feinberg, predicted our second child was going to be another boy, to my wife's disappointment; she so much also wanted to raise a dainty girl. When she got to the hospital she was told the baby's arrival would not be for a while, so they sent me home and told the doctor he could continue his house calls—they did house calls in Ellenville. The baby started to arrive sooner than anticipated and the doctor rushed fast to the hospital. He came into the delivery room in his shorts, too late to help with the delivery. My wife didn't care. She was so elated, it was an unexpected girl! Ten days later we got our second family jolt—my father passed away. After rushing to New York City to see him just as he passed away, I rushed back to Ellenville and arranged for the babysitter who had just taken care of my son while my wife was in the hospital having our daughter to watch my two kids for a week. The next day, my wife and I drove back to New York City for the funeral and stayed there for the seven-day mourning period.

Channel Master had been generous with essentially yearly raises, but in the fall of 1959 the president, Harry Resnick, informed the staff that he was not in position to give any raises that year irrespective of the quality of work performed. I saw that as a bad sign for the future with the company and started looking for a new job by advertising for job opportunities in the *New York Times*. After taking several interviews, I was offered and accepted a position in Hudson, NY, with a firm that manufactured rubber mats and carpets for car trunks. I gave Channel Master three weeks notice. The company had production lines similar to some extent to what I worked on at Channel Master, so I felt comfortable with the technical aspects of the position. I went back for a trial visit and took my wife along. I found the personnel I was to supervise and work with very cold; they evidently didn't like the idea of working for a newcomer, expecting someone within the company to replace the owner's son's management position that I was taking over. The owner's wife showed my wife around town; it depressed my wife. The horse-hitching post in the center of town did it. It seemed like we were leaving a small town to go to a *smaller* town. Because we both became concerned about the move to Hudson, I decided to look further for a new job and went back to the responses to my position-wanted advertisement in the *New York Times*. I called US Industries Inc., which was offering a mechanical design position in Silver Spring, MD, that previously I hadn't responded to because I was reluctant to work in the south. I took an interview the next Monday, accepted the position on the spot, and started to work for US Industries the following Monday. So for one week, I had three jobs.

I later learned that the Channel Master professional work environment continued to deteriorate for the professionals; several of my co-worker friends left over the next few years. The Resnick owners sold the aluminum fabrication part of Channel Master to a European aluminum company and sold the antenna and electronics business to the Avnet Corporation, requiring the remaining professional staff to move to South Carolina. More of my co-workers left within two years after their move there. Looking back at this history later, it made me feel all the more satisfied with my bold move to leave Channel Master when I did.

US Industries Employment

The Robodyne division of US Industries Inc., a large conglomerate, hired me. This division was established to design robotic equipment for more efficient parts handling in manufacturing processes. They also envisioned it to being applicable for mail handling.

I interviewed on a warm Monday morning in February 1960. The temperature was about 70°, but with the nervousness over the interviews that were held at different locations, it felt like 80°. I thought I was moving to a hot Southern climate. They hired me with generous terms—an increase in salary, payment of moving expenses, putting our household belongings in storage, and putting the family up in a motel until we found a suitable place to live in.

The moving process was an annoying experience. The mover told us to get out of the house on Friday so he could load our furniture; we stayed at a local motel that night, came back to the house the next morning before leaving town, and found the mover had gone to the local bar the previous night, got somewhat drunk, and never started loading our furniture that night. He slept in our bed and we had to sleep in a motel. His story was that he couldn't recruit moving help that night. When we eventually got our furniture out of storage two months later, we found that the mover left all the food in the warm refrigerator to rot and smell.

I finally got a break with respect to driving violations. I was driving down to Silver Spring on a main highway at a modest speed with my three-year-old son sitting on my lap, *helping me to drive*, when I was stopped by a state trooper. This time I probably deserved a ticket but I only received a warning.

My wife was thrilled driving into Silver Spring with tree-lined streets, nice homes along the road, and a large city-type shopping center in downtown Silver Spring. Dinner at a Chinese restaurant that Sunday night made her feel comfortable. We were put up in a nearby motel with a mini kitchen; the two infants played happily with each other in the room all day. Under these conditions, my wife didn't find it too hard staying at the motel for the next two months.

The Robodyne business objective was to develop a line of robotic systems to be used in the assembly of different small mechanical devices through the robot's movement programming capability. Management also envisioned a robotic application for the US Postal Service mail-sorting process and had some exploratory understanding with the Postal Service. The basic design consisted of a swiveling extendable twenty-four—to thirty-six-inch arm with a movable hand and articulating gripping devices at the end. Considerable progress had been made with the robot arm design before I started working. I worked on the internal mechanisms and the assembly stands to demonstrate the use of the robotic arms. There were even plans in place to build the product line manufacturing plant in an industrial park just outside of White Oak, MD, a suburb of Silver Spring.

Deciding whether to rent or to buy a house was the dilemma. I got a lot of advice from my new co-workers encouraging me to buy a house. The typical $130-150 a month rental rate in the Silver Spring area compared to the $70 a month I was paying in Ellenville when I left helped persuade me to buy. I found a new house for $25,000 in a new housing community located in the White Oak area not far from the planned factory location—a perfect location from that standpoint. Our ability to get the size mortgage and second mortgage needed to finance our purchase encouraged us. After we visited our potential neighbors, who were raising families with kids our own kids' ages, we got enthusiastic and proceeded to buy the house. My family thought it was a dream house; none of my three sisters owned a home or a car. The house came with a large backyard, where I soon learned to grow a vegetable garden, two more steps outside of that Lower East Side restrictive web. A picture of my house and a king-size six-inch tomato I grew is shown below.

I went to work that Monday after closing the purchase of the house, eager to tell everyone about my decision to buy a house. Instead of the congratulations I anticipated, I got a disturbing response from my immediate supervisor. He said, "Why did you do that. Jobs around here are not very stable." He was prophetic. About four months later the company ended the Robodyne operation. The robotic design was successful, but the technology application was premature, and there was little business to sustain the operation. However, I was very fortunate in that Chief Engineer Sid Weiser was allowed to develop a new research and development (R&D) group to go after military contracts and he asked me to join his small five-person staff. Led by Weiser, who was a photography and projection equipment expert, the new group developed a photo-interpretation training system with applications primarily for the air force's Rome Air Development Center. The basic system consisted of a booth where the photo interpreter would look at new film taken that was projected on the back of the viewing screen and would be able to call up interpretation aides from a library of aides to identify what was in the subtle or camouflaged image. I spent a lot of time looking at different sites in the Baltimore Harbor for details that the interpreter should be able to extract from the aerial photographs of the area that were displayed in the training system we built. I learned two political lessons on a business trip in the summer of 1991. I had accompanied my boss, Sid Weiser, on a business trip to an old line aerial photography company in Philadelphia in conjunction with our photo-interpretation business. Sid asked the owner what he thought of the recent presidential election. Kennedy had defeated Nixon, and Kennedy planned on a large increase in federal spending to get out of the recession the country was in at the end of the previous Eisenhower administration. The owner responded with the Republican Party's theme that year; he proceeded to rant about the Democratic president Kennedy's economic policies being too liberal and wasteful with his spending plans. When next asked how business was, he commented that he hoped some of Kennedy's spending would result in business for him. This was a lesson that people can be two-faced about government spending when it comes to their personal impact. I heard this inconsistent view expressed repeatedly in the 2012 election year. I also learned an economic lesson in the early 1960s; Kennedy's government-spending plan took the country out of the recession. In the summer of 2012, the Republican Party presidential candidates' viewpoint had no tolerance for considering increased government spending to avoid going into a recession or as a step to get the country out of a recession if it developed later that year. They were called too socialistic in order to rally the Conservative vote.

The new company operation was very successful, obtaining several contracts and tripling the staff. The following October the company sprung a surprise. Our group's corporate vice president decided to relocate this operation, which was profitable, and combine it with his Westchester, NY, group that was in the red so that his pet Westchester group would then be in the black. I was offered the opportunity to move to the Westchester operations. From my earlier knowledge of the Westchester area, living there didn't appeal to me. When my boss, Sid Weiser, decided he didn't trust the VP and wasn't moving, I also turned down the offer. We had two months to train the new staff, which involved several flight trips to Westchester. They also generously gave us a month's severance pay, which gave me until February to find a new job.

My family did very well in our new home. My wife made good friends with several neighbors having kids the same ages as ours; the mothers were busy raising the kids in a comfortable, trouble-free environment. It was the start of several long-lasting family relationships. Most notably, my wife has continued to have lunch with Helen Sandler every Friday afternoon for the past thirty years; I kept a friendship with Seymour Gould and Fred Loeb until their deaths many years later. This pleasant mood was disturbed in the summer of 1961. While I was at the Rome Air Development Center on contract business, I got a call from my sister Frances telling me that my mother, staying with her at a bungalow in the Catskills (popular primarily Jewish resort area 125 miles north of New York City), had terrible stomach pains. I gave her the name of an internist to see in Middletown some thirty miles away; Ellenville had no medical specialists. I had known the doctor from my Ellenville days. She was diagnosed with incurable cancer. A few months later, while in Cleveland with my in-laws for the Rosh Hashanah holiday, I got the sad call that my mother had died. My wife and I flew to NY for the funeral. My wife stayed a couple of days and flew back to Cleveland. I spent the weeklong mourning period in New York City with my sister Frances.

Transitioning to NASA Goddard Space Flight Center Employment

After deciding to leave US Industries, I took a dual path to find new employment in the local area because my wife and I both preferred to remain in our present home. My boss, Sid Weiser, decided to establish his own research and development operation with the primary objective of getting work with the Department of Commerce. He asked me to be part of this operation, and I spent some time helping him set up an office in Washington DC and develop marketing material. However, this new business venture sounded too risky, so I also pursued looking for new employment with the private industry or with the National Aeronautics and Space Administration (NASA), which had established the Goddard Space Flight Center (GSFC) in Greenbelt, MD, to conduct unmanned satellite development and operations. My job hunting was unsuccessful. I was beginning to get worried and considered looking for employment opportunities away from the Washington area but had no clue as to how to approach this consideration. The Washington area had little need for my industrial engineering experience and no need for my recent projection-display equipment experience. The small industries here did not need industrial engineers. The government agencies and the applied physics labs were looking for theoretical mechanical engineering experience, which I did not possess, and my photographic-display equipment experience seemed to be the worst loser for me. Then by a stroke of luck, my job hunting misfortunes turned favorable when my *useless* photographic display equipment experience actually landed me a career job with the Goddard Space Flight Center as the Nimbus spacecraft operations manager described in Chapter 3. I obviously quickly recognized that I made the right decision to drop working with my previous boss doing consulting services and to work for NASA. Sid called me about ten years later to tell me I made the right decision about going to work for the government and that he wished he had done the same. He subsequently took a job with the National Bureau of Standards.

STX Employment

Prior the effective date of my retirement from NASA, I checked with the GSFC legal department to see what limitations I had with respect to any postretirement employment. I could not work as a NASA-retired employee without specific authorization from NASA Headquarters, and for two years I was restricted from working on a contractor task supporting GSFC. My Nimbus science support contractor STX hired me under these conditions.

STX president Dr. Ashok Kaveeshwar told me that he hired me because he was convinced that I would apply my talents productively on other areas of the company business—I had to live up to my reputation and worked hard at it. Twenty-five years later, I am again supporting Ashok in his capacity as vice president of the Science and Technology Corporation, this time as a consultant on proposals for NASA support services contracts.

For the first several years I worked primarily on three different corporate activities. the development of a company commercial product which was a small airplane beacon landing support system to be used at small airports, pursuing several FAA contract opportunities, and company business development strategizing and planning. The first area turned out to be a major task for me. I initially supported the quality assurance manager in monitoring the tests being conducted at a small San Diego airport by the STX subcontractor responsible for the location guidance software development and conducting the system testing. My assessment of the test conditions for the tests that I monitored suggested that the subcontractor's software wasn't being tested for the full range of the aircraft-approach conditions. Based on my assessment comments, I was authorized to go to San Diego to conduct my proposed exploratory test under a new set of test conditions using towed balloons instead of aircraft to keep the cost down. The new test results revealed a significant hole in the software; it didn't support airplanes that had to fly over a wide central area over the airport before coming in for a landing. It took the subcontractor several months to fix their software, which was followed by another system test that I witnessed as a quality assurance representative. The testing was successful, demonstrating full coverage of an airport landing zone, and the company had a product line.

The two major activity areas for the balance of my time with Hughes STX consisted of working as a systems engineer on a systems engineering support task with the new GSFC Earth Observation System (EOS) Program and supporting all the company proposals for government contracts. On the former support effort, I helped incorporate effective systems engineering principles into the many interfaces being designed into the EOS program based on my twenty-year experience on the Nimbus Program. For the latter proposal support area, I developed quite a reputation critiquing proposals; they were penetrating, challenging, and constructive, contributing to improved proposals. I supported all proposals as a writer, specializing in three areas: (a) writing the past performance of previous contracts to show relevance to the work to be conducted on the proposal contract, (b) reviewing and guiding the writing of the resumes written by the candidate personnel to show strengths applicable to the contract work areas, and (c) responding to sample tasks that represent scenarios for different contract support areas. The latter effort was the most challenging. Depending on the individual scenario details, it could require a description of the technical approaches to specific planning procedures, analyses and trade studies to be conducted, devices to be designed, fabricated and tested, all in order to meet the objectives and achieve the performance specifications. This information is complemented with the identification of the skilled personnel required, and a detailed work activity schedule to meet the delivery schedule. The proposal that I had the most fun with involved STX teaming with prime contractor IBM located in Clear Lake, Texas. This proposal activity exposed me to the NASA Houston operations in Clear Lake and to the pleasures of that part of the country, which included several interesting nearby Galveston restaurants, trips to famous, exciting New Orleans restaurants, an introduction to Mexican food, and an exposure to Texas two-step dancing. The impact I made reviewing STX proposals is summed up by the outfit they had me wear at the very nice retirement party they gave me, shown in the picture of me, "The Barking Dog," with my boss, Ashok Kaveeshwar.

My GSFC contract work and STX coworker interaction contributed to a most unusual, remarkable success story. I helped the new STX co-worker software specialist Frank Islam to understand the satellite aerospace environment by arranging for him to support the systems engineering task that I was on; I became his aerospace mentor. A few years later, his new knowledge of the aerospace field enabled him to start the QSS Corporation and, twenty years later, to sell QSS to Perot Systems for $300 million dollars.

STX was a private company owned by Sharad Tak and Porter Bankhead when I was hired. It was purchased a couple of years later by the Hughes Division of General Motors, and the organization was renamed Hughes STX. I worked for STX-Hughes STX for nine years and received this very complimentary Certificate of Appreciation upon retirement.

Certificate
of Appreciation

PRESENTED TO

Ralph Shapiro

For nine years of quality service and loyalty to Hughes STX.

Ralph has an impressive ability to perform a diversity of tasks—from the simple to the complex—and do so reliably and on time. He approaches each job with dedication, becomes an expert in the subject, and completes the project in its entirety. Like the postman, neither rain, sleet, snow, nor dark of night will delay Ralph from completing his assigned project.

We wish him all the best in his retirement.

Ashok Kaveeshwar
President, Hughes STX

HUGHES
AIRCRAFT

HUGHES STX CORPORATION

QSS Employment

The QSS owner, Frank Islam, personifies the true entrepreneurial spirit. After some disappointing assignments at Hughes STX, where we worked together, he left STX to start his own company. He scraped together enough money to buy a minority-owned small business company that had a three-person contract, which immediately gave him the credentials as a minority small business contractor that enabled him to go after this category of government work. Frank was from India, which qualified him as a minority for government business. While still working for STX, I got their approval for me to support Frank as his proposal representative on his prime teammate's proposal review and editing effort; I made some significant suggestions for proposal improvements. The proposal won, and Frank had his first contract earned through a proposal effort. I didn't charge Frank for my proposal effort because I knew he had little money and because I was kept on the STX payroll for the time I worked on the QSS proposal, which would have been unethical as a double payment for my time.

After I retired from Hughes STX in 1995 I, started to support Frank Islam as a QSS proposal consultant. In view of his poor financial condition, he offered me a rate that was half the going rate for proposal consultants, and I accepted it. I was instrumental in his winning NASA, NOAA, and Coast Guard contracts. I wrote several of his qualification statements that enabled QSS to compete and then led the proposal-planning efforts and wrote many management and technical proposal sections. My first proposal-support effort was on a proposal already underway for a large GSFC business administration division contract. I identified several proposal weaknesses and offered a strategy to strengthen the proposal. I then worked with Frank over the long Fourth of July weekend to revamp the key parts of the proposal and incorporated my recommendations; it became a winning proposal. His next proposal was for the Coast Guard in Rhode Island. He was still having financial difficulties, so he offered to pay me at a rate of one quarter of my proposed hourly rate. I offered for him to *double my rate or nothing*. He thought he had inside knowledge that he was the favored competitor, so his proposed labor and overhead rates were not competitive. He lost the contract on a cost basis but learned a lesson that contributed to his future successes. He *sharpened his pencil* and learned to bid very competitive overhead rates and to keep the company's actual overhead rates close to what he bid so that contract actual costs didn't escalate due to overhead rate growth that many companies experienced. This rate proposal and actual rate-handling reputation was a factor in many later proposal wins.

There were two very standout QSS winning proposal efforts to which I contributed very creatively and substantially, one with NASA and the other with the Coast Guard.

Without having any corporate engineering capability, QSS wanted to go after a new very large GSFC engineering contract, the Multidisciplinary Engineering Development Support (MEDS) contract. I wrote the QSS capability statement to be able to compete and then recruited the Orbital Sciences aerospace company to be his engineering teammate and write the technical section of the proposal. I wrote the management sections and led the technical proposal review effort. I even helped the GFSC lawyers nullify the award protest arguments. QSS developed quite a good reputation after this win.

The next effort QSS pursued was a contract for the renewal of a Coast Guard management support effort conducted at Martinsburg, WV. Frank Islam recruited the incumbent personnel to work for him after contract award to QSS and to support writing his proposal. Frank and I went to Martinsburg to review the proposal effort. My assessment was that the proposal was noncompliant. The incumbent writers were convinced that the QSS proposal would win because Frank had the employment tie with the incumbents, and they wrote a shallow proposal that didn't respond to the specific instructions; it just described what services were required. I convinced Frank that the incumbent staff had nowhere to go if QSS lost, and they would go to work for whoever won the contract; the government proposal team surely understood this and would award the contract on the basis of the quality and merits of the proposal response to the detailed proposal instructions. I took over managing the proposal effort at the home office, which involved educating the incumbent writers to address the specifics of all proposal requirements by providing descriptions of how the work will be performed, which they inherently knew because the required services were services they were actually providing. QSS won the contract based on the highest technical score.

Frank gave me two other large proposal challenges. He had a proposal consultant spend two months in Cleveland working with his Cleveland subcontractor teammate to write the proposal for a NASA Lewis contract. He took me with him to Cleveland to review the proposal and came out of the meeting room shrieking, "The proposal is awful!" After I agreed with his assessment he threw the burden of taking over the proposal on me, with no help offered. I recruited one of the original writers, a specialist in handling the risk-handling area, and I wound up writing the rest of the proposal essentially by myself—the proposal won. The other challenge had a different twist. It was for a NASA Ames proposal for scientific-type support, and the QSS scientist writing the proposal's science effort had no imagination to respond meaningfully to the proposal support requirements. I traded my engineering hat for my Nimbus program science hat and created science requirement responses that the proposal review team endorsed—this proposal also won.

My relationship with Frank Islam is an example of how a Jew and a Muslim can fraternize harmoniously even under challenging circumstances. I had been Frank Islam's personal friend at our common place of employment, STX, helping him to retain employment with STX after he failed to bring in IT business, which was the objective and condition for his being hired. I was essentially his only friend and mentor at STX, teaching him about satellites and their operations, which he knew nothing about before. He later made use of this information to help his new small company grow and applied his intrinsic entrepreneur talent to enable QSS to become one of the most successful minority companies in the nation.

I also helped Frank Islam on a personal basis. As his company grew he was under severe emotional pressure caused by the financial challenges of the growing company and by some company personnel issues. Until then, he had little need for medical support and thus didn't know how to contend with the poor medical support he was getting from his company's health services provider, the Kaiser HMO medical organization. I wound up taking him to many a physical exam, providing him an understanding of the physician's diagnoses and recommendations, and providing advice on contending with the poor HMO support conditions. I finally convinced him to see my personal physician, who helped Frank to better understand his problems, which were emotionally induced false symptoms, and he started feeling better. Frank still sees my personal internist, Dr. Jerome Schnapp, as his personal physician. When his company prospered, he still considered me his friend. We ate lunch together very frequently; I was basically his only lunch companion. We discussed the Near East among many political subjects. We had a common view regarding Israel and Palestine. The State of Israel had a right to exist without being threatened by the Arabs. The Palestinians needed a state of their own with some measure of economic stability to avoid continued unrest and further agitation against Israel. Although his Moslem family in India suffered financially and morally when British rule over India ended and India became independent, Frank only expressed bitterness over the harsh treatment he remembered from his youth and accepted the reality of the new political environment in India.

I recently met Frank for lunch and learned about his fantastic growth in the political world. He has become an economic advisor to President Obama and his cabinet, friendly with Democratic congressional leaders, and has the promise to be appointed as an Ambassador should Obama win reelection; an aspiration he expressed to me when we first met 25 years ago and he barely kept his job because of lack of accomplishment. He also has a small TV interview program. We reminisced how I gave him advice on how to handle his first TV interview after he won his first big GSFC contract. His achievements after coming to this country penniless and now constructing a seven building mansion complex as his new home in Bethesda, MD is for the story books.

Postretirement Independent Consultancy

After I retired from full-time employment I undertook a variety of part-time volunteer efforts that were described earlier. I was also asked by former co-workers who started their own businesses and by consultant proposal managers to support their proposal efforts on a part-time basis and managed to fit in both activities. My involvement in this activity was explained in the previous section. I have consulted for six different companies, generally serving as a compliance reviewer and section writer, with a knack for past-performance sections and with broad experience to address sample tasks that represent the type of work to be performed on the contract. I also conducted a review of the overall proposal for consistency of themes/approaches and to incorporate strengths and avoid weaknesses, which very few reviewers can do. One such contribution was acknowledged by Analex proposal manager Joe Broadwater, who wrote me a letter calling me his hero. I was supporting his teammate subcontractor Jackson and Tull on the proposal and went to the prime's office in Virginia only to refine Jackson and Tull's input, if required. While I was there, I convinced Joe and another sub, Wylie Inc., that their proposal inputs were too shallow and staffed incorrectly and offered improvements/corrections that they accepted. The proposal won, with the areas I improved cited by NASA as being very good. I have continued on as a proposal consultant to Jackson and Tull on several opportunities.

I find that this consulting work very stimulating mentally, keeps my old mind from decaying. It is financially rewarding and also personally rewarding and encouraging to know that at my age I can still make meaningful contributions to complex technical and management proposal efforts for NASA and NOAA technical services contracts. I still have the ability to sharply understanding the proposal requirements and whether the response is compliant and a skill to recognize inconsistencies of a subject described in different sections of the proposal. I recently reviewed a 150-page proposal and was thanked for all the errors in compliance and inconsistencies that I found.

Chapter 3

Working for NASA

We had been living in Silver Spring for two years when I had to decide on whether to stay with US Industries and move to Westchester, NY, or look for a new position in the Washington DC general area, which would have enabled us to remain in our house. After we decided to try to remain in the area, despite the fact that I had little relevant experience and poor prospects for employment there, through most unusual circumstances I got a job with NASA that developed into a most wonderful career, more than I anticipated and as good as anyone could ask for. For about twenty years I worked on an Earth resources satellite program called Nimbus in the capacity of spacecraft operations manager for seven Nimbus spacecraft that had different instruments making different types of scientific measurements. It provided the ultimate job satisfaction, new technical challenges with an opportunity to be creative for the benefit of society, and working with a large group of very competent support personnel.

Joining NASA Beats the Odds

The Washington DC general area in 1962 had little industry, so my search for machine design engineering opportunities was not fruitful. The Goddard Space Flight Center in nearby Greenbelt, MD, was rather new, and there was not much publicity about its activity. However, the new Russian Sputnik satellite and the US follow-up satellite activity in the news sounded exciting, so I decided to explore opportunities at Goddard. I submitted the standard employment application form and received one interview. It was for a mechanical engineering theoretical analysis position; I had no college training or experience in this field. The position was offered to the other applicant who had the relevant mechanical analysis experience working on aircraft design. Later, I chatted with my neighbor Herb Meyerson about my difficulties finding employment. He worked at GSFC on the space science Voyager program as an electrical engineer. Sympathizing with my plight, he offered the names of three GSFC supervisors to call as long shots; he had no specific knowledge of any job opportunities.

The first contact I called was Bill Stroud. He was a GSFC mid-level supervisor overseeing Earth-viewing satellite programs that included the TIROS program and the new Nimbus satellite program that NASA was developing to replace the TIROS satellites. He asked about my experience, and learning from my previous GSFC interview that my industrial engineering experience had little value at GSFC, I dwelled on my recent experience developing photographic display equipment for photo interpretation. It struck a bell. He went on to explain that the new Nimbus satellite being developed was going to take worldwide pictures of clouds, and a display system was required for meteorologists to view the pictures for analysis of the clouds in conjunction with their weather forecasting. He told me to call Harry Press, who was the Nimbus Project Manager, and tell him Bill Stroud said he wants him to hire me for the Nimbus cloud picture display system development. I called Harry Press and gave him that message. His answer was to call Moe Schneebaum, the Nimbus Program engineering staff manager, and tell him that Harry Press told me to call him and tell him to hire me for the Nimbus cloud picture display system development. Moe Schneebaum was the one who gave me my earlier failed interview and grudgingly hired me. He offered me a GS-12 position at an $11,000 salary, which was $1,000 less than I was earning. With no other job prospects in sight, I naturally accepted. The exciting work that I visualized was ahead eliminated salary as an issue for me, but my wife had some apprehension. I did very well salary—wise over my twenty-four-year span at GSFC. In appreciation of my high-quality work and accomplishments, I received multistep increases and grade advances such that I bottomed out at the top GS-15 step several years before I retired.

There were several ironies to my being hired. First, the task of developing the Nimbus photographic display equipment, which was the only reason why I was hired, never even got started because the Weather

Bureau dropped out of the Nimbus program. Second, Mr. Schneebaum, who hired me, had a negative reaction to being forced to hire me and probably wouldn't have hired me by his own choice. This attitude was evident when two months after he hired me I asked for advance leave to attend my mother-in-law's funeral and he turned me down (approving advance leave for extenuating personal needs was very common). Third, Bill Stroud, who initiated my hiring, became my antagonist after the first Nimbus spacecraft launch. And finally, the dim prospect of my working at GSFC because I essentially had only industrial engineering experience was emphasized by the GSFC Employment Office's return of my employment application six months after I started working at GSFC. My application came back with the note that there was no prospect for me finding work at GSFC with my industrial engineering background, so they didn't want to keep it on file. I fooled them by working at GSFC for twenty-four years and getting a NASA Headquarters Exceptional Service Medal and a GSFC Exceptional Performance Award.

Initial Nimbus Program Role

The Nimbus Program had contracts with the RCA Astro-Electronics Division in Hightstown, NJ, for several Nimbus satellite subsystems and for the companion ground systems. I was assigned to be the technical officer on the ground systems contract. There were three major subsystems involved, a system in the Nimbus Control Center to process the cloud video data, another system to process the related time code data, and an electronic demultiplexer system to separate the combined (multiplexed) science data signals transmitted from the spacecraft that was used at the NASA tracking sites that received the satellite data. RCA had subcontracts with two companies for creating photographic displays from the Nimbus spacecraft Advanced Vidicon Camera System (AVCS) electronic signals. One company was the well-established Consolidated Electrodynamics Corporation (CEC) in Pasadena, CA, that was to use their commercial system for plotting medical examination signals to plot out the AVCS cloud pictures. The other was a relatively new company, Photomechanisms Inc., in Huntington Station, NY. Their system was to create developed negatives of the AVCS high-resolution pictures using a technique similar to the Polaroid camera technique that didn't require a darkroom to develop the picture.

My first challenge was to address the CEC subcontract, which was not proceeding well. The CEC display approach, conceived by the GSFC Nimbus spacecraft concept initiators, was to apply the CEC stylus writing system used for medical encephalograph analysis to create cloud pictures. CEC was having difficulty implementing this design approach, and RCA was having difficulty getting their government-designated subcontractor to make real progress. I made an early trip to CEC with the RCA subcontract manager, John Sternberg, to get the status of the development. There was little satisfactory progress. CEC offered to develop a new development plan for our review in three weeks. When we returned, I spent the first day critiquing the CEC plan presented, which turned out to be weak. The project manager agreed to develop a new plan for making design changes to overcome the deficiencies identified at the review and have the plan ready for a meeting the next afternoon. When we met the next day, I expected to hear the plan. Instead, the manager said, "Although I agreed to come up with a plan last night, this morning I don't agree to come up with a corrective plan at this time." After this shocking statement, I abruptly left the meeting. From what I had learned the previous day, I was convinced there was little prospect of the CEC stylus technique making quality cloud pictures. It was time to turn off the contract and save the Nimbus Program money. I also felt comfortable with this decision because the alternate Photomechanism Company technique was already showing very good prospects. I told the RCA subcontract manager with me that I was going to advise my boss to allow RCA to terminate the contract—he endorsed my decision wholeheartedly. I went outside and called Moe Schneebaum on a public phone, offering why the contract should be terminated, and he agreed. John Sternberg was so relieved and thankful that he took me to dinner at the famous Lowery Steakhouse in Hollywood.

My next challenge was to help the GSFC contracting officer, Ed Rossette, negotiate the ongoing ground system contract with RCA. I took the unusual step of asking RCA to provide in advance a listing of all the design and fabrication tasks required and that they would be presenting for the cost negotiation. They could do this because the contract had been active for at least three months and the conceptual detailed designs were completed. I applied my experience at Channel Master doing somewhat equivalent designs to come up with my own time/cost estimate for each work element RCA was costing, although I had no experience with the actual detailed electrical designs required. At the negotiation I challenged the time required for many individual tasks, and RCA had difficulty refuting most of my challenges. After some give and take, the contract was negotiated at $3.5M, down from the proposed $5M. On the way out of the negotiation RCA marketing manager Jerry Cohen said, "Ralph, you are killing us." That statement laid the challenge on me to avoid having the contract overrun the negotiated cost. I spent the next eight months visiting RCA essentially every two weeks, helping them resolve design issues quickly and making certain that personnel were taken off the task when their work was completed. I was a pain to them with my intrusion in their work management effort, but I wanted to take steps to contain the cost within the negotiated amount by avoiding unnecessary costs. At the spacecraft pre-vacuum thermal test party the Nimbus program office held for the major participants in the program at the General Electric spacecraft integration site in King of Prussia, PA, RCA VP Frank Hogan greeted my wife with, "How do you put up with that SOB husband of yours." When the RCA equipment was finally delivered, the actual total cost was within the negotiated cost—it was personally very rewarding that the contract cost I negotiated was realistic.

The ground system RCA was developing processed the spacecraft digital data consisting of the cloud pictures taken by the AVCS instrument on the Nimbus spacecraft. The ACVS daytime camera took sharper (higher resolution) pictures than a similar-type camera on the satellite in orbit, called TIROS, that was operated by the U.S. weather service agency. The Nimbus camera system had several other advantages over the existing TIROS system. There were three AVCS cameras on Nimbus vs. one camera on TIROS so that the AVCS picture covered three times the area of an equivalent TIROS picture. The TIROS spacecraft spun around, whereas the Nimbus spacecraft was controlled to look straight down on Earth without spinning in any direction, which made the Nimbus pictures much clearer. Nimbus had another great improvement. There was a tape recorder onboard the spacecraft so cloud pictures could be taken anywhere around the globe, whereas the TIROS pictures could be only be taken in areas where there was a ground station to receive the electronic picture.

In the early winter of 1963, Gerald (Gerry) Burdette, the Nimbus Project AVCS contract technical officer, told Bill Stroud, "We have a problem, Bill. Lancaster forgot how to make vidicon tubes." Three of these

TV camera-type tubes were used in the spacecraft AVCS camera system (it had three cameras), but five new vidicons were required for each spacecraft model (two spares to have available in case of test failures), and there was a prototype model, flight model, and a spare camera system built to meet the new summer of 1964 launch date, so twenty vidicons were required. All vidicons in a fabricated lot had to pass the tests for any vidicon in the lot to be acceptable. It wasn't happening—there was a low useable output. Stroud panicked and called a big review at RCA covering the flight system that included the vidicon procurement and the companion ground system that I was responsible for. We were taking advantage of the year launch slip to incorporate some improvements in the ground system. At the review in Hightstown, NJ, Bill Stroud came down hard on RCA for their production problems and on Gerry Burdette and me for our management failures. I wasn't too concerned because I felt the ground system was not in the bad shape Stroud declared it to be in, but the comments were disturbing. However, Gerry Burdette was affected badly. On the way home, driving on a road in the middle of no-where in New Jersey, he stopped the government car he was driving and told me to take over driving. He said he was troubled over Stroud's comments and was not up to driving. It turned out to be quite an experience for me. I didn't pay attention to the amount of gasoline in the car tank, but it was essentially empty. After driving a short distance I heard the car start to sputter and pulled off to the side of the road. I had no idea where the nearest gas station was but planned on walking as far as I needed to and told Gerry to stay in the car and continue his resting. The driver of a large trailer truck behind us saw us pull off the road and thoughtfully pulled up ahead of us to see what was wrong. He knew the road and offered to drive me the almost twenty minutes to the nearest gas station ahead. I had the new experience of an uncomfortable jerky ride in the cab of a big truck, but was I thankful—I wondered how the driver could take the rough rides for their long trips. An attendant at the gas station offered to take me back to the car with a can of gasoline—another blessing. When I got back to the car, Gerry was gone. He woke up while I was gone and decided to walk in the opposite direction—I never figured out why he left the car. I turned the car around and drove until I found him walking, picked him up, and I reversed again back to the gas station to fill up. I drove home for two more hours with Gerry sleeping most of the way home.

In addition to the RCA ground system responsibility, I was appointed contract technical officer on two other ground system contracts. One was with the Westrex Corporation in NYC to develop a facsimile machine to create films of the infrared (IR) radiometer instrument cloud pictures taken in orbit and recorded for playback to the NASA ground station. Although the resolution was not as good as the daytime AVCS camera, the IR system had a full-orbit daytime and nighttime picture-taking capability, which was beneficial to the meteorologists. This device was developed with little input from me. The other contract was with the Fairchild Camera Company in Farmingdale, NY, to create a facsimile system for the local area daytime cloud pictures received from the spacecraft Automatic Picture Taking (APT) system. The APT system had a special type of TV vidicon camera. It had a memory device on the vidicon so the signal could be read out slowly and transmitted to the ground at a very low rate that enabled commercial facsimiles to make the cloud pictures. The local cloud pictures covered approximately 1,500 miles and became the source of local cloud pictures displayed on TV news channels; it was a big hit. By the launch of the second Nimbus spacecraft that also had the APT camera system, the number of APT stations grew to over three hundred, located in forty-three countries. These two contracts each required my periodic trips to the factories to monitor the developments, resolve the few issues that surfaced, and witness the acceptance tests. These two contractors were very capable and efficient. I had no issues with either company. After some experience with the equipment, the RCA service company operator of the Westrex facsimile in the GSFC Nimbus ground station recommended a change to improve the equipment maintainability, which Westrex incorporated.

Nimbus Spacecraft Operations Manager Role

The Nimbus ground facility located in the basement of GSFC Building 3 consisted of two elements. One element, called the Meteorological Data Handling System (MDHS), processed the satellite instrument (science) data and the satellite health information (telemetry data) coming from all the spacecraft components. It also sent the electrical signal commands (such as instructions to change the status of the equipment or to take a camera picture) to the tracking sites for their subsequent transmission as a radio signal to the satellite. The other element was the Nimbus Control Center

(NCC) that scheduled the spacecraft operations in response to the mission requirements by sending commands to turn the Earth-monitoring scientific equipment on and off at the scientist's prescribed times, and managed the spacecraft data-recording systems and their later transmission to a ground station. NCC also monitored the spacecraft health and status information (telemetry) on chart recorders and analyzed the computer-processed telemetry data to assess the health of the spacecraft and instruments, and to send the appropriate commands in reaction to any problems observed.

Except for the large data-processing computers in MDHS bought directly from the computer vendor, the MDHS equipment was supplied under the companion spacecraft equipment vendor and operated by their respective field service technicians. Five different contractors covering command, telemetry, data-signal processing, computer processing, and picture generation were involved in operating and maintaining the MDHS—all managed by the GSFC Code 500 MDHS manager. Three months before the initial launch scheduled in the summer of 1963, the MDHS system equipment was being connected (integrated), and there were operational problems. Some signals from the sending equipment to the receiving equipment were not flowing properly, indicative of an interface electrical design problem. The GSFC Code 500 MDHS government managers couldn't get their operator/maintenance services contractors to own up to any responsibility for fixing the several interface problems that were found. The two Nimbus Project representatives, Bernie Trudell and Dick Ormsby, could not succeed at breaking the impasse. When Harry Press, the Nimbus Project Manager, became aware of this situation, he became alarmed and concerned that ground system readiness delay might cause a launch schedule delay, and decided to appoint me as the Nimbus Operations Manager. He advised the MDHS manager and his supervisor of the sense of urgency to correct the MDHS problems and told them that I had his authority to make independent autonomous decisions as appropriate to get the ground system ready for launch. Press appointed me because he was impressed by my earlier handling of the contractors I worked with and thought I had the systems understanding and managerial toughness to break the impasse.

I quickly undertook my new assignment, convening a working group of the hardware system managers. We laid out a plan to assess each interface individually, and I assigned an interface manager for each interface with the responsibility to address the problem identified with that interface and to design a fix. Some interfaces required a fix of the equipment at both sides of the interface (i.e., signal-sending and signal-receiving equipment). When a particular system maintenance manager had a problem designing the required type circuit, I found someone in the ground system with the right skills to help. The little knowledge of electronics that I had picked up in my earlier work at GE and Frankford Arsenal, and at a community night school in Schenectady, NY, was sufficient to equip me to understand the nature of the interface technical problems and their solution requirements such that I was able to provide effective leadership for quickly resolving the interface issues. The MDHS ground system was ready to meet the 1963 launch schedule.

When I took on the role of spacecraft operations manager, another not-well-advertised problem surfaced. The two Nimbus Project representatives were having problems with the General Electric (GE) Company manager of the NCC contract and with the GE manager of the NCC support software development. GE was to build the spacecraft structure, integrate all the spacecraft and instrument equipment, and test the entire spacecraft for operational performance. Therefore, they were given those two spacecraft-related flight operations support contracts. After I had a chance to review and fully understand the problems, I had the GE corporate-level Nimbus program manager make two changes. Benny Palmer, who was second in command of NCC, was given full responsibility for the NCC operations management. Morrie Gunzberg, who I learned had been doing a commendable job managing GE software development at the NASA tracking site in Fairbanks, AK, was brought down to be the overall GE manager of both the NCC and the related software development contracts. Both changes brought immediate positive results, with better launch-readiness planning, improved relations between the Nimbus Project representatives and the NCC managers, improved relations within the NCC staff, and NCC software development progress to the satisfaction of the government software contract monitor, Lloyd Green. The delay in the launch that occurred was very helpful, giving us time to get the control center staff better prepared with more software tools.

It turned out that the spacecraft test conducted to see how the Nimbus spacecraft would operate in the vacuum of outer space and at the anticipated spacecraft temperatures for the cold outer-space conditions where the spacecraft will operate (i.e., five hundred miles above Earth) had to be stopped when two identical electronic items failed, and it was determined that a bad lot of this electronic item was released by the vendor and they were used in several spacecraft components. This caused a one-year launch slip to replace the failed items in all the affected spacecraft components, and then the acceptance retest of the components containing the replaced items, followed by an acceptance retest of the entire spacecraft. Had a singular item failed, it would have been replaced, and then the box it was in would be retested, and the spacecraft thermal vacuum test would be conducted, causing only a several-month delay. As a consequence of this one-year delay, the Department of Commerce cancelled their agreement with NASA to buy the next two production versions of the first Nimbus spacecraft for their operational use. This turned out to be very fortuitous for the nation and for me personally. The Nimbus program was changed from a weather satellite production program to a research and development Earth satellite program that resulted in the development of many new satellite instruments for measuring Earth's atmospheric, oceanic, and land behavior over a twenty-year period. These new categories of information about Earth's behavior, coupled with the new tools and processes for weather forecasting, environmental monitoring, and Earth resources assessment that were developed, resulted in many benefits to the public and commerce. Not planned initially, seven satellites with essentially the same structure but with different instruments making new types of measurements were built, and I had an intense involvement in each.

Spacecraft Problem Management Role

I applied a hands-on involvement with spacecraft problems compared to most other government mission operations managers (MOM) working along with me on other programs. My intense involvement with the Nimbus Control Center data analysis planning and my detailed knowledge of each Nimbus spacecraft as it was being developed and became operational equipped me to do that. A call at three in the morning was infrequent but not unusual, and I drove quickly (an hour's drive) to the Nimbus Control Center to coordinate the understanding of the problem and to help develop the corrective measures, if required. My wife got used to these calls over the many years of my Nimbus operational support.

Preparation for the Next Nimbus Spacecraft Operations

There were several phases of preparation activity required to get the information tools prepared and personnel ready. The spacecraft (s/c) and instrument command telemetry information was obtained from the integration contractor, GE, and used to create the command database, telemetry brush chart displays, and computer analysis program evaluation parameters. Long-term telemetry analysis programs were also developed. Software was developed to create the science data products for the scientific analysis to be conducted by the scientists to accomplish the particular Nimbus s/c scientific objectives. For the first six spacecraft this was done by each instrument principal investigator, who essentially owned the respective instrument data (standard practice). This was changed for Nimbus-7. The Nimbus Operations Processing System (NOPS) was created under my leadership for project processing and distribution of the data. Nimbus Experiment Teams (NETs) of three to five members were established for each instrument; they were national and international experts in the science disciplines related to the instrument. The NET members defined the instrument data products and developed the algorithms collectively so the production algorithms represented the best approach. The science data became available to all interested scientists after the data quality was validated by the respective instrument team of scientists.

The personnel preparation for each new spacecraft had three phases. The operations staff was trained to send the commands to match the instrument operations in accordance with the scientist's objectives and within the constraints of the s/c power system, and to evaluate the real-time telemetry and the full orbit telemetry stored on the spacecraft and played down to a NASA ground station once on orbit. To be sure the ground system command signals were compatible and the orbital operational scheme was sound, the Nimbus Control Center at GSFC took over the testing of the spacecraft in the GE thermal vacuum chamber at Valley Forge, PA, running typical orbits by sending commands and receiving telemetry back over telephone lines.

The last training effort related to the launch and first few orbits support readiness. Because the planned orbit required Nimbus to cross the equator northward at noon, the two-stage Thor-Agena rocket lifting Nimbus into orbit is launched southward from Lompoq, CA, crosses over the South Pole, and heads northward. The spacecraft is separated from the launch vehicle over South Africa, then crosses over Spain,over England, continues toward the North Pole and then heads southwards over Alaska. Each spacecraft was launched from California at approximately 3:00 a.m. GSFC time. I wanted the telemetry evaluators in the control center that included Nimbus project and GE engineering subsystem specialists to be experienced while comfortably working in the middle of the night, so the practice exercises using tape data of simulated orbits created during spacecraft development vacuum-thermal testing were held starting at ten at night and ran through midnight or so; it was my compromise not to hold them at three in the morning. To soften the pain, we generally had a nice dinner together each practice night at a nearby restaurant. The practice involved looking at telemetry data that was fixed to have problems, expecting the evaluators to catch them and call out the appropriate alarm. This practice was initiated with the second spacecraft. I was at the NASA/ GSFC tracking station in Fairbanks, AK, for the first launch because the Nimbus Project management didn't trust the many (about sixty) microwave telephone relay stations between Alaska and Maryland, which hadn't been used operationally before to bring the telemetry data to GSFC. I was a novice at the business of evaluating spacecraft and so was everyone else on my evaluation team of project subsystem engineers that joined me there. I describe the exciting days activating a Nimbus spacecraft for the first time in Chapter 7.

Managing the Second Nimbus Spacecraft Assembly and Testing Effort

Because of the two-year period after authorization required to build the next Nimbus spacecraft with the new instrumentation planned, NASA Headquarters also authorized the building of a Nimbus spacecraft similar to Nimbus-1 that failed after a month of operation, one that could be built rather quickly, at a reasonable cost, in less than a year, and provide the exciting data that Nimbus-1 generated. The use of a Nimbus spacecraft structure left over from the original concept of building three identical spacecraft for NOAA operations and using a new instrument planned for Nimbus-1 that wasn't ready in time to be included in Nimbus-1 made the short Nimbus-2 schedule realistic. The Nimbus Project technical staff was needed to support the ambitious instrument program for Nimbus-3 that included three new-concept instruments, two new technology systems, and two repeat instruments. So Project Manager Harry Press found me with no spacecraft operations to manage, and he appointed me Nimbus-2 spacecraft manager with the responsibility of managing the General Electric Company effort to build and test that quick-turnaround Nimbus-2 spacecraft. I had three NASA engineers that worked at the GE factory where the spacecraft is assembled and tested to support me. Since I had no other work to do and never resisted learning new technologies and techniques required for new work tasks, I took on the assignment with no objection.

It turned out to be a remarkable opportunity. With the cooperation of the very capable General Electric Company Nimbus Program Manager, Sheldon Haas, who deserves the credit for the effective, efficient GE Nimbus-2 development program, the three resident NASA employees, George Meehan, Seymour Leibowitz, and Ed Wright, a couple of GSFC engineering specialists, Edwin Stengard and George Hinshelwood, and the GE staff in general, the spacecraft was built, tested, and launched in a little less than a year, with no problems in-between. My major task was to work with the GE program manager to maintain an efficient schedule. I applied what I learned from my Nimbus-1 ground equipment development management experience working with RCA. We created a detailed schedule, looked at what was ahead when the current task was completed, and made sure the required equipment and right manpower would be available to start the next activity on time. We resolved all open issues early enough so they didn't cause schedule delays. I got involved with technical areas I knew nothing about. For example, I had to decide on the alternative option to approve for a new vibration equipment feature that would avoid (notch out) vibrating the complete Nimbus spacecraft at the Nimbus solar array paddle natural low frequency that would cause it to resonate and break. I found vibration and stress analysis expert George Hinshelwood at GSFC to help me make the decision. Another major technical area challenge was handling the testing of the spacecraft solar array that converts the sun's rays into electrical power. The solar array paddle motor drive on Nimbus-1 froze because there was no way to radiate the rotor heat away from the ball bearings, so the grease dried up. There was no air in space to conduct the heat away the rotor, and the rotor metal was natural light colored, which doesn't radiate heat well. This was determined by array fabricator RCA in Hightstown, NJ, by running a similar drive in a vacuum chamber at their factory and monitoring the device with an infrared thermometer.

The fix was to blacken the rotor so it could radiate the rotor heat to the housing in vacuum and to change the grease to one that worked better in space, whereas the original motor was a commercial design not made for operating in space. I found mechanical engineer Edwin Stengard available at GSFC to help me plan the testing program with RCA to validate the fixed array. Another challenge for me was the handling of the addition of a new instrument on the spacecraft. The new Medium-Resolution Infrared Radiometer was built for Nimbus-1, but it didn't make it on time to be included in the spacecraft assembly and test effort. It required the addition of RF electronic isolators to avoid RF interference with the other RF equipment; I needed to learn a lot of electrical engineering in a hurry to help understand communication circuit-design and help make design option decisions. Planning the vibration testing was another new world for me. The development and test schedule was accomplished as planned and at a relatively low cost for this elaborate spacecraft.

Managing the Nimbus spacecraft development effort required me to travel to King of Prussia, PA, for a few days almost every other week and all week during the long thermal vacuum tests. I mixed the transportation method to make the trip more interesting. Flew to Philly, took the train to Philly, and drove there a variety of ways. I sampled every restaurant between King of Prussia and Camden, NJ, and stayed in every cheap motel in the area. It became routine; my family hardly complained about my being away.

The results were very gratifying. The satellite operated for thirty-two months, achieving good scientific results and practical applications. The nighttime infrared picture-taking system was broadcast to the local weather forecasters, giving them the first broad view of the area clouds at night and provided the temperature patterns of lakes and oceanic areas of interest to shipping and fishing industries. The high resolution TV camera system on Nimbus-1 that was a boon to the weather forecasters worked equally as well on Nimbus-2. For my comprehensive efforts to manage the integration and test effort with a small support staff that helped deliver the spacecraft within one year and at a cost within the low $20M budget, and in view of the successful spacecraft operations, NASA Headquarters honored me with the NASA Exceptional Service Medal in 1969.

Operational Software Development Coordination

Each new Nimbus had new instruments with their own complement of commands and telemetry data covering the components in the respective instrument design that had to be incorporated into the operations computer database along with their telemetry calibration tables and out-of-limit values. Plots of results had to be generated. The orbital power balance computations had to be adjusted for the new satellite orbital parameters. Displays of the instrument science signals needed to be generated, some requiring photo-generation software. Due to the attitude control system design changes, software computing the spacecraft three-axis attitude needed to be developed.

Unofficial Use of Nimbus Data to Support Government and Commercial Operations

My employment goal on all my previous jobs was to be as productive as I could, a temperament carried over from my youth. It carried over to my Nimbus Operations Manager role. The Nimbus-1 spacecraft was originally prompted by NOAA (known as ESSA then) to be their improved operational satellite because of its higher quality AVCS cloud pictures and the remote area picture-taking capability compared to their TIROS satellite. When the Nimbus development program required a one-year delay due to development problems, NOAA dropped out of the Nimbus program. Nevertheless, the agencies had an agreement to have NOAA receive the AVCS digital data played down from the spacecraft recorder, and I as the operations manager set up an arrangement with NOAA that their liaison representative Jeff Albert would advise my staff as to where in the world we should take pictures (the recorder had a limited picture recording capacity). That arrangement was working fine until an incident with Bill Stroud, who was the one that essentially hired me to work at GSFC on the Nimbus Program. That year, Labor Day was late and the Jewish New Year religious holiday, Rosh Hashanah, was early; they coincided. Since my two deputies took Labor Day off, I sent my wife to synagogue with my neighbors and I went to GSFC to conduct the picture-taking planning with Jeff—the national need let me justify my missing the religious services. By coincidence, the large Orbital Astronomical Observatory (OAO) satellite was having a problem, and I was asked to stop in to the OAO Control Center to provide some aid/advice based on my Nimbus experience, which I did when I first got to GSFC. While I was in my office working out the picture-taking schedule, Bill Stroud stepped in and learned what I was doing. He got angry and ordered me not to schedule any pictures with Jeff and the planning ended. His bitterness over NOAA's cancellation of the Nimbus satellite production deal hadn't gone away a year later. A couple of days later I worked out an arrangement with NOAA to have someone else at NOAA daily call into the control center the locations where they would like to see pictures taken—I was determined to put the picture-taking capability to good use. The problem with Stroud didn't end with his instruction about picture-taking coordination with NOAA. He then asked me who was managing the Nimbus Control Center, and I told him it was the very capable GE manager, Bennie Palmer. He shouted another irrational instruction: "Don't let your deputies (Trudell and Ormsby) take the Jewish holidays off again!"

Nimbus-3 carried an experimental atmospheric temperature measurement instrument called the Satellite Infrared Spectrometer (SIRS). The instrument was proposed by two NOAA meteorological scientists, Dr. William Smith and Dr. David Wark. This was the instrument that revolutionized weather forecasting by providing daily worldwide temperatures at different levels of the atmosphere that are absorbed in a software model to predict the weather. There were two basic scientific challenges—figuring out how to convert the different spectral (signal frequency) categories of raw measurement signals into temperature and to develop this new software model that integrated the information and made weather predictions. Smith and Wark had different approaches to these challenges and were conducting parallel developments. The conventional approach was to collect data tapes at the Nimbus ground station and send weekly batches of tapes to the scientists. When I initially planned this delivery process with Dr. Smith, he explained that the lag in delivery and the batch delivery would blunt the timeliness of any prediction. I took the initiative to have an error-correction tape transmission arrangement developed by a Code 500 Group at GSFC that could send these signals to NOAA over low-data-rate telephone lines that existed then shortly after the data was received from the satellite. This transmission arrangement was conducted for about two years, enabling NOAA to have their forecasting model working almost operationally with data from the new NOAA satellite that contained an instrument similar to SIRS. It took a lot of work for Smith and Wark to have the National Weather Service (NWS) get over the inertia that resisted change in the weather forecasting process. Six months after the NOAA researches were into their modeling to absorb the SIRS data, the head of NWS publically remarked that this satellite data will never be good enough to replace the current source of atmospheric temperature data (which consisted of sparse balloon and rocket instrument atmospheric temperature data).

The Nimbus-5 Electrically Scanning Microwave Radiometer (ESMR) provided a new field of Earth measurements from space, microwave measurements. After the scientists developed the ability to distinguish between snow, ice, and water in ESMR pictures generated in the Nimbus ground station, I went to the NOAA/NAVY Joint Ice Center in Suitland, MD, to make arrangements with the admiral in charge for them to routinely receive the polar-area ESMR pictures generated in the Nimbus MDHS for this application, to be delivered by a Nimbus courier. They used these pictures operationally to route ships through the Arctic's ice-free sea channels identified in the pictures for almost ten years until ESMR operations ended.

Nimbus-7 carried an instrument, the Coastal Zone Color Scanner, referred to as CZCS, which opened up the measurement of the oceans, shorelines, and other water bodies. The scientists learned that the CZCS instrument could measure water temperature accurately. The commercial tuna fishermen off the California coastline knew that tuna liked to feed where the ocean temperature changed sharply from cold to warm. This information was used to develop a practical, commercial application for CZCS. The Nimbus Control Center determined when Nimbus was over the California coastline and scheduled the instrument to take measurements and the CZCS data to be transmitted to the local ground station in real time. This schedule was coordinated with the Scripps Research Institute in La Jolla, CA. This oceanographic institute received the CZCS data transmitted from the spacecraft, processed it to locate the areas where the sharp temperature gradients were occurring, and faxed the locations to the commercial fishing fleets.

Supporting Other GSFC Satellite Programs

There were several opportunities for me to support other GSFC programs while I was still engaged as the Nimbus Operations Manager. I essentially undertook them on my own initiative.

A few months before the new NOAA spacecraft launch, Jack Sargent, my former co-worker on the Nimbus Project had become the project manager of a new GSFC project to build the next series of NOAA satellites based on the technology demonstrated by the early Nimbus satellites. He also served as my Nimbus attitude control expert before he became project manager. He and his wife became family friends. His predecessor had failed to incorporate in the GSFC control center the equipment required to handle the new telemetry data format and the spacecraft attitude control information. This satellite's ground system at GSFC was used to activate/ check out the spacecraft before turnover to NOAA. When he told me his troubles, I met with my ground system team to see what we could do for him. We were able to adapt the Nimbus telemetry processor to handle the NOAA data and had an RCA attitude control specialist develop the software to process the attitude control data in a standby Telemetrics computer. I arranged to have the NOAA satellite signals sent to the Nimbus ground system. I overlooked the ground system development and then the NOAA spacecraft operations support in the Nimbus Ground Station to make sure they were proper. Everything worked like charm, except the reaction from Jack and the Nimbus Project Manager, Stanley Weiland, another family friend. I was caught in a catch-22 situation. Each one complained to me periodically that I wasn't giving their respective ground operations system proper support, without being specific. They really had nothing to complain about—there was no delinquent support of their projects, everything was ready for launch for their respective satellites, and the long activation went smoothly.

I supported the Applications Technology Satellite project for two different conditions. After a GSFC panel review of the project status concluded that the Fairchild Company in Germantown designing a new ATS satellite was not well organized, I joined a GSFC review group that spent a few weeks at the plant reviewing their plans to come up with a get-well plan. Another ATS Project had a new camera instrument onboard its geosynchronous satellite that was to take pictures of the full Earth sphere. They neglected to have a ground system to quickly process the data to see if the camera system worked on turn-on. I arranged to have the computer processing/display system in the Nimbus ground system process the ATS data. (This processing system's task was to quick process the new Nimbus ocean color instrument CZCS) data.) Seeing the first picture of the full Earth globe with all its clouds come out of the processor was a thrill. The Earth globe illustration is a production version of this first ATS view of our planet.

NASA ATS III MSSCC 18 NOV 67 150303Z SSP 49.16°W 00.03°S ALT 22240.59 SM

First picture of the Earth globe taken by a satellite.

My former Nimbus co-worker Gerald Burdette was appointed project manager of the Hubble Space Telescope project after the project responsibility was moved from the NASA Marshall Space Flight Center to GSFC. The new project was shorthanded, so I helped him with systems engineering support for several months until he acquired additional support.

The TIROS-N project was established to develop a new operational spacecraft for NOAA that incorporated the new meteorological instruments developed by the Nimbus program. Rudy Stampfl, the project manager, asked me to support him by providing operational insight to the design process. I didn't let his long lingering irritation with me over the Nimbus-1 activation episode get in the way of supporting him.

Helping Initiate the Earth Observing System (EOS) Replacement to Nimbus

Every new Nimbus satellite had a new Project Manager (PM) responsible for the development of that new spacecraft. They had little interest in the older ones operating in space, so I was essentially on my own managing the spacecraft operations. A few months after the launch of the last Nimbus, number 7, in October 1978, the Nimbus Project was disbanded. Charles MacKenzie was established as Project Manager of the Satellite Operations Project responsible for the operations of Earth-viewing satellites, five satellites including Nimbus and an old Landsat satellite. I was his Deputy PM-Technical. I turned the Nimbus operations over to Michael Forman, who years earlier worked in the Nimbus ground system developing a sophisticated data system for the Infrared Interferometer Spectrometer (IRIS) instrument system. He ran a very successful Nimbus operations conducted by essentially the same General Electric crew (with new additions) under Bennie Palmer starting with Nimbus-1, conducted until the last Nimbus wore out in 1995. Michael was instrumental in replacing the room full of big computers processing the Nimbus data with a PC—representative of how advanced electronics had become in ten years.

In 1982, Burt Edelson, NASA deputy administrator for space science, envisioned a satellite that would be a follow-up to Nimbus. He called it System Z. Why this name, I don't know. He arranged for a group of Earth scientists to collaborate on developing a set of Earth science measurement requirements to be taken by the new satellite and the concepts for instruments to make those measurements. This group, led by NASA headquarter scientist Dr. Dixon Butler, included well-recognized scientists from the top national universities around the country representing all aspects of Earth science. The task was assigned to Goddard and turned over to the Satellite Operation Project for management. As the project's technical deputy manager I had the responsibility to support Dr. Butler, arranging his meetings, attending the meetings and keeping the minutes. I also helped to put together the final report by Dr. Butler. The final report included the requirement and instrument concept for every type of Earth science measurement the group selected to propose for the new Earth science satellite program to be undertaken by NASA, except for a radar-type instrument proposed by the JPL scientist that was estimated to cost as much as all the other candidate instruments.

The science study effort was followed a year later by the initiation of an EOS development project led by Mackenzie, with me as his deputy. It started with design studies to be conducted by TRW in Redondo Beach, CA, and by RCA in Hightstown, NJ. This assignment exposed me to a new set of equipment design considerations—and lots of travel again. The trips to California had a side benefit. I got opportunities to see my son, David, and my uncle Nat and his family. My relationship with TRW was poor. Their designs had many deficiencies regarding accommodating the instrument support requirements, and they were not open to suggestions. I sensed they were not interested in this effort, believing the program had no future. It had not yet been established as a firm new program. After the second design review by GSFC, the TRW design effort was terminated. On the other hand, I had a very effective, congenial working relationship with the RCA design group. I met with each subsystem design group and was able to offer suggestions for improvement, many coming from my colleagues at GSFC. A major contributor was Seymor Kant, a multitalented engineer who was the attitude control expert and systems engineer supporting all Nimbus satellite developments and Nimbus and Landsat spacecraft operations. His extraordinary talent was such that in his last ten or so years at GSFC before retirement they allowed him to pick his own advanced studies subject to get involved with. He likely set a record for years of civil service employment as an engineering professional with sixty-four years of government service that included 13 years at the Naval Gun Factory located in the Washington Navy Yard. When the RCA engineering study group heard of my retirement and quick departure from NASA, they got together to take a group picture that they gave me annotated with best wishes from all in the picture.

RCA EOS study team posing for picture they sent me.
Picture frame, not shown, annotated with good wishes.

This exploratory design effort later evolved into what is known as the EOS Program consisting of three large Earth-observing satellites, 1) Terra, measuring the Earth's environment and changes in the climate system; 2) Aqua, measuring the Earth's water properties, and 3) Aura, measuring atmospheric Ozone.

NASA Space Station Concept Development Team Participation

In November 1983 I was appointed to represent GSFC on the Space Station Concept Development Group that met downtown in Washington DC, requiring me to be a subway commuter. My role was to see how servicing of NASA satellites could be incorporated into the mission of the space station being conceived by the group of engineers from the various NASA centers. The design was completed and presented with an $11 billion cost estimate to NASA administrator Jim Beggs in April 1864, which I sat in on. Beggs listened and had one comment—"The cost is $9 billion"—and walked out. That was evidently all the budget could afford. The actual space station design followed this group's modular design concept, but the space station activities widened and the size expanded to about five times larger. It became an international space station. The total United States cost through 2012 was approximately $150 billion. I received this relevant cartoon with a complimentary comment from Luther Powell, who led the concept development group.

Cartoon sent to me by Luther Powell, Concept Development Group Manager.

The space station system through the space shuttle element did accomplish satellite servicing. The highlight was the several repairs to the Hubble Space Telescope satellite, which received good news coverage. This spacecraft and instrument servicing extended the life of Hubble many years, enabling it to continue to operate after successive failures several years apart. It is still operative NN years after it was first launched. The Jackson and Tull (J&T) engineering company in the Washington DC area supported the Goddard Space Flight Center organization with the servicing responsibility. J&T had the major role in developing the unique servicing systems for each Hubble-servicing mission. Coincidently, I had been providing proposal development consulting support to J&T for several years, and as recently as I was completing this book.

Retirement from NASA

In May 1986 I had reason to consider retirement from government service. Congress had passed a law starting in June not allowing an individual to receive both a government pension and Social Security benefits, which is called double-dipping. If I kept on working, I had to lose the Social Security benefits based on my eighteen years of commercial employment prior to working for NASA. I had the necessary longevity with government employment to get a full retirement at age sixty-two, which I achieved that May. Besides this financial consideration, the GSFC work environment had become somewhat uncomfortable. The EOS program was becoming an attractive program for the younger engineers in my division to want to get involved with, and a couple took an active role in trying to take over my position as EOS technical manager. (One chap apologized to me years later.) For these two reasons, I decided to retire. My retirement did not last long. I submitted my retirement application to be effective the last Friday of May. I started work for STX the next Monday morning.

For someone who didn't have the experience or even academic training at the start of my GSFC employment, I left GSFC feeling very content that I earned my keep there, having made many contributions particularly to the success of the Nimbus program. This was reflected in the NASA Headquarters' Exceptional Service Medal and the GSFC Exceptional Performance Award, the several GSFC cost-savings awards, and the grade raises I received. I was extremely appreciative of the opportunity to work there. I look at the information about NASA that I present in this book as payback for that wonderful opportunity. I am working with the GSFC Center Directorate to develop a Nimbus accomplishment publicity program in connection with the 50th anniversary of the first Nimbus spacecraft launch coming up in August 2014.

Chapter 4

Nimbus Satellite Program Benefits

Unmanned Earth-observation scientific satellites orbiting Earth since 1960 have had a profound impact on everyone's lives in so many respects that go unrecognized by the general public. The scientific study of the data derived from the many US and international satellites operated has been able to significantly advance many public services, including weather forecasting (accuracy and time duration), tornado warnings, climate knowledge, environmental assessments (air pollution, ozone protection, shoreline protection, land and ocean/lakes/river oil-spill pollution control), global land mapping, agricultural planning, human safety, Arctic Sea ship navigation, and more. The continuing improvements in these services resulted from several factors: (1) the ability to make worldwide, daily, and timely measurements; (2) the advancement in the technology required to measure the chemistry (e.g., O_2, O_3, H_2O, CO) and physics (temperature, wind speed) of the air, oceans, and land component characteristics; (3) ability to get the data in a timely fashion to address time-critical problems; (4) advancement in scientific knowledge regarding obtaining new types of measurements resulting from the use of satellite data; (5) cooperation of international agencies and scientists; and (6) the availability of large, fast computers to efficiently conduct the processing of large amounts of data.

Nimbus Benefits to Society

As a result of the Nimbus meteorological developments we now have more accurate, three-to-five-day-duration global weather forecasting as opposed to the previous regional, less-accurate, one-day-duration weather forecasts. Prior to the weather satellites, temperature and wind measurements required for the weather prediction were taken only in the lower atmosphere sparsely around the country by rocket-launched or balloon-launched instruments; airplane pilot weather reports were the only meteorological inputs over the oceans. Today, as a result of the Nimbus program's meteorological measurement advances, many more atmospheric parameter measurements are taken over the full height of the atmosphere globally and taken multiple times daily by various NOAA operational satellite systems, and by international satellites.

Worldwide environmental protection was another major Nimbus program benefit. The importance of ozone (O_3) gas in the upper atmosphere (stratosphere) to limit the harmful ultraviolet sunlight that causes skin cancer from getting to Earth was becoming more understood. After the new Nimbus atmospheric ozone measurement instrumentation in conjunction with a ground system for taking these ozone measurements discovered that this ozone protection layer was being reduced significantly over populated areas of the world, chlorofluorocarbons (Freon) refrigerants that destroy the ozone were banned internationally; an international satellite program is in place that measures the stratospheric ozone to identify any new human health threat.

Another Nimbus benefit, and probably the most important benefit because of all of the lives being saved annually, is the satellite search and rescue system that was developed on the Nimbus program. Not being scientific, this benefit gets little recognition. Since the search and rescue system location computational technique was developed and demonstrated by a Nimbus satellite instrument in 1977, an international search and rescue (SAR) system has been in place, supported by international search and rescue satellites and now by the Global Positioning Satellites (GPS). This SAR system that locates downed small aircraft and wrecked boats is reported to have saved twenty-seven thousand lives worldwide since its inception.

Nimbus Contribution to Science

One of the most important scientific contributions of the Nimbus missions was their measurements of Earth's radiation budget. For the first time, scientists had direct global observations of the amount of solar radiation entering and exiting Earth's energy system. The observations helped to verify and refine the earliest climate models and are still making important contributions to the study of climate change. As scientists consider the causes and effects of global warming, Nimbus radiation budget data provides a base for long-term analyses and made change-detection studies possible. The Nimbus technology gave rise to current radiation-budget sensors, such as the Clouds and Earth's Radiant Energy System (CERES) instrument on NASA's latest large Earth observation satellites, the Terra and Aqua satellites.

Weather Forecasting Revolution

When it comes to weather satellites, it is not a stretch to say that nearly everything that the present-day instruments are capable of measuring about Earth's atmospheric behavior has its roots in the pioneering technology developed by the third Nimbus satellite. Today, anyone with an Internet connection and even the slightest interest can pull up the latest satellite image showing the weather over his or her hometown. But fifty years ago, the idea that we could measure something as intangible as air temperature using a satellite orbiting hundreds of miles above Earth was revolutionary. With each Nimbus mission, scientists broadened their ability to collect atmospheric characteristics that improved weather forecasting, including lower-atmospheric and stratospheric temperature profiles, cloudiness, water vapor, rain, and oceanic temperatures and winds. The global coverage of these meteorological parameters provided by Nimbus satellites made accurate three-to-five-day forecasts possible for the first time.

Prior to satellites there was sparse information about the condition of the atmosphere that affects the weather. There were personal observations of cloudiness and wind motion from meteorologists around the United States and called in by commercial pilots while flying over the oceans near the United States. Some weather data were also obtained by meteorological instruments on balloons and radiosondes (measured temperature) and rawindsondes (measured winds) carried by rockets during times of the day when it was thought this information had the maximum impact on weather-forecasting models. This expendable equipment system was labor intensive and thus rather expensive for the relatively small data points collected. With this sparsity of information, accurate one-day forecasts were real challenges.

More accurate, longer-term (three to five days) weather forecasting is now realistic because weather satellite systems are capable of measuring global atmosphere and stratosphere temperature, and moisture vertical profiles under clear and cloudy conditions. Rainfall can be measured. Cloud coverage can be collected for determining wind speed and direction. Multiple weather satellites operating at different times of the day collecting similar types of data enables the weather-forecasting models to be more accurate. Satellites that are high enough to stay positioned over the same Earth location (a geosynchronous orbit) provide continuous weather data for the weather-forecasting models.

Climatology

Climate behavior and climate change prediction is a subject of current interest in relation to the profound subject of global warming. Where does natural climate change fit in? Is it a driver of global change, or is climate change a result of the world's environmental behavior, or a combination of both? Without satellite data, the climatology field scientists who use worldwide models of the atmospheric phenomenon that drive the climate conditions from which to forecast potential climate changes would have little information with which to conduct their analyses of the climate changes. Earth's climate is an Earth-sun-coupled energy system tied to the sun's input, the energy radiating away from Earth, the ocean energy behavior, the atmosphere behavior and the cryosphere (polar ice and ocean iceberg areas). Only satellites are in position to collect the various data sets necessary to conduct climatology studies. The related worldwide concern about the possibility of human-induced global warming would have remained subdued without the availability of satellite data to support the global warming research studies.

Environmental Protection

Environmental protection is another major public concern that feeds off satellite data of another kind, global atmospheric chemistry measurements. This concern blossomed after satellite data confirmed that there were large-size (measured in millions of square kilometers) ozone holes (amounts of ozone below what is considered normal and safe values) in the upper atmosphere (stratosphere). The ozone layer protects humans against the sun's extreme ultraviolet exposure that causes skin cancer. Initially it was discovered over Antarctica by ground instruments in place to monitor the ozone layer because of the importance to human health. When the Nimbus satellite global ozone data revealed these detrimental holes existed over heavily populated areas of the world, the worldwide governmental community took corrective action. They mandated the elimination of CFC (chlorofluorocarbons) refrigerants that contributed to the formation of the ozone holes. This life-threatening ozone-hole impact on the world population was severe enough to result in the US and Soviet governments committing to a collaborative effort to continuously operate a satellite ozone measuring system to monitor the ozone distribution in the stratosphere around the world.

Oil Spill Control

For the past thirty years, almost every year there has been a ship oil spill discharging millions of gallons of oil that has contaminated coastlines. Perhaps the most-reported spills are the Exxon Valdez spill, which spilled 11 million gallons off the coast of Alaska in 1989, and the Amoco Cadiz spill, which spilled 68 million gallons off the coast of France in 1978. Depending on the circumstances, oil spills can be very harmful to marine birds and mammals and also can harm fish and shellfish. You may have seen dramatic pictures of oiled birds and sea otters that have been affected by oil spills. Oil destroys the insulating ability of fur-bearing mammals, such as sea otters, and the water-repelling abilities of a bird's feathers, thus exposing these creatures to harsh elements. Many birds and animals also ingest (swallow) oil when they try to clean themselves, which can poison them. Several techniques have been developed to clean the spills, but the tracking of the spills that start to cover a vast area as the ocean currents carry the thinned-out oil slick can only be accomplished through the aid of satellites taking pictures of the contaminated areas.

Reacting to Disruptive Volcanoes

The occasional explosive eruption of active volcanoes not only causes great destruction on the ground but can also potentially have a devastating effect on jet aircraft; the volcanic plumes are destructive to jet engines. The winds carry the volcanic-ash trails for thousands of miles crossing aircraft flight paths. The affected areas are too large to be monitored by aircraft. Fortunately, the detection of the sulfur dioxide and volcanic ash spewed out by the volcanoes can be detected by the same satellite instrumentation that monitors the ozone in the atmosphere. Operational plans are in place to use the US operational satellites with these instruments to determine the path of the volcanic plumes as they erupt and to reroute commercial aircraft away from the contaminated areas.

Hurricane Warnings

Over the past few years, the United States suffered much damage as a result of hurricane winds and the follow-on flooding that frequently occurs. Much of the property damage that occurs can't be avoided, but many human lives have been saved thanks to the hurricane warning systems in place that rely on satellite information. The Nimbus program started the picture-taking capability that first detects new hurricanes spawning in the eastern Atlantic Ocean, tracks its motion until landfall, and measures the intensity of the winds. You will learn how these capabilities were developed in the discussions of the accomplishments of the individual Nimbus satellites.

Oceanographic Studies

The vast oceans that cover 80 percent of Earth's area can only be studied effectively through the use of satellite data. Oceanographic behavioral knowledge contributing to water-basin preservation and shoreline protection, hydrologic data supporting water conservation, cartography with improved land and snow cover mapping, and many other related field studies rely on measurement taken by satellite.

Technology Transfer

Nimbus-3 flew two devices that were the forerunners in their technology fields. One was an experimental gyroscope pressurized to support an air bearing design that gave the instrument a sharper signal output than the models with standard ball bearings. This design became the standard for space flight applications. The other was a small nuclear electrical power generator device, the Radioisotope Thermoelectric Generator (RTG), a design that was used to power spacecraft going to deep space where there is too little sunlight to power the spacecraft.

Nimbus-3 and 4 carried a system that interrogated a platform around the world and computed its location based on the signal Nimbus received back from the platform, and collected platform data. This technique was advanced for the Nimbus-6 satellite, which carried a system that collected data and located a remote platform without the need to interrogate the platform. It is the system used for the international search and rescue system and to track animal and ocean fish migration. It was instrumental in saving the lives of two balloonists and another adventurer described in the book's Preface.

Chapter 5

Satellite Systems Basic Tutorial

I anticipate that most readers of this book have little knowledge about satellites. In this section, I attempted to provide a tutorial on this subject that is not very technical for the benefit of this category of reader. It provides an opportunity to understand the basics of satellite systems and to better comprehend my experience narratives involving satellite technology.

Understanding Scientific Satellites and Their Operations

Jules Verne, the French author, pioneered science fiction with novels such as *Twenty Thousand Leagues Under the Sea* (1870), *Journey to the Center of the Earth* (1864), and *Around the World in Eighty Days* (1873). He wrote about space travel long before practical means of space travel had been devised. It wasn't until the post—World War II cold war period between the United States and the Soviet Union that rockets developed for military applications had the capacity to put objects in space. In 1955, the USA announced plans to put a scientific satellite in orbit in 1957/58 as a part of the International Geophysical Year (IGY) activity. The International Council of Scientific Unions (ICSU) established the IGY in 1952, with the objective of conducting a comprehensive series of global geophysical activities to span the period of July 1957-December 1958, which coincided with the peak of the sun spot activity (electrical radiations that affect global communications). The US government actually undertook to develop a satellite program to study the Earth's upper atmosphere. The satellite program was called Vanguard and was assigned to the Naval Research Laboratory (NRL), which was basically considered to be a scientific rather than a military organization. By assigning it to NRL, it emphasized the nonmilitary goals of the satellite program, avoiding public discussions as to whether it was legal to conduct overflights of foreign countries by satellites.

On October 4, 1957, the Soviet Union surprised the world with the successful launch of Sputnik 1. The satellite, about the size of a basketball, weighed approximately 185 pounds, and took ninety-six minutes to orbit Earth. It embarrassed the United States. The first two Vanguard satellite launch attempts before Sputnik were failures. The next two hurry-up, catch-up attempts were also failures. The first successful Vanguard satellite was launched on March 17, 1958. It weighed 3.3 lbs. and was 6 inches in diameter. Both Sputnik and Vanguard were simple demonstrations of satellites being placed in orbit around Earth by sending radio beacon (transmitter) signals. Sputnik was battery powered and lasted three weeks. Vanguard, the first satellite to be powered by solar cells, operated for eight years. Vanguard-1 also transmitted the first satellite engineering (telemetry) information, the satellite internal temperatures, providing some insight as to how thermal control systems worked in space.

The US scientific community reacted to the Sputnik and Vanguard space news with new concepts for satellite applications for both civilian and defense applications. The defense and political communities first responded, creating the Advanced Research Projects Agency in February 1958 to serve as a high-level Department of Defense organization to execute research and development (R&D) projects. It later became the Defense Advanced Research Projects Agency or simply called DARPA. On July 29, 1958, President Eisenhower formally brought the United States into the space race by signing the National Aeronautics and Space Act, creating the National Aeronautics and Space Administration (NASA), which was to take on the responsibility for developing civilian scientific satellites and the manned satellite programs. In 1960, the responsibility for civilian-application satellite operations was assigned to the Department of Commerce's Environmental Satellite Service Administration (ESSA), later designated as the National Oceanographic and Atmospheric Administration (NOAA). As the name implies, NOAA operates satellites that monitor the condition of the nation's oceanic shores and Earth's atmosphere to support the nation's weather-forecasting system. NASA retained the responsibility for developing new concepts for operational satellite instrumentation and building the new application satellites for NOAA.

Scientific satellites provide information for the scientific study of Earth's dynamic atmospheric, oceanographic, and land behavior affecting Earth's climate, weather, and environmental control. Satellites also measure the sun's behavior to further understand Earth's behavior because of the direct relationship of the sun's energy radiation and Earth's heat balance. Astronomy, the study of the celestial bodies, and astrophysics, the study of the physical properties of the universe, are also conducted using data taken by satellite instrumentation.

These unmanned research satellite systems all have three major components designed to meet the satellite mission objectives, the space component (spacecraft and the instruments on the spacecraft that make the measurements), the ground component (the satellite control center and data collection system), and the science research component that makes use of the data to study Earth's climate, improve weather forecasting, support environmental issues, and more.

The space component includes the launch complex, where the satellite is attached to a launch vehicle (large rocket), the big tower that supports the rocket until it blasts off into space and the rocket that places the satellite into the desired orbit going around Earth or to the moon or planets. The manned space shuttle, which recently ended operations, also served as the launching platform for small satellites and the satellite repair service station (such as the Hubble Space Telescope satellite) for the past twenty years.

Earth viewing satellites are placed into two categories of orbits (a rotation around the Earth), low Earth orbit (LEO) and geostationary (GEO). LEO satellites are either: 1) equatorial (circle the Earth over the equator) or at a varying inclination up to 70° inclination to the equator, or 2) sun-synchronous (orbit plane in line with sun's rays), which puts the satellite in approximately a 90° inclination orbit that crosses close to the North and South poles. The satellite is kept being pulled down by Earth's gravity, which counters the satellite velocity trying to move the satellite away from 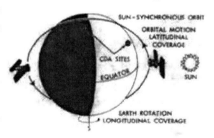 the Earth, thereby keeping the satellite in orbit. The orbit can be designed to be circular (generally for Earth science satellites) or eccentric (generally for atmospheric science satellites). The Launch vehicle has to have enough power to lift the particular satellite's weight to the desired altitude and then fire again at the desired altitude with a lighter force sufficient to overcome the Earth's pull in order to circularize the orbit. The satellite is then pushed off the launch vehicle and goes into its orbit around Earth while the launch vehicle orbit altitude rapidly decreases and returns to Earth under controlled, relatively safe reentry conditions (avoid populated areas). LEO altitudes are basically below 600 nautical miles (1100 km) above the Earth's surface. At this altitude the orbital period to circle the planet is approximately 100 minutes and there are approximately fourteen orbits each day before the pattern repeats. The lower the orbit, the shorter is the orbital period. The orbit can cross the equator during daylight going northward, called an ascending node, or cross southward, called a descending node. A GEO orbit is a circular orbit at an altitude of 22,236 nautical miles (35,786 km) above Earth's equator following the direction of Earth's rotation. An object in such an orbit has an orbital period equal to Earth's rotational period of one day; and therefore, to ground observers, it appears motionless at a fixed position in the sky.

Almost all of the US satellites in low Earth orbit (LEO) and inclined to the equator were launched from the NASA Kennedy Space Center at Cape Canaveral off the east coast of Florida. Launching the rocket eastward over the Atlantic Ocean represents a low hazard by not flying over populated areas. Very recently, NASA successfully initiated launching small satellites from the Wallops Flight Center launch facility at Wallops, VA, previously used for launching non-orbiting rockets carrying atmospheric probes. Sun-synchronous, polar orbit satellites are launched southward from the Vandenberg Air Force Base at Lompoc, CA, going over the Pacific Ocean for the same safety objective as for equatorial satellites.

The ground component is supported by the NASA institutional worldwide data acquisition sites and the NASA satellite-tracking and data-acquisition system (known as the Tracking and Data Relay Satellite System, or TDRSS) for sending spacecraft-operating instructions (command signals) from the spacecraft control center to the spacecraft and receiving the science and spacecraft engineering data from the spacecraft. The data acquisition sites send data and receive commands through high-speed ground communication links with the respective satellite control centers.

The science research and application segment represents the mission purpose and objective of each of the satellite program. The science research is generally conducted by teams of government and national and international institutional scientists. The application of the data to the services provided to the community is accomplished by governmental agencies and more recently by commercial enterprises.

In the early years of the satellite programs, the United States and the Soviet Union were the only countries with the personnel resources and technical capability to build and launch satellites. Many countries now have this capability to build, launch, and operate satellites for conducting their own scientific research and applications, generally in collaboration with scientific research conducted by worldwide scientists.

The following sections are intended to convey a general understanding of how Earth-viewing satellite programs operate and what influences their design. Although the descriptions apply to Earth-resources satellites, the concepts described basically also apply to astronomy and astrophysics satellites. Similarly, although the references are to the US satellites and ground support infrastructure, these concepts generally apply to the satellites launched by the international community of nations.

Satellite Design Concept: Satellite Overview

An Earth science satellite is fundamentally a factory in space. The spacecraft housing is akin to the factory building. It is shaped to both accommodate the requirements of the manufacturing equipment on the spacecraft, which are the scientific instruments that measure some aspect of Earth's performance and behavior, and provide the spacecraft utilities that support the manufacturing process and business communications. It has an electrical power system that derives its power from sunlight and provides battery power when the spacecraft is in darkness. It includes some form of a thermal control system to keep the spacecraft components from getting too hot or too cold. There is an information system that collects, stores, and retrieves the data for transmission to the ground through a communication system that both sends the data to the ground and receives the command instructions on operating the instruments and the satellite itself. A distinctive additional component of this satellite factory is the system that controls the factory from tumbling like a top due to gravity and keeps it in the right position for the instruments measuring Earth to look at Earth (or sun, moon, or stars). It is called the attitude control system. The instrument that makes the measurements has its own control system that varies in motion for each instrument, depending on what the instrument wants to look at. It can look straight down, scan from one side to the other, cover a small area or large area of the ground (e.g., 1,500-mile swath), or look at an angle when it looks at the limb of the Earth. The instrument looks at Earth in a special signal frequency, depending on what it wants to measure. This characteristic is explained in the electromagnetic spectrum, Section 5, page 188.

Nimbus Satellite Design. The ten-foot-tall Nimbus spacecraft illustrated in Chapter 7 has the attitude control system (on top) separated from the five-foot-diameter sensory ring (bottom of spacecraft). Spacecraft and instrument electronics fit into the fourteen sensory element compartments; instruments were mounted under, inside, and on top of the sensory ring. The three-axis stabilization, Earth-pointing attitude control system (a technological first for civilian spacecraft) maintained the attitude within one degree of pointing accuracy and with low jitter. The satellites operated in a noon, ascending node (i.e., crossed the equator northbound at noon local time), near-polar sun-synchronous orbit, and at a 900-1100 km altitude that resulted in thirteen to fourteen orbits per day. The orbit around Earth is shown in the illustration. The polar orbit inclination is set to be more than 90 degrees, such that the slight motion of the orbit plane matches the rotation rate of Earth about the sun, and the orbit repeats daily over the same Earth location. Depending on the particular Nimbus altitude, it ranged between 98 and 99 degrees. This sun-synchronous orbit, a first for meteorological satellites, provided both daytime and nighttime local coverage every twenty-four hours, repeated at the same time daily. Equatorial locations received twice-daily coverage; higher latitudes received more daily coverage as the orbits all converged to cross the poles, but the instrument viewing swath width remained the same. This polar orbit provided global data that was very beneficial for weather-forecasting models and became the norm for operational meteorological satellites. Beginning with Nimbus and its contemporary TIROS satellites, weather forecasters were able to move beyond the relatively sparse airplane and ship reports, and the meager radiosonde and rawinsonde atmospheric temperature and wind data.

Power System. The standard source of satellite power is sunlight, which is converted to electrical power by solar cells—originally developed for the initial US satellite program but now common as a source of residential and commercial facility power. Solar cells are mounted on the satellite platform's outer body to generate electric power from the sun in the daylight portion of the orbit. Since the portion of the spacecraft structure viewing the sun is constantly changing around the orbit, each solar cell views the sun only during a small portion of the daylight period. A more efficient use of the cells is to mount them on paddles that track the sun during the entire daylight portion of the orbit, such as on Nimbus spacecraft. Solar cell output degrades after a few years, representing a limiting factor in the longevity of the satellite. For sun-synchronous satellites, another solar input factor is the orbit plane alignment to the sun. Due to Earth's uneven diameter at the equator, this bulge applies forces that cause the orbit plane to drift away from alignment to the sun, causing loss of power as a function of the cosine of the orbit plane alignment angle.

The power system includes a power regulation and conditioning system that converts the raw electricity from the solar cells to DC power at a stable voltage level, generally 24V DC, and frequently converts the power to lower-voltage levels as required by many electronic circuits, e.g., 6V DC.

Batteries supply power to the spacecraft and instruments when the satellite orbit takes it behind Earth and hidden from the sun's rays. The power system also includes the circuitry to manage the battery system, controlling the battery-recharging rates at safe levels and interfacing the battery outputs to the voltage control/regulation system. Multiple batteries are generally incorporated into the battery system to provide more system reliability. Nickel hydrogen is the primary type battery, followed by Nickel Cadmium. Longer-life, more efficient batteries for spacecraft operations are under continual development.

Spacecraft that go to the outer planets can't generate enough power from the dim sunlight that far from the sun. Low-level nuclear-powered devices, radioisotope thermoelectric generator (RTG) systems, are used to provide the power for these applications.

Command and Data Handling System. The command and data system serves several functions. It handles and distributes the instructions from the ground, receives status (e.g., on/off state, component mode that is operative), and engineering/health information (e.g., operating temperature, electric currents and voltages, motor speeds) from all the spacecraft and instrument subsystems in a coded data word format called telemetry. The telemetry and scientific instrument output data are stored in the spacecraft computer memory device or on tape recorders for later relay to the ground. It also provides the timing signals that synchronizes the equipment and provides intercommunication between all the spacecraft elements. This clock signal and its derived spacecraft frequencies are developed from a precise, stable crystal oscillator. It is also used to develop a clock to time tag the science and telemetry data.

Attitude Control Spacecraft Stabilization and Pointing System. For non-spinning spacecraft, the attitude control system keeps the spacecraft in the desired stable orientation rather than tumbling like a top when it loses its control due to gravity and the forces of the sun in the atmosphere where the spacecraft is, which works even at the high altitude above Earth. It keeps the spacecraft from moving ever so slightly (stable) so the instruments can point at their ground targets precisely and repeatedly. Earth-horizon-scanning devices on both sides of the spacecraft provide signals that are used to adjust the roll (side to side) and pitch (front to back) attitudes of the spacecraft within the required pointing accuracy. A sun scanner provides the signal to adjust the spacecraft yaw attitude within the required pointing accuracy. Spacecraft with celestial instruments have star trackers programmed to look at select bright stars in the area of the stars to be examined to keep the spacecraft attitude stable and the instruments pointing at the sky area or star of interest.

Communication System. The communication system operates at different bands like AM and FM radio channels. It receives the command instructions from the spacecraft control center that are uplinked from the ground tracking stations (or from TDRSS) and downlinks to the ground tracking stations (or through TDRSS) the various streams of spacecraft and instrument data that are generated with each particular spacecraft. The downstream signal serves another purpose. It is used to track the position of the satellite for generating a mathematical model of the satellite orbit (called an ephemeris) that is used to position the ground station antennas to accurately point to the satellite passing overhead when communicating with the satellite. This ephemeris is also used to generate the Earth location of the science data in the data-processing system. Many spacecraft now carry a Global Positioning System (GPS) device that continually computes the spacecraft location in real time from signals received from the multiple US GPS satellites that orbit Earth; this location data is transmitted to the ground with the other spacecraft data. A backup spacecraft ephemeris is computed by the Air Force's NORAD system derived from the system's radar tracking data taken for all satellites and junk space objects in near-Earth orbits.

Thermal Control System. The outer-space temperature seen by the satellite when not looking at Earth or the sun is very cold, -273°C. Thermal-insulating blankets are wrapped around the sides of the spacecraft to keep it from cooling off to low temperatures at which it could not operate. For areas that don't permit effective use of these thermal blankets, electric heaters or heated liquid circulating in small tubing are used. Conversely, if the equipment needs to be cooled, radiator panes are opened to look at deep space to cool the equipment, or the technique of liquid flowing in tubing is used but the liquid is cooled rather than heated. The electric power consumed in operating the equipment is an inherent source of heat. The scientific measuring device (sensor) in a scientific instrument generally operates at a specific low temperature, requiring a special thermal control device/system to maintain that particular temperature.

Payload. Unique designs are required for the instrument's mechanism that scans Earth to suit the instrument's Earth coverage objectives and for instrument optical element telescope-type design that look at a large area of Earth or the sky and images what it sees onto a very small measuring device (sensor) that puts out an electrical signal proportional to the intensity of signal it is measuring, or for taking a picture of the land, oceans, or clouds.

Satellite Earth Science Basics

Earth science covers four areas of Earth's dynamically active elements that everyone has an interest in—the atmosphere, which affects our weather and climate; the ocean, which affects our shorelines, where the fish live, and which also affects our climate; the land masses, where the vegetation and trees grow; and the polar ice masses, also known as the cryosphere, which affect our climate and is also affected by Earth's climate. These activities interact as one ecological system. Another area of Earth science that is mostly of scientific interest is the geological history of Earth and how Earth's geological formations are slowly moving.

Satellites offer an extremely beneficial method of measuring Earth's behavior in these areas. These measurements can be taken globally, which would otherwise take prohibitive, enormous human and instrumentation equipment resources. Measurements can be taken over sparsely traversed oceanic areas. Short-term detailed data is now available to understand short-term phenomena, such as hurricane behavior. Long-term data is now available to understand long-term phenomena, such as climate change and related global warming concerns.

Scientists have developed methods of remotely detecting the wide range of physical properties associated with Earth science, such as atmospheric chemistry discriminating water vapor, ozone, and other species; oceanic content such as chlorophyll and living organisms that fish feed on, such as phytoplankton; and types of trees and vegetation growing. They have used the same basic approach to remotely measure the accurate behavior of these physical properties that is so important to societal services, such accurate atmospheric temperature at all levels of the atmosphere essential for accurate weather forecasting, quantities of crop growth for agricultural management, and ocean temperature for hurricane-formation prediction and climate change research.

Measuring Earth's Behavior from Satellites

This common approach to the remote sensing and measurement of Earth's behavior is based on the fundamental behavior of all natural objects; they either transmit or reflect light. In this remote-sensing context, light is the full electromagnetic spectrum of radiation, visible light being only a very narrow, small element of the full spectrum.

Electromagnetic Spectrum. The electromagnetic spectrum includes bands of radiation that everyone is familiar with, such as visible light from the sun or electric bulbs, AM and FM radio channels, telephone and television communication channels, infrared used to create heat, microwave that domestically is used to heat food, x-rays for examining bones and teeth, and ultraviolet light coming from the sun that we protect against with sunscreen to avoid skin cancer. Some may be familiar with the gamma ray band that the star universe emits but also radiates from nuclear power plants.

These same channels of electromagnetic radiation are used in a much different manner to measure Earth's physical properties and behavior. For example, there are channels in the infrared range that radiate as a function of atmospheric temperature. It is more precise than that. There are narrow bands within the wide infrared band that radiate more sensitively to particular temperature ranges and with sensitivity to water vapor in the atmosphere. In view of the normal atmospheric behavior, whereby the atmospheric temperature level varies with altitude, satellite instruments that measure atmospheric temperature use a combination of these temperature-sensitive infrared bands to accurately measure temperature over the full atmosphere altitude. Other narrow bands within the infrared channel are sensitive to water vapor in the atmosphere. These bands are used to detect clouds.

Another example is how ozone is measured in the atmosphere. The sun radiates ultraviolet energy, which is reflected back by the ozone layer in the upper atmosphere, protecting Earth from this deadly radiation. Ozone radiates in the ultraviolet band. Satellite instruments that measure ozone in the atmosphere measure the level of ultraviolet radiation reflected back from Earth's atmosphere in relation to the level of the atmosphere's sun radiation that is measured at the same time.

The instrumentation on the seven Nimbus spacecraft took measurements in five different spectral regions—visible, infrared, far infrared, ultraviolet, and microwave—with Nimbus-6 and Nimbus-7 covering all five spectral regions.

Frequency of Radiation. Each band in the spectrum vibrates, i.e., the signal level goes up and down like ocean waves at a uniform, smoothly increasing and decreasing rate. For example, home electricity vibrates at sixty cycles per second. However, the frequencies in the electromagnetic spectrum are at very much higher cycles-per-second rates. The rate-per-second expression is commonly designated as hertz (Hz), in honor of the German physicist Heinrich Hertz who is recognized as the first to prove the existence of electromagnetic waves. Because of the extremely large frequencies involved, the size of the frequency is annotated in a compact mathematical expression of large numbers known as 10 to a power, which represents how many times you have to multiply ten to arrive at the actual number. For example, the AM radio band has a frequency band of five thousand cycles, or 10^5 Hz; the infrared band has a multimillion frequency ranging from 10^{11} to 10^{14} Hz.

Who Builds Satellites

The NASA satellites are built by the NASA Goddard Space Flight Center (GSFC), by university NASA-affiliated organizations, such as the Applied Physics Laboratory (APL) and the Jet Propulsion Laboratory, and by commercial organizations such as General Electric, Ball Brothers, and Orbital Sciences. The instruments are built by GSFC and a wide variety of commercial organizations. GSFC is responsible for building the NOAA operational weather satellites.

How Satellites Are Tested

The satellites are designed and analyzed to survive the very harsh launch forces applied to the spacecraft by the rocket that lifts it from the ground and puts it into the intended orbit in space. To assure that the spacecraft can survive the launch forces, it is tested on the ground. It is mounted on a vibration machine that applies a wide range of vibrations that simulate the forces and vibrations the satellite would see during launch, which shakes the spacecraft violently, applying forces equal to many times the gravity force.

The satellites are designed to operate in the vacuum of space and be kept warm enough to survive the almost-absolute zero outer-space temperature. On the other hand, some of the instrument components, such as the instrument sensors (detectors), need to be kept cold by looking at outer space. For testing the satellite's behavior under these conditions, this tricky combination of vacuum and temperature conditions is achieved in a thermal vacuum chamber, which comes in all sizes. Nimbus was tested in a thirty-six-foot-diameter chamber. Vacuum pumps slowly evacuate the chamber with the satellite inside to achieve the required vacuum level, with electrical connections through the chamber wall to connect cables to the ground equipment sitting outside the chamber that runs the tests and cables from the wall to the spacecraft to interconnect with the ground equipment.

Cryogenically cooled walls and cold plates and heated panels provide the combination of required temperature conditions. The tests are run for several days with the spacecraft at the expected operating temperature and at higher and lower temperatures to demonstrate a safety margin. During this period (or when the instrument undergoes these tests by itself before being installed on the spacecraft), the instrument looks at targets with the scene characteristics the instrument will see when it operates in space in order to accurately calibrate the data (i.e., the relationship between the data values and the measured physical parameter values.)

Satellites have RF communications systems onboard to send data to the ground, receive commands from the ground, and generally as part of an instrument onboard the particular spacecraft. Tests are conducted to assure that there is no interference between the RF signals and that the RF signals do not contaminate the instrument measurements. These tests are conducted in a chamber that has special material to avoid RF signal reflections (anechoic chamber) or conducted in isolated fields to avoid external inputs or artificial reflections.

The expected lifetime of a satellite and its equipment early on in the satellite world was two years. With improved electrical components and improved knowledge of how to keep moving parts from seizing, the lifetime of satellites is generally five years. Life test are conducted on parts that do not have a heritage of demonstrated long-life capability.

In addition to the vacuum and cold temperature conditions, the satellite equipment is exposed to categories of sun radiation and particles that are not seen on the ground because Earth's atmosphere blocks these solar outputs. New electronic devices are subjected to the assortment of the sun's rays and articles to demonstrate they do not degrade and have the required lifetime before they are qualified for space applications.

Satellite Operations

Satellite operations vary with the nature of the instruments onboard the spacecraft. Some instruments operate full time day and night, whereas other instruments only operate during the daylight portion of the orbit. Some instruments are operated to view discrete targets and have to be commanded on at the right time. When there is insufficient solar power input to operate in the normal full-time mode, the instrument operations are shared with duty cycles according to the individual spacecraft's project scientist's instructions. Satellites that have equipment that can address international emergencies get the high priority to support emergency operations and ground station access for special commanding and data retrieval on the ground.

Ground System Operations

There are two components to a satellite's ground system operation. One is the NASA network of spacecraft data acquisition and commanding stations and supportive international stations that communicates with a spacecraft nominally once an orbit to receive the spacecraft data and send commands. The basic system is the Spacecraft Tracking and Data (Acquisition) Network (STDN). The major STDN station is in Fairbanks, AK, a site I have fond memories of from my Nimbus-1 first orbit operations management experience there in 1964. The newer system is the NASA Tracking and Data Relay Satellite System (TDRSS), which is a network of American communications satellites called Tracking and Data Relay Satellite (TDRS). Scheduling and operational control of both of these networks is conducted by the Network Operations Control Center (NOCC) at the Goddard Space Flight Center in Greenbelt, MD. The second ground component is the respective project data center, where the scientific data processing, data archival, and data distribution takes place, which can be distributed at multiple locations.

Control Center Operations

The control center is the facility that manages all facets of the spacecraft operations. It schedules acquisition contacts with the respective satellite with NOCC, sends commands to the spacecraft via STDN/TDRSS, and evaluates the spacecraft and instrument telemetry. The staff reacts to all observed spacecraft anomalies, generally with the assistance of the project technical expertise. The spacecraft operations are conducted within the power constraints of the satellite and within the project scientist's guidelines. It involves computing the power coming in from the sun via the spacecraft panels of solar cells is greater than the power being consumed by the spacecraft to assure the spacecraft batteries don't run down after a few orbits. This condition would cause the spacecraft to tumble out of control, preventing communications and resulting in the loss of the satellite.

Large spacecraft have their own large control center. Smaller satellites generally share a control center at GSFC. Some satellites are managed by outside organizations with the respective control center located at the organization's facility.

Chapter 6

Nimbus Satellite Program Overview

August 28, 2004, was the fortieth anniversary of the launch of Nimbus-1. I arranged for a symposium and party event held at GSFC to commemorate that event. I invited the primary scientists involved in the Nimbus project scientific program to offer a review of their accomplishments, and the majority did attend and made presentations of their major Earth science findings. Many charts showing Earth geophysical and weather-related parameters that were uniquely derived the first time from Nimbus data were presented. Professor Tom Vonder Haar of the Colorado State University was so impressed with the information presented that he had me arrange with the GSFC public relations office to compile the presentations and put them on the Internet so they could be used as college educational tools at his university. Other educators at the symposium shared his view.

In conjunction with the fortieth-anniversary celebration I put together the Nimbus Program History document, which is available on the Internet under my name. It provides a history of how the Nimbus program evolved, who the program drivers, leaders and primary scientists were, the design heritage, major accomplishments, and more. It also presents an overview of the instruments flown on each of the seven Nimbus satellites and their accomplishments. Since the document is available on the Internet, I only described here enough information to give the reader a basic understanding of the Nimbus Program History and its accomplishments.

Nimbus Satellite Program Heritage

The initial challenge to develop the first meteorological satellite, TIROS, was given to the Army Signal Corps in Fort Monmouth, NJ. The responsibility was transferred to the new NASA facility, the Goddard Space Flight Center, in Greenbelt, MD. The design team came along. The members included engineers and scientists that continued on to have a long, meaningful role on the Nimbus program and on other GSFC programs, such as Bill Stroud, Rudy Stampfl, Rudy Hanel, Bill Bandeen, and Bill Nordberg. The first TIROS satellite with its large area pictures of clouds ushered in a new era in meteorological operations. TIROS was designed to spin like a top so it wouldn't tumble in space; however, the spinning action degraded the pictures. The engineers came up with the Nimbus design that had an attitude control system that kept the spacecraft always looking down at Earth, with little motion. This enabled clearer cloud pictures to be taken. This stability also accommodated other instruments planned for measuring the atmosphere. It had other improvements, paddles that tracked the sun, generating electrical power more efficiently, and had room for many instruments. It was to fly in a polar orbit, circling Earth from pole to pole rather than an equatorial orbit to see higher latitudes. NASA was to build three, the first one with their funds as a research program. NOAA, then called the Environmental Satellite Service Administration (ESSA), would fund the next two operational satellites. It was a completely new design, with a new-concept three-axis stabilized attitude control system that couldn't be tested on the ground before it was launched to verify that the design worked. A large air-bearing test platform was built, but it did not work to nullify the effect of gravity, and it was abandoned. After a major problem building the first Nimbus that caused a year's delay, ESSA dropped out of the arrangement and Nimbus was converted to an Earth meteorological research satellite program, funded by NASA.

NASA Headquarters Program Management

Richard Haley, Burton Schardt, and Douglas Broome served as the Nimbus program managers. Their role was to establish the science objectives for each spacecraft, coordinate the selection of the instrument to make the required measurements, arrange for funding, and arrange for the support by external organizations. Charles (Chuck) Matthews, the NASA Headquarters Associate Administrator for Applications had the significant role in headquarter approval of continuing the Nimbus program at all the crucial decision points in the program. ESSA administrator Dave Johnson, with the vision to see the benefits to weather forecasting the proposed new Nimbus instrumentation offered, used his authority to support these Nimbus research efforts that indeed vastly improved meteorology.

Project Management

The Nimbus Project was set up to manage the design, fabrication, testing, launch operations, and flight operations. Harry Press, who was an air force senior meteorologist, joined NASA to become the first Nimbus Project manager. Bill Nordberg became project scientist, and Bill Stroud became the division chief overseeing the Nimbus Project. Moe Schneebaum was the engineering branch manager. Harry Press served as project manager for Nimbus-1, 2, and 3. He played a key role in convincing NASA Headquarters to continue Nimbus-1 after the NOAA dropout and to undertake Nimbus-3 with its experimental instruments. His persuasive promotional efforts for the proposed future measurements to be taken contributed to Nimbus-4, 5, and 6 becoming new missions. Stan Weiland moved up from the Nimbus-3 integration and test manager to project manager of Nimbus-4. Each subsequent spacecraft had a new project manager, including John Boeckel, Don Fordyce, and Ron Browning. Browning was the Nimbus-7 project manager who very effectively managed the very ambitious technical challenges of developing instruments for measuring atmospheric and oceanic properties never measured before from space and supported the arrangement of a project data system with the participation of the broad science community to enhance the usefulness of the data by making it rapidly available to the research community. Ron is the president of the Goddard Retirees and Alumni Association (GRAA), having led this organization's interesting monthly meetings covering new and old GSFC program activities for many years.

I spoke to Harry Press before going to press with this book. He is living in a condo in Portland, OR. He says for a ninety-two-year-old he is doing well healthwise. His wife, Sylvia, passed away two years ago. He has a lady friend who helps keep him going. Harry retired from GSFC in 1968. For his retirement party, several Nimbus Project staff members put together a tongue-in-cheek version of the actual Nimbus-1 news press conference held after the successful launch and spacecraft activation described in Chapter 7. The skit parlayed the problems encountered during Nimbus-1's first week of activities. Ed Mason portrayed himself, Stan Weiland was himself, Bill Redisch represented Harry Press, Chuck Cote was Art Johnson, Dave Beiber was Harry Goett, and Chuck Thienel a questioner. The Nimbus Project was blessed with two guys who contributed the humor to counter all the seriousness, Dave Beiber and Joe Toz. Dave Beiber was famous for his ubiquitous, "How are you doing, Bubie?". Joe was the bard at all the parties. He put together a ditty for the Nimbus twentieth birthday party that tells the story of the agony surrounding the first orbits of Nimbus-1, when nothing seemed to go right. I put together all this humor and a collection of famous Nimbus quotes from 1963 to 1970 in a 1989 Nimbus Memorabilia document that was circulated to the Nimbus staff.

Project Staff

The Nimbus Project had very large staff of engineers that were the technical officers overseeing the contractors building the spacecraft structure, spacecraft components, and instruments. They managed flight operations and the ground software development, provided quality assurance oversight, interfaced with the launch vehicle developer/operator, conducted project financial management, and performed public relations. This staff included Wilbur (Bill) Huston, who served as deputy project manager for all Nimbus spacecraft, Geoge Abid, Joe Arlauskus, Ed Baden, Dave Beiber, Chuck Bolton, Sol Broder, Tom Cherrix, Phil Crossfield, Dick Devlin, Bob Drummond, Gerry Burdette, Gene Delio, Paul Feinberg, Art Fihelly, Mike Forman, Joe Gitelman, Harold Goldberg, Lloyd Green, George Hogan, Peter Hui, Seymor Kant, Seymour Leibowitz, John Lesko, Jim Lynch, Chuck Mackenzie, Ed Mason, John Meehan, Brice Miller, Herb Mittleman, Earl Moyer, Ron Muller, Helen Newman, Harry Nichols, Rick Obenschain, Dick Ormsby, Harvey Ostrow, Bill Redisch, Ben Schlachman, Joe Schulman, Ralph Shapiro, Ed Stengard, Jim Strong, Jim Taylor, Chuck Thienel, Bernie Trudell, Stan Weiland, Lou Wilson, and honorary member Joe Toczalowski (Toz), the RCA battery system caretaker who kept the Nimbus launch crews in stitches.

The Nimbus Project members were very grateful to these three office managers who kept the Nimbus houses in order and helped make the work environment pleasant—Wilma Evans in the Nimbus Project Office, Josephine Aldrich in the NCC, and Doris Schacte in the MDHS.

Spacecraft Developers

The General Electric Company in King of Prussia, PA, was contracted to build the spacecraft structure, attitude control system, thermal control system, and communication antennas, and to integrate and test all the instruments and other spacecraft subsystems. They adapted the Nimbus-1 structure to accommodate each new spacecraft's instrument complement and the instrument particular viewing requirements, avoiding significant structure design costs. They conducted the environmental testing of the completely assembled spacecraft with their large thirty-six-foot-diameter vacuum-thermal chamber and large vibration-shaker tables. Credits have been given to Lou Michelson, Joe Turtill, and Fred Drummond for leading GE's technical development and test activity. Sheldon Haas, the GE Program Manager starting with Nimbus-2, had a significant role in GE accomplishing the integration and test of each spacecraft with its different complement of instruments and with only one set of improved spacecraft attitude control system and data/telemetry system design changes, all within cost and schedule.

The RCA Astro-Electronics Division in Hightstown and later in East Windsor, NJ, was responsible for the power subsystem, the cameras and their power supplies, the science data tape recorders, and the communication electronics, all having complex requirements. Dr. Jack Keigler and Irv Stein had commendable roles in the RCA efforts. CalComp Inc. built the command system and Radiation Inc. built the telemetry system. Instruments were built by electronic companies such as IT&T, Texas Instruments, Ball Brothers, General Dynamics, and by universities such as JPL and MIT nationally, and internationally by UK's Oxford University.

Scientist Organization

Dr. William Nordberg was the first Nimbus Project Scientist. He had a profound impact on the project. He promoted the meteorological objectives and scientific benefits that sold the continuation of the Nimbus Project after ESSA pulled out of the first Nimbus Program. His vision for future instrument capabilities and the values they would offer was vital to the acceptance of the new categories of instruments on the next three Nimbus spacecraft. Nordberg's visions became a reality with the application of the data from the instruments he advocated.

Dr. William Bandeen took over as project scientist after the untimely death of Bill Nordberg. He led the complex and productive science programs for Nimbus—4, 5, and 6. He moved on to a higher position at GSFC, and Dr. Albert Fleig became the project scientist for Nimbus-7. He managed the new Nimbus-7 science program, the Nimbus Experiment Team (NET) that involved teams of scientists developing the scientific algorithms to derive the science output from the instrument Earth measurements—a departure from the tradition of the instrument principal investigator (PI) "owning the data".

Scientists from various organizations get credit for the success of the instruments on the seven Nimbus spacecraft, as indicated in the table.

Scientist	Nimbus	Instruments	Data Products
		Goddard Space Flight Center (GSFC)	
Charles Cote	3,4	Interrogation, Recording, Location System (IRLS),	Platform locations, data collection
	6	Tropical Wind Energy Level Experiment/Random Access Measurement System (TWERLE/ RAMS)	Tropical wind studies, animal tracking, platform locations, data collection
Per Gloersen	7	Scanning Multi-channel Microwave Radiometer (SMMR)	Rainfall, global sea-ice concentrations, sea surface temperature and winds

Rudolf Hanel	3,4	Infrared Interferometer Spectrometer (IRIS)	Vertical profiles of temperature, ozone, chemical species, interferograms
Donald Heath	3,4	Monitor of Solar Energy Ultraviolet (MUSE),	Solar radiation not viewed from Earth
	4	Backscatter Ultraviolet Spectrometer (BUV),	Atmospheric ozone profiles,
	7	Solar Backscatter Ultraviolet Spectrometer (SBUV)	Ozone profiles in lower atmosphere
Arlin Krueger	7	Total Ozone Mapping Spectrometer (TOMS)	Total ozone in stratosphere and troposphere, volcanic ash clouds
William Nordberg	1,2,3	High-Resolution Infrared Radiometer (HRIR)	Day and night global cloud cover; full swath
John Theon	4,5,6,7	Temperature/Humidity Infrared Radiometer (THIR)	Day and night global cloud cover and water vapor mapping
Thomas Wilheit	5,6	Electrically Scanning Microwave Radiometer (ESMR)	Global sea ice concentrations, snow cover, water vapor, rainfall

<u>Langley Flight Research Center (LARC)</u>

Pat McCormick	7	Stratospheric Aerosol Measurement II (SAM II)	Global concentrations of aerosols and optical properties in stratosphere

<u>National Oceanographic and Atmospheric Administration (NOAA)</u>

Warren Hovis	5	Surface Composition Mapping Radiometer (SCMR),	Surface mineral mapping, identification
	7	Coastal Zone Color Scanner (CZCS)	Oceanic temperature, productivity
Herbert Jacobowitz	6,7	Earth Radiation Budget (ERB)	Incoming and outgoing radiation measurements for energy balance

William Smith	3,4	Satellite Infrared Radiometer Spectrometer (SIRS),	Atmospheric temperature profiles
	5	Infrared Temperature Profile Radiometer (ITPR),	Atmospheric vertical temperature
	6	High Resolution Infrared Spectrometer (HIRS)	Full-swath atmosphere temp. profiles
David Wark	3,4	Satellite Infrared Radiometer Spectrometer (SIRS),	Atmospheric temperature profiles
	5	Infrared Temperature Profile Radiometer (ITPR)	Atmospheric vertical temp. profiles
National Center for Atmospheric Research (NCAR)			
John Gille	6	Limb Infrared Inversion Radiometer (LRIR)	Earth limb temp., ozone, water vapor
Massachusetts Institute of Technology			
David Staelin	5	Nimbus Experiment Microwave Spectrometer (NEMS),	Atmospheric temp in presence of clouds
	6	Scanning Microwave Spectrometer (SCAMS)	Global rain, hurricane imagery
U.K. Oxford University			
John Houghton	4,5	Selective Chopper Radiometer (SCR),	Temp. of six layers of atmosphere
	6	Pressure Modulated Radiometer (PMR),	Stratospheric temp. and chemicals
	7	Stratospheric and Mesospheric Sounder (SAMS)	Temperature and gas concentration in stratosphere and mesosphere

Center Recognition

The annual GSFC awards program honors two major contributors to the Nimbus program, Bill Nordberg and Moe Schneebaum. The Nordberg award is for scientific achievement; the Schneebaum award is for engineering achievement. Dr. Nordberg had the vision to see the value to meteorology of several Nimbus instruments and proposed the infrared imagery for nighttime cloud cover, an infrared system for measuring the temperature of the atmosphere, and a microwave system for measuring the atmospheric temperature in the presence of clouds. Schneebaum led the large GSFC instrument team that worked with the contractors building the Nimbus spacecraft equipment. They contributed to the design of the new-technology equipment, the thorough testing of the equipment, and resolving problems.

Nimbus Ground System

There were three elements to the Nimbus ground system. The place where the spacecraft operations are conducted is called the *Nimbus Control Center* or NCC for short. The facility where the Nimbus spacecraft data is processed for NCC operations support and for sending spacecraft commands was given the title *Meteorological Data Handling System* or MDHS for short. This facility was located adjacent/connected to the NCC. They were located in the basement of Building No. 3 at the Goddard Space Flight Center (GSFC) in Greenbelt, MD. The third element was the worldwide *STDN Tracking and Data Network,* managed out of GSFC Building 14.

Nimbus Control Center. The NCC staff was responsible for scheduling the spacecraft and instrument operations, evaluating the spacecraft health data called telemetry, and reacting to spacecraft and instrument problems. They also had to manage the power consumption against the power generation from the sun by solar cells, which changed as the spacecraft orbit plane drifted away from being in line with the sun, and degradation of the batteries and solar cells. NCC was operated twenty-four hours a day, seven days a week—no vacations. The operators had brush charts of telemetry to look at. A picture of a simulated operational orbit telemetry observation is illustrated below. Computer printouts of the telemetry data checked against acceptable values were generated in the MDHS computer system for additional engineering analysis.

Bennie Palmer was the head of NCC since just before Nimbus-1 was launched and continued that role until almost the end of Nimbus flight operations. He is an electrical engineer graduate from the University of West Virginia. Bennie and I had the same work disciplines and temperament; we collaborated very effectively as a government/industry team. We even had the same family background in two respects. His parents were hardworking immigrants from Italy (mine from Russia) and had a name change because the immigration official couldn't pronounce his lengthy family name (my father in-law had his name shortened to Pierce under the same circumstances). In addition, his jobs before the NCC position didn't equip Bennie for his NCC role any more than mine did for the operations manager position, as I explained earlier. Bennie and I remain friends. *Bennie*, Mike Forman, who took over my operations manager role, Dick Stephenson, one of Bennie's right-hand man, and Seymor Kant and me had a Christmas period lunch every year until illness interrupted this gathering. The Nimbus Project was extremely grateful for Bennie's superb leadership of this vital operation, which never required a reprimand.

The NCC staff consisted of engineers and technicians with experience and training to operate the satellite, monitor the various types of equipment on the spacecraft, and to conduct analyses of satellite equipment malfunctions. They normally operated two Nimbus satellites at the same time and once handled three operative Nimbus satellites. A picture of a large segment of the well-integrated staff is illustrated below. I am third from the right. Bennie Palmer, NCC manager, is the fourth from the right (back row). My deputy Dick Ormsby is the fifth from the left (front row). Chester Eddington, superb GE software programmer of so many software systems supporting Nimbus operations and science data processing, including the complex attitude determination system, is second from the left (front row). Josephine Aldrich, NCC office manager, is in the center with the white blouse. Lloyd Green, not shown in the picture, was the project software manager overseeing the GE software development.

NCC staff at telemetry brush charts.

Major NCC staff members.

Meteorological Data Handling System. This system was operated by the RCA field services organization and supported by electronic technicians from five different companies that developed their respective equipment. It was also a 24/7 operation. There was an overall RCA on-site MDHS manager, several over the long program, Ray Balon being one of the standouts, and a shift manager coordinating the shift operations. This activity was under the very effective general management of Bill Powell, who helped to maintain a well-organized operation staffed to keep the equipment operative. John Sheehan was the primary government MDHS manager and Dale Fahnestock provided Code 500 oversight.

STDN Tracking and Data Network. It consists of facilities around the world that have communications equipment (antennas, receivers) to receive spacecraft radio signals of spacecraft data, and have communications equipment (antennas, transmitters) that send the command signal to the spacecraft. Three STDN sites were equipped with the special Nimbus electronic equipment (demultiplexers) that separated the individual data signals from the spacecraft downlink signal that contained several of the data signals combined (multiplexed) together. This was the Nimbus high-volume data channel. They were at Fairbanks, AK, at Rosman, NC, and at Goldstone, CA. Nimbus was in a polar orbit, so it essentially crossed the North Pole every orbit. With Fairbanks being at a 65° latitude, several orbits crossed Fairbanks while the spacecraft was going north, and several other orbits crossed Fairbanks when the spacecraft had crossed the pole and was heading south. There were generally at least eight orbits a day when the data was played back at Fairbanks. Goldstone was the secondary station. The other small STDN stations were used to collect real-time, low-volume data to look at telemetry for safety monitoring. Example stations were Winkfield, UK, Guam, and Hawaii. GSFC Code 700 managed the STDN network from their control room in building 14 at GSFC.

Chapter 7

Nimbus Program Satellite Operations

There were seven Nimbus satellites operative from 1964 to 1994. Summaries of the individual satellite accomplishments are presented below. An eighth Nimbus satellite, known as B-1 (Nimbus satellites were designated alphabetically until successful in orbit and then designated numerically), was destroyed at launch. The circumstances that caused the failure are presented.

Nimbus-1 Satellite: Twenty-Eight-Day Operation Kick-Starts Satellite Earth Science

(08/28/1964-09/23/64)

Nimbus-1, the first civilian three-axis earth-pointing satellite, was designed to be stabilized within one degree in each axis, with low jitter. This arrangement was very effective for the 800-line resolution, 0.5-7 um Advanced Vidicon Camera System (AVCS) that provided high-quality cloud pictures that could be taken around the world and recorded for playback on a wideband tape recorder (new technology for space application). Three side-by-side one-inch vidicons (camera lens) covered the full 2,300-km swath width. This gave the US Weather Bureau an improved capability to study weather phenomena outside of the United States that influenced the weather over the United States. On the third day of operations, this camera system provided an exceptional clear picture of Hurricane Cleo and subsequently tracked another hurricane and a Pacific typhoon. In addition, the AVCS pictures enabled cartographers to correct inaccuracies on relief maps and supplied better definition of the Antarctic ice fronts. Nimbus went into the first of its several semi-operational modes during the program's lifetime. The scheduling of the limited AVCS cloud picture recording capability was coordinated with a Weather Bureau operational representative to cover worldly weather features of timely interest to the Weather Bureau.

Another major success was the Automatic Picture Taking (APT) system. This instrument also had 800-line resolution, but it used a special 1-inch, 0.5-7 um vidicon that stored the image for a slow readout (low data rate transmitted to the ground) that was compatible with the commercial facsimile image recorders available for displaying the pictures received at the local weather stations. The local cloud pictures that covered approximately 1,500 miles thrilled the world's meteorological community. They could receive this weather data from this high-resolution camera system at about the same time daily by using a small inexpensive antenna/receiver and a commercial facsimile recorder.

The third instrument was the High-Resolution Infrared Radiometer (HRIR) that operated in the 3.4-4.2um spectral interval with a rotating mirror for scanning horizon to horizon. It provided the first nighttime cloud pictures from space, a boon to the meteorologists. It provided global daytime and nighttime cloud coverage. A facsimile recorder that produced high-resolution negatives from the electrical data signals was developed by the Westrex Corporation. Daily mosaics of worldwide clouds were produced for global cloud behavior and related weather analysis. Shown is a remarkable image of twin cyclone storms taken on the same day by the instrument. It shows the natural phenomena that cyclones north of the equator rotate counterclockwise and those below the equator rotate clockwise.

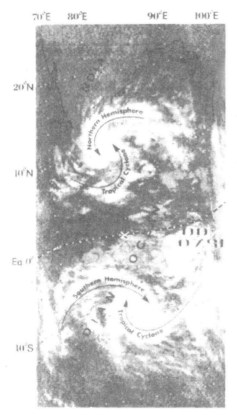

Twin tropical storms on the same day taken by HRIR.

Nimbus-1 was launched on August 28, 1964, and failed after twenty-eight days of operations due to the seizure of the solar array drive motor. The array designers overlooked the absence of convection in the airless outerspace environment when they selected a small commercial motor for the array drive speed-reduction mechanism early in the Nimbus development program, a case of learning how to accommodate the unique aerospace application conditions. The rotor was bright colored instead of radiative black and could not radiate sufficiently to compensate for the lack of convective rotor cooling in the operational vacuum environment. The rotor heat could only be dissipated through the motor's small half-inch ball bearing, causing the bearing grease lubricant to dry out.

The spacecraft failure impact on the operations staff had to be addressed. With a replacement Nimbus in the works, I was able to convince my management to continue funding the NCC staff so everyone was retained. However, with the next launch over a year away, Code 500 reduced the

MDHS funding so we were only able to retain the senior, highly skilled MDHS personnel (about half).

Remembrances of Exciting Nimbus-1 Activation. Gerry Burdette, Peter Hui, Ben Schlachman, and Chuck Bolton from the Nimbus project came to Fairbanks to assist me with the initial operations. In addition Rudy Stampfl, who helped create the Nimbus design concept, took leave from his sabbatical teaching job and volunteered to be there too. We heard the lift-off dialogue indicating everything was okay and, later, on time, confirmation from Johannesburg that there was a launch vehicle second burn. However, there was no Nimbus beacon signal acknowledgement from the next station, Winkfield, Great Britain, so we knew something was wrong. At the expected spacecraft arrival time the Fairbanks antennas were put through the search routines planned, but no signals were heard. My inquiries brought no satisfactory answer. About a half hour later I was told three Minitrack stations equipped with wire-type, very-wide-angle receivers that are used to determine satellite orbits had received the Nimbus beacon signal. I was also informed that they later looked at the launch vehicle telemetry at the Joburg tracking site and concluded there was no launch vehicle second burn, so Nimbus was in an elliptical orbit. I shouted over the communications network to George Harris, my Code 500 coordinator at GSFC, to get Dr. Joe Siry, the GSFC orbital computations expert to look at the Minitrack data and predict the orbit Nimbus was in. Whether by computer or manually, somehow in this short time he did establish the orbit, and the antennas were programmed by his orbital parameters correctly for the Fairbanks antenna to receive the Nimbus beacon signal at the horizon on the next orbit. I was advised ny Dr. Stampfl to keep the telemetry data off the beacon signal at launch to make it easier to capture the signal on the first pass, so before the second pass was to arrive I consulted with my advisors about whether to turn on the telemetry signal. They all passed on giving me advice except Dr. Stampfl, who insisted that it was best to do nothing for another orbit. I thought it over and concluded we needed to know the status of Nimbus in case we had to take corrective action and made plans to turn the telemetry on. We did turn it on and were thrilled to see the spacecraft's three axes stabilized. However, with no instrument loads on the power bus, the batteries were being overcharged, which could be harmful. We turned on auxiliary loads and protected the batteries from damage. This incident of not listening to him irritated Dr.

Stampfl and he kept the grudge against me for several years. It didn't matter to him that that turning on the telemetry enabled taking steps to avoid damaging the battery system.

This false concern occurred. The first APT picture received was not a cloud picture, so the instrument was turned off. Further examination of the picture showed it was a picture of the launch vehicle spacecraft attachment structure. Evidently the APT system suffered a turn-on glitch during separation and took the picture that was stored on the camera vidicon until the system was first turned on. There were a couple of other activation false problems (that I can't remember), which helped make the activation more exciting.

Three days after spacecraft activation, I received a call from John Miller at the University of Alaska in Fairbanks with this inquiry: "Is anyone interested in a tape of the Nimbus first orbit?" Wow. It turned out that while I was deliberating with the Fairbanks antenna people on how to adjust their search mode, command operator Ralph Owen followed the plan I laid out to send the tape recorder playback command five minutes before the nominal end of the interrogation period since the attitude control information after the spacecraft separation from the launch vehicle would be lost with the endless loop telemetry recorder having a one orbit storage capacity. Peter Hui, the attitude control expert helping me, rushed to the university to look at the data. He came back disappointed. The spacecraft ejection during separation from the launch vehicle was so gentle that he couldn't tell anything about the attitude control system's capability to stabilize under bad separation conditions.

Lessons Learned. The Alaska University used a smaller antenna with a wider beamwidth and was able to capture the Nimbus beacon signal even though the antenna wasn't pointing at the spacecraft, whereas Fairbanks used large antennas with a narrow beamwidth and failed. The Fairbanks command signal transmission antenna was a small, wide-angle beamwidth antenna; so the command signals were received by Nimbus even though the antenna wasn't pointing correctly.

Nimbus-1 Press Conference. Five days after Nimbus activation and the value of Nimbus data was already recognized, a news conference was held at GSFC that I missed because I was still in Alaska. At the conference Bill Nordberg had this to say: "The future meteorological satellite program will move from cloud mapping to measuring parameters of the atmosphere such as temperature profiles, pressure, and winds. We will put all of these parameters into a model and run it in a huge computer to grind out the prediction of what the weather will be." As it turned out, Nordberg certainly had the right foresight.

Three years ago there was a solicitation to contribute Nimbus artifacts to a museum to be opened in Bill Nordberg's hometown in Austria with a room dedicated to him. Nimbus PM Ron Browning had given me a twenty-four-inch model of Nimbus-7 that he received from GE as Nimbus PM, saying I was Mr. Nimbus and deserved it. I proudly displayed it in my house den. I thought Dr. Nordberg deserved the model for his foresight that expanded the Nimbus program leading to its many scientific achievements and responded to the solicitation by sending the model to the museum.

Other Remembrances Associated with Nimbus-1. There were several personal activities associated with the Nimbus-1 launch that I can't forget. I went to Alaska three times. The first time was to get acquainted with the people I was to work with and to get familiar with the equipment used during the first orbit activation of the spacecraft, and to evaluate their preparedness—the activation process was almost as new to them as it was to me. Just flying that far and to Alaska was exciting, as was climbing up the base of the station's eighty-five-foot antenna to be used to communicate with Nimbus. There was nothing impressive about the city except the disappointing situation regarding the native Eskimos—lots of unemployed drunken males in the run-down bar area of town that reminded me of the Bowery in NYC when I was a youngster. I wasn't smart enough to take in the beauty of Alaska as other GSFC visitors did, but I did take a short trip to the North Pole. It was a small town about twenty miles north of Fairbanks with a post office that stamped US mail, North Pole. They sold lots of Christmas gifts. I did make one very beneficial connection in Fairbanks—Ralph Owen, a CalComp employee who was the lead command operator and CalComp equipment maintenance person. He hosted me at his home and broke me into eating caribou meat. We developed a friendship that continued when he transferred to MDHS at GSFC.

The day before I was planning to leave for my next trip to Alaska two days before the scheduled launch, an unknown chap stopped into my office at GSFC and asked if I would take the box he had to the Alaska STDN site. He said it contained transmitter spare parts, so I was glad to do it. The next day I was enjoying lunch on the plane to Alaska when the pilot announced lunch just ended and we were making an emergency landing in Cleveland. I was not very comfortable seeing the runway lined with fire engines as we landed. We were taken to a hangar where it was explained that someone called in from Washington DC, where the plane first left from, advising that a soldier was carrying a bomb on the plane I was on. I was to tell the attendant the nature of the electronic equipment I brought on board. While I was waiting my turn, I felt awfully uncomfortable having to explain I didn't know anything about the electronics I checked in. As we started to discuss this, an announcement was made that the emergency was called off. I found out later that the caller evidently read the name of the presumed bomb carrier off a soldier's nameplate. The soldier had gotten off at BWI with his luggage, so they called it a bomb scare, common then.

On the third visit, the satellite launch was successful and I was very appreciative of the spacecraft activation help given me by the project team of experts who were up there in Fairbanks with me. So the night before we left, I invited them for a dinner on me at the fancy Switzerland restaurant outside of town. Of course we couldn't settle for dinner alone, so we each started buying a bottle of champagne. We had quite a few. By the time we were ready to leave the restaurant I was feeling so good I left a blank check to pay the bill. The restaurant was considerate; they called me at the motel to ask if they could fill in the check for about $300. I was feeling no pain so I said okay. The only unhappy one at the party was my assistant, Bernie Trudell. He had just about stepped off the plane to join the party. He was to take over my active role of managing the operations on the network and confessed he was too nervous about that to relax and enjoy.

During the few hours when there was no satellite interrogation in Alaska, I went to the hotel to take a nap and relax a little. Peter Hui helped here; he broke me into enjoying a Moscow Mule, a mix of vodka, special beer, and who knows what, served in a copper cup.

One afternoon while in the hotel lobby I heard a tour guide tell his group of elderly women tourists who had just arrived in Fairbanks what the exciting activity of the day was—a little league baseball game. That describes how exciting Fairbanks was then.

Personal Reprimands Received. With all the pressure I had managing the spacecraft activation, which went well, management at GSFC had these three reprimands to give me.

Bill Stroud called me to reprimand me for not listening to Dr. Stanpfl about keeping the telemetry off the beacon during the second orbit interrogation. Never mind my decision was right; turning the telemetry signal onto the beacon was safe, and it enabled us to put the spacecraft in a safer condition with respect to the power system.

After the HRIR system was turned on, Dr. Nordberg lashed out at me for allowing the HRIR facsimile system operator to keep a copy of the first HRIR picture taken. He said that as principal investigator, he was the sole owner of this data. It didn't mean anything to him that this guy was the one that helped improve the design of the facsimile equipment that made these HRIR pictures and operated the equipment that made the first picture. I let him keep the picture. This fellow actually had a license plate "NIMBUS," which he gave to me years later when he changed plates. He said I was Mr. Nimbus and was entitled to it. I had it displayed in my old house den.

My wife was kept informed of my progress in Alaska by Bennie Palmer. When I made plans to return, I called her on the government nonoperational SCAMA phone line to tell her my return plans. I was coming home on Friday, and we were going to Art Fihelly's wedding the next day. He had postponed his wedding plans twice because of two previous launch plans and told PM Harry Press, "Sorry, Harry, I can't postpone my wedding again, or I'll get divorced before I ever get married." Bennie Schlachman had me tell my wife to have his wife make reservations at a motel near BWI and meet him there; he was away from her too long. So this important call didn't mean anything to the network division director, he called me to reprimand me for making a personal call on a government line. I was informed much later by a friend in the SCAMA office that this director made three personal calls to his home during a recent boondoggle trip to a STDN station in Australia.

Nimbus B-1 Satellite Launch Failure

This satellite was the same as described below for Nimbus-3. It was all set for launch with the Nimbus Control Center and MDHS trained to handle it. During the countdown to the launch firing of the rocket there were erratic signals showing up for the rocket gyroscope. The telemetry analysts couldn't tell if it was in reaction to the strong winds at the launch complex or due to a faulty gyro so the launch director stopped the launch. The gyro was removed from the launch vehicle and tested. When it was determined that the gyro was okay, it was reinstalled and the launch proceeded. The launch vehicle behaved erratically shortly after liftoff so the safety officer sent the destruct command, sending the launch vehicle and Nimbus parts into the nearby bay. Since it contained a nuclear power supply, a few weeks later, divers extracted the power supply from the wreckage.

A failure review committee was established to determine the cause of the failure, which shockingly turned out to be needless. To remove the gyroscope from the electronics box it was attached to, the mechanic had to remove the dowel pins that were put in to make sure it was attached to the box properly. When he reattached the gyro after it was tested, he neglected to use the dowel pins and installed the gyroscope 180° backwards. After installation, the mechanic had hit the left side of the gyro and there was no response. However, when there was a response after he hit the right side of the gyro, the launch director decided the gyro was OK. Too bad the mechanic decided to hit the right side of the gyro, the launch would have been scrubbed.

It was a depressing night for everyone involved with the launch. My wife and a few other Nimbus members' wives were in the GSFC launch control room's viewer room at three in the morning expecting to be excited to witness the launch over closed-circuit TV. Instead they went to Jack Sargent's house where wife Mickey had a "Nimbus death" reception.

Nimbus-2 Satellite: Author's Cradle-to-Grave Responsibility

(05/15/1966-01/18/1969)

As indicated earlier, with no operating satellite to manage after the early failure of Nimbus-1 and with the Nimbus Project team devoting their time to the Nimbus-3 developmental challenges, I was given the responsibility of managing the fill-in Nimbus-2 development effort except for the launch phase, when I put my operations manager hat back on.

At the same time that Nimbus-3 was authorized, NASA Headquarters authorized Nimbus-2 in order to provide a continuation of the Nimbus-1 application benefits to the meteorological community and provide data to support the scientific research initiated by Nimbus-1 until the next

Nimbus with more advanced instrumentation was to be available. With minor design changes to accommodate a third instrument that didn't make it to the Nimbus-1 spacecraft integration schedule, Nimbus-2 could be built rapidly at a relatively low cost.

Nimbus-2 contained four instruments: three identical to the Nimbus-1 complement (APT, AVCS, and HRIR) and one additional instrument, the Medium-Resolution Infrared Radiometer (MRIR). It was produced using a spacecraft structure residual from the original Nimbus Project plan to build three identical spacecraft. It required the incorporation of RF isolators to avoid RF interference with the addition of the new MRIR data stream to be included in the VHF communication link.

Continuing the Nimbus-1 experience, the APT pictures were exploited by the worldwide local forecasters and TV stations. The capability of transmitting local nighttime cloud pictures from the HRIR instrument was added to the real-time transmission system capability. This feature provided a nighttime view of local cloud conditions and other benefits, such as temperature patterns of lakes and oceanic areas of interest to shipping and fishing industries. The high-resolution AVCS pictures that gave insights to storm patterns were of continued interest to the research community.

The new instrument, Medium-Resolution Infrared Radiometer (MRIR), measured radiation emitted and reflected from Earth in five wavelength intervals from visible to infrared (0.5-29 um). MRIR data was used to study the effect of water vapor and ozone on the Earth's energy balance.

I kept watch over Nimbus-2 until it was turned off because it was no longer useful and not to interfere with Nimbus-3 operations management. Nimbus-2 operated for thirty-two months.

Nimbus-3 Satellite Revolutionizes Weather Forecasting

(04/14/69-01/22/72)

The Nimbus-3 observatory was the first of the line of Nimbus spacecraft with experimental meteorological and other science instrumentation built under the renewed Nimbus charter as a meteorological research satellite program. Nimbus-3 operated for thirty-two months.

Nimbus-3 carried nine instruments compared to three for Nimbus-1, covering twenty-eight spectral channels compared to three for Nimbus-1. Seven instruments were science experiments, including five that were completely new. One, the Satellite Infrared Spectrometer (SIRS) instrument inaugurated a new era in weather forecasting by the use of satellite instrumentation to make the basic meteorological temperature measurements required for weather forecasting. Two instruments were technology experiments. One new experiment provided a breakthrough on the weather prediction modeling techniques that resulted in improved forecasting accuracy. Another new experiment was the forerunner of satellite search and rescue technology by demonstrating satellite collection of remote platform data and the capability to locate remote platforms. Another new experiment, the Infrared Interferometer Spectrometer (IRIS), served as the forerunner of the instruments that measured the temperature and chemical composition of the outer planets using infrared interferometer technology, e.g., the mission to the planet Mars.

SIRS was a grating spectrometer with eight channels in the 11-15 um spectral interval, which pointed to the nadir with a 12-degree angular field of view. Nimbus SIRS data provided the first daily measurements of atmospheric temperature profiles suitable for numerical weather prediction that covered the globe. The new SIRS data presented a major challenge to the meteorological community. They needed to develop techniques of converting the raw radiance measurements to temperature profiles and develop robust global numerical weather prediction models that could absorb and integrate this new type of information. This high volume of global data replaced the relatively sparse radiosonde and rawinsonde temperature and wind data essentially collected by US weather forecasters only over the United States and by a few ships at sea. SIRS data was delivered to NOAA/NESDIS in near real time in a pseudo-operational mode for two years. This cooperative routine enabled NOAA to develop the raw data temperature inversion algorithms, to develop the techniques for integrating the large volume of computed data into their weather forecast models, and to refine the forecast models. These algorithms and processes were adapted to handle data from the upcoming NOAA satellite carrying the operational Infrared Temperature Profile Radiometer (ITPR) instrument that was patterned after SIRS.

The Interrogation, Recording, and Location System (IRLS) demonstrated the feasibility of using polar-orbiting satellites to locate and collect data from remote instrumented platforms around the globe. Environmental data was collected from balloons and buoys for wind studies and ocean current studies. Animal and large fish migration was studied using signals received by IRLS from transmitters attached to the animals and fish to compute their locations at the Nimbus Control Center. The platforms on the animals/fishes were programmed to transmit their signal every five minutes and stay on if it received a signal from the spacecraft. It was necessary for commands to be sent by NCC to IRLS to interrogate the platform before the platform would activate to send its data. The computation of the platform location was performed for the experimenters by a computer program developed by the Nimbus Project and operated in MDHS.

The Infrared Interferometer Spectrometer (IRIS) instrument was a modified version of the classical Michelson Interferometer. It was nadir looking, covered the 5-25 um spectral interval and had a built-in self-calibrator. The interferograms created by IRIS on the spacecraft were converted on the ground to thermal emission spectra. This data yielded vertical profiles of temperature, water vapor, ozone, and other chemical species. Another IRIS flew on Nimbus-4. Other versions of interferometers based on the successful Nimbus IRIS design flew on the Voyager spacecraft to Jupiter, Saturn, Uranus, and Neptune and on the Mars Mariner 9 mission, and on the Cassini mission to the outer planets. They measured the planet's atmospheric temperature and determined the elements or compounds in the atmosphere and multispectral reflectance. All versions of this spectacular instrument were managed by the Nimbus IRIS principal scientist, Dr. Rudolf (Rudy) Hanel.

The Monitor of Ultraviolet Solar Energy (MUSE) experiment measured solar radiation previously undetectable on the Earth's surface because of the atmosphere's screening effect. The primary objective was to look for changes with time in the ultraviolet solar flux in five broad bands in the 1120-3100Å range. MUSE looked at the setting sun as the spacecraft crossed the terminator in the Northern Hemisphere. It discovered that there is a pronounced periodic variation in solar ultraviolet radiation that corresponds to the twenty-seven-day solar rotation period that could affect upper-atmosphere ozone concentrations.

The Image Dissector Camera System (IDCS), which demonstrated the new electrically scanned imaging radiometer technology for space applications, replaced the AVCS visible sensor. It took 800-line resolution daytime cloud-cover pictures that were stored on the high data rate recorder for playback at the tracking and data acquisition sites. It also replaced the APT system; it had a slow scan readout mode for the APT-type real-time data transmission system. The IDCS frame covered approximately 2,500 kilometers with a pixel resolution of 4 kilometers.

Two technological experiments flew successfully on Nimbus-3, the Radioisotope Thermoelectric Generator (RTG) and the Rate Measuring Package (RMP). The RTG demonstrated a nuclear electric power generation capability designed for operating in space. The RTG design was later adapted for several deep-space missions going beyond the reach of sunlight. The RMP was an experimental gyroscope, pressurized to support an air-bearing design that would result in lower gyro signal noise and extended longevity. It demonstrated the efficacy of a gas-bearing gyroscope that later became a standard design for space applications.

HRIR, with a 0.7-1.3 um channel added and a copy of the Nimbus-2 MRIR instrument completed the instrument complement.

Nimbus-4 Satellite: Breakthrough in Earth's Upper-Atmosphere Knowledge

(04/08/1970-09/30/1980)

Nimbus-4 carried nine instruments; three were new instruments. The Backscatter Ultraviolet Spectrometer (BUV) and the Selective Chopper Radiometer (SCR) were breakthroughs in providing knowledge of Earth's upper atmosphere; the Filter Wedge Spectrometer (FWS) never operated successfully. Six instruments that were repeats or improvements of instruments previously on Nimbus-3 were included to continue the scientific research (IDCS, IRIS, IRLS, MUSE, SIRS, THIR). The spacecraft design incorporated two new spacecraft major subsystems, the Versatile Information Processor (VIP) computer system, and an improved Attitude Control System (ACS). Nimbus-4 operated for ten years.

The Backscatter Ultraviolet Spectrometer (BUV) experiment was a twelve-channel grating monochromator spectrometer in the 2500-3398Å range, capable of measuring Earth radiance to six orders of magnitude. BUV initiated our understanding of ozone patterns in the atmosphere. It operated for ten years, providing data that showed time-changing ozone profiles that varied around the world. The unanswered questions that came out of the BUV data analysis and the area coverage limitations provided the basis for later flying the Nimbus SBUV ozone profiling instrument and the Total Ozone Mapping Spectrometer (TOMS) instrument on Nimbus-7 that measured the global total ozone rather than the single-point ozone profiles measured by BUV. BUV is the instrument with the most continuous use in satellite applications. A slightly modified version was flown again on Nimbus-7 in 1978 and has been on NOAA satellites continuously since 1984.

The Selective Chopper Radiometer (SCR) experiment was developed jointly by the UK's Oxford and Reading Universities under the leadership of Sir John Houghton. It determined the temperatures of six successive 10-km layers of the atmosphere from absorption measurements in the CO_2 band from 2-200 um, which yielded an innovative and meteorological-beneficial set of data. In measuring the stratospheric temperature, it was discovered that there were sudden warmings of the winter stratosphere near the North Pole that adversely affected global climate. Monitoring stratospheric temperatures became new data points of interest to the meteorological community for weather forecasting.

The Filter Wedge Spectrometer (FWS) intended to measure the vertical distribution of water vapor and carbon dioxide was the first instrument with a detector that was radiantly cooled by looking at deep space. It failed due to icing that built up on the detector after launch that could not be removed. It provided a lesson learned to other instrument designers. Because of its failure, all future instrument radiant coolers were designed with either a cooler door or heaters to evaporate any frozen condensation on the detector or cooler interior as the spacecraft entered deep space after launch and before the instrument activation. In addition it became standard practice to allow a lengthy period of time for the cooler chamber to outgas before activation.

The SIRS instrument was modified to scan 35° across the swath and six channels were added, which greatly enhanced the meteorological forecast models.

The THIR instrument, which replaced the HRIR instrument that flew on Nimbus-1-3, had a 6.7 um water vapor channel and a 10-12 um long-wave channel. The former, designed to show moisture distribution in the stratosphere and upper troposphere, provided vivid portrayals of jet streams and large storm systems. The 10-12 um channel where there is virtually no sunlight eliminated glint problems often seen in the HRIR data and provided pictures of unusual clarity and contrast.

The Versatile Information Processor (VIP) was a state-of-the-art computer processor designed to operate in space. It was designed to handle all spacecraft telemetry and the low-rate instrument science data with a 4 kbps data rate. It had precision sample and hold circuitry for digitizing the input analogue telemetry and had the capability to be reprogrammed to change the sampling rate of the input telemetry/science data and reprogrammed from the ground to provide this capability to change telemetry sampling rates to aid in diagnosing in-flight problems. It proved invaluable in being able to accommodate the integration of the data from new complements of low-rate instruments on Nimbus-5, 6, and 7 with a small software effort, which was a significant cost saving to the program.

The Attitude Control System (ACS) system was modified to include improvements that provided greater stability and more accurate attitude information to improve the quality of the science data and provided improved ACS and spacecraft reliability. The changes included a finer sun sensor for improved azimuth attitude determination and a set of magnetic torquer bars for backup momentum control, which proved to be an asset for extending the life of the spacecraft. Nimbus spacecraft ran well beyond their design life and the ACS momentum control system's pneumatic capacity limitation would have curtailed the spacecraft lifetime. This system was used for all spacecraft as they aged, starting with Nimbus-4. Nimbus-7 operated for fifteen years, the magnetic torquer system for momentum unloading was used exclusively for the last seven years of operation. Seymor Kant was the ACS expert who provided the guidance on how to successfully use this new, tricky momentum control system.

Nimbus-5 Satellite Initiates New Technology for Earth Remote Sensing

(12/04/1972-03/29/1983)

Nimbus-5 carried just six instruments. Two instruments, the Nimbus Experiment Microwave Spectrometer (NEMS) and the Electrically Scanning Microwave Radiometer (ESMR), introduced a new realm of technology to satellite remote sensing, the use of the microwave frequency spectrum. A third instrument, the Surface Composition Mapping Radiometer (SCMR), expanded the Nimbus experimental program into terrestrial research. A fourth instrument, the Infrared Temperature Profile Radiometer (ITPR), was an improvement on the predecessor SIRS atmospheric sounding instrument. A fifth instrument, the Selective Chopper Radiometer (SCR), was also an improvement of an earlier instrument. THIR was the sixth instrument. Nimbus-5 operated for a little over ten years. Nimbus-5 was turned off to eliminate competition with Nimbus-7 for data acquisition site coverage. It had marginal science utility at that time and was being operated to provide spacecraft-longevity engineering data.

The Nimbus Experiment Microwave Spectrometer (NEMS) was the first microwave sounding device. It was a Dicke superheterodyne microwave radiometer, operating with five channels between 20-60GHz with a 10° beamwidth. It had the capability to probe through dense clouds to provide atmospheric temperature profiles. NEMS was the first to provide multispectral measurements that separated humidity and cloud water contributions. It was also the first to provide extensive global observations of ice microwave spectral signatures, indicating sea-ice age and snow depth and snow accumulation rates over Antarctica. NEMS was the forerunner of the Advanced Microwave Sounder Unit (AMSU) on the NOAA operational satellites.

The Electrically Scanning Microwave Radiometer (ESMR) was the first microwave device to map global radiation from Earth's surface and atmosphere. It had an electronically scanning Dicke-switched phased array antenna (74°) operating at 19.35 GHz with a beamwidth of 1.1°. ESMR had the capability to distinguish rain over the oceans and between snow and ice. The latter capability revealed errors in ice canopy maps and enabled clear shipping channels in the Arctic ice fields to be identified. An operational arrangement was set up to deliver ESMR ice field pictures generated at the MDHS to the Joint NOAA/Navy Ice Center in Suitland, MD, for their operational use in routing ships through the ice-free Arctic sea channels.

The third new instrument was the Surface Composition Mapping Radiometer (SCMR). This imaging radiometer/spectrometer introduced the technology of mapping Earth's mineral resources from space. The SCMR technology evolved into the Multispectral Scanner System (MSS) instrument on the Landsat satellites that made similar measurements with far greater resolution and accuracy. SCMR had three data channels

(0.8-1.1um, 8.3-9.2um, 10.5-11.3um) and scanned horizon to horizon (86°) with an angular resolution of 0.75°.

The Infrared Temperature Profile Radiometer (ITPR) had an expanded spectral interval compared with the Nimbus-4 SIRS instrument that it was patterned after, i.e., 3.8-15 um vs. 11-15 um, a field of view sharpened to 1.5 degrees, double the number of sensors and double the Nimbus-4 SIRS scanning range (76° vs. 35°). ITPR was operative until shortly before Nimbus-5 was shut down.

THIR was carried as the sixth instrument to provide a global cloud reference for the other instrument data.

Nimbus-5 presented an opportunity to learn about the Attitude Control System (ACS) Earth acquisition and stabilization capability. In its eighth year of operation, the combination of solar array degradation and orbit drift out of the sun plane reduced the array output to marginally support the operating power load. A sudden loss of a small array string was enough to upset the power balance, and the cumulative negative power balance caused an undervoltage of the voltage regulator sufficient to shut it down. I developed a plan to try to reactivate the spacecraft consisting of the Alaska tracking site, when in daylight, routinely repeatedly sending a command sequence that would put the spacecraft in the absolute minimum spacecraft condition, including turning the THIR motor off. The perseverance paid off. After about three months, the spacecraft beacon reappeared. Although the spacecraft had gone into a tumbling mode, the solar array orientation became aligned to the sun sufficiently long enough to activate the voltage regulator to accept the commands, and the ACS reacquired the Earth's horizon and stabilized. There were no new failures, and the THIR motor ran normally after being turned back on. The spacecraft operated with ITPR and THIR for approximately another year before the spacecraft was turned off.

Nimbus-6 Satellite: Profound Impact on Meteorology and the International Search and Rescue Program

(03/12/1975-03/29/1983)

Nimbus-6 had a profound effect on meteorology akin to the Nimbus-3 impact. The type and quality of measurements taken by three of its instruments enhanced the robustness and sensitivity of the worldwide meteorological forecast models, extending weather prediction accuracy to three days and beyond. It had nine experiments with a total of sixty-two spectral channels. Nimbus-6 operated for eight years. Nimbus-6 was turned off to eliminate competition with Nimbus-7 for data acquisition site coverage at the time when Nimbus-7 was operating at its peak.

The High-Resolution Infrared Spectrometer (HIRS) was a temperature sounder based on the SIRS temperature sounder technology. It had additional channels (seventeen total) selected to cover the depth of the atmosphere (0.7-15 um), and scanned 72° to cover the breadth of the orbital swath.

The Scanning Microwave Spectrometer (SCAMS) produced temperature profiles, oceanic humidity, and rain data. SCAMS produced the first global microwave imagery characterizing fronts and hurricanes. It was the first to reveal a hot spot near the eye of a hurricane and the first to be a good indicator of hurricane wind strength. It was a mechanically scanning radiometer, with five channels operating in the 20-60GHZ range, having a 7.5° beamwidth and scanning 86°.

The Pressure Modulated Radiometer (PMR), developed by Oxford University, UK, was an advanced design of the earlier SCR instrument that measured stratospheric temperature up to 85Km altitude and chemical species. Data from PMR was routinely delivered in near real time to the British Meteorological Service for their operational use. PMR had two channels operating at 15 um that scanned 15°.

Data from these three instruments was routinely provided to NOAA for developing algorithms for deriving their meteorological data and for modifying their forecast models in anticipation of the future NOAA satellites that would generate the equivalent data. The positive impact these three instrument data sets had on weather forecast models was demonstrated during the yearlong First GARP Global Experiment (FGGE) in 1978 that was conducted by the major national and international meteorological modeling centers. The Nimbus-6 data contributed to more accurate five-day forecasts compared to the other data sets that were tried. The types of measurements made by these three Nimbus instruments were incorporated into the TIROS Operational Vertical Sounder (TOVS), which has become NOAA's standard operational atmospheric measuring system for their polar-orbiting satellites. TOVS consists of three elements, HIRS/2 (High Resolution Infrared Spectrometer/2), SSU (Stratospheric Sounding

Unit), and MSU (Microwave Sounding Unit). NOAA developed their algorithms for deriving the meteorological products from these instrument data by using the equivalent Nimbus data as proxy data sets.

Another Nimbus-6 experiment, Tropical Wind Energy Conversion and Reference Level (TWERLE), had a profound impact on the search and rescue methodology used worldwide. The basic instrument research objective was to measure winds by locating platforms attached to balloons that circumnavigated the globe near the equator. Ocean currents and ice movements were also to be measured by the same technique. During the first year of operation, thirty-one investigators representing seven countries had activated over seven hundred platforms. The TWERLE design eliminated the need for the platform to interrogate the spacecraft that was required by the predecessor Nimbus-4 IRLS location system. TWERLE/RAMS had the ability to receive and locate signals from two hundred platforms within the spacecraft view. These features proved excellent for small aircraft and boat search and rescue purposes. TWERLE first became prominent in this regard with the rescue of the two balloonists, Ben Abruzzo and Max Anderson, trying to cross the Atlantic in their Double Eagle balloon in 1977. The TWERLE platform that the balloonists at almost the last minute decided to carry enabled the Nimbus Control Center to locate them after their balloon was downed by a violent storm off Newfoundland and they were lost at sea because there was no airplane tracking them on this mission. This rescue was followed by the rescue of the Japanese polar adventurer Naomi Uemera on his first attempt to dogsled solo to the North Pole. He fell into a crevasse in the Canadian Northwest Territories, out of view of airplane search parties. He was found through the Nimbus TWERLE platform that he carried. These life-saving accomplishments were preceded by British aviatrix Sheila Scott, who was convinced that for her safety, she should carry a Nimbus-4 IRLS platform (which included a distress signal feature) on her attempt to be the first person to solo fly a light aircraft across the North Pole and then around the world. The Nimbus Control Center unofficially tracked the aircraft flight for her safety (her safety responsibility was officially assigned to the US Navy) by computing the IRLS platform locations, thereby confirming that her plane crossed the pole. These successful lifesaving efforts led GSFC to promote the use of the IRLS location technique in a satellite search and rescue program (SARSAT). It became an international satellite program, now in place for over twenty years locating downed aircraft and ships in distress, credited with saving hundreds of lives annually. Another TWERLE feature of automatically collecting environmental data from unattended remote platforms was broadly demonstrated through environmental platform data collection and animal-tracking exercises. This capability evolved into a French satellite data collection system that was later replaced by a standard NOAA satellite operational capability for US data collection requirements.

The Limb Radiance Inversion Radiometer (LRIR) experiment had an unconventional remote-sensing method of viewing the atmosphere. By viewing the limb of Earth (10° in 0.2° slices) it was able to see the layers of the atmosphere directly as opposed to the normal method of looking down at the top of the atmosphere and inferring the altitude from the measurement characteristics. LRIR measured temperature, water vapor, and ozone in 10-km slices from above Earth to space. The design demonstrated the capability of low-temperature detectors to handle very low radiation signal levels; the detector was cooled to 63°K by a two-stage solid-cryogen cooler. The cryogen requirement gave the instrument a nominal six-month lifetime, which it achieved. This instrument was followed by the Limb Monitoring of the Stratosphere (LIMS) on Nimbus-7, which also required a cryogen-cooled detector because of the low signal levels viewing a small section of the Earth's limb.

The Earth Radiation Budget (ERB) experiment initiated the comprehensive scientific study of the balance between the solar incoming radiation and Earth's outgoing radiation, essential to understanding climate changes. This research was continued with the Nimbus-7 ERB instrument and expanded later with two ERBE satellites carrying a suite of instruments dedicated to studying the Earth's radiation balance. ERB measured shortwave radiation from 0.2-5 um, longwave radiation from 5-50 um, and total radiation from 0.2-50 um. It measured solar radiation between 2000Å and 50 um. It had a total of twenty-two scanning and non-scan channels.

The ESMR instrument was included on Nimbus-6 to continue producing quality global microwave data, previously produced by the Nimbus-5 ESMR, for supporting long-term cryosphere ice formation, land snow cover, and rainfall analysis. This ESMR had a conical scan with horizontal and vertical polarization at 37GHz, which made it effective for measuring wind speed over the ocean surface.

The THIR instrument was included to provide daily global cloud images that served as a meteorological background reference for the other experiment data.

The Tracking and Data Relay Experiment (T&DRE) was a technology experiment to demonstrate the technique for a low Earth-orbiting spacecraft to transmit data to the ground via the Tracking and Data Relay System (TDRS) geosynchronous satellite that was going into operation at a later date. Another purpose of the experiment was to gain information on the use of such a link for range and range-rate communications for satellite geodetic purposes. This experiment provided the Nimbus portion of a communication link from the Nimbus spacecraft to the data-acquisition site to the NCC through ATS-6.

Nimbus-7 Satellite: Program Climax with Many Earth Science Accomplishments

(10/24/78—02/14/1995)

The objectives of the Nimbus-7 mission represented a new an ambitious challenge. In addition to the development of instrument sensors to measure atmospheric and oceanographic features never measured before from space, the program goal was to broaden the participation of the science community and to enhance the utility of the data by making the data products rapidly available to the research community. The latter goal required a departure from the traditional Principal Investigator (PI) method of experiment, science data management, and the implementation of a new Project data ownership and processing data management regimen.

These objectives were achieved with outstanding success. Nimbus-7 carried nine instruments that generated the largest data set of any previous satellite program. Teams of scientists (Nimbus Experiment Teams) collaboratively developed the data product requirements and specifications, the algorithms for converting the measurements into geophysical parameters, the calibration of the sensor data, and the validation of the data products to initiate the data production mode. The nine-instrument data products were routinely processed by a Nimbus Project managed facility and by three other institutional facilities and distributed to the large number of scientists and scientific organizations (over forty-five) engaged in the

Earth science investigations and the applications of the data. This new data management arrangement is described in the Nimbus-7 data system section that follows.

Two new instruments, SBUV and TOMS, made a distinctive impact on scientific knowledge of the Earth's environment and how to react to this knowledge for humanity's benefit.

The Solar Backscatter Ultraviolet (SBUV) instrument was similar to the BUV on Nimbus-4, with an improved diffuser plate configuration for relating the incoming UV radiation to the reflected UV radiation. It measured ozone profiles in the stratosphere and total ozone along the orbit track. The SBUV was mounted together with the TOMS instrument, sharing the solar-illuminated diffuser plate used for calibration. An operational version of this instrument, SBUV/2, has been carried on NOAA's afternoon polar-orbiting spacecraft since 1984, which have the necessary sun angle for seeing the backscatter radiation.

The Total Ozone Mapping Spectrometer (TOMS) that measured total ozone in the atmosphere alerted the international community about the stratospheric ozone degradation resulting in a public awareness of this concern and international agreements to curtail the cause of the degradation. TOMS had the capability to measure the ozone and total sulfur dioxide, and aerosols (smoke, dust, and ash) in a column of air through the atmosphere as a function of the backscattered ultraviolet radiation. The radiation, sequenced by a chopper, was measured at six wavelengths between 312 to 380 nm, with a 0.2 second exposure to the sensor at each of thirty-five cross-track scan positions. The TOMS scanning mechanism took measurements across the orbital swath with a 50 x 50km resolution at nadir. The TOMS science program took on international interest after Nimbus TOMS data revealed the existence of ozone holes (large areas where the ozone level is below normal, safe levels) in the stratosphere that led to a twenty-five-year and ongoing international TOMS data-collection program because of the concern about the impact of stratospheric ozone holes on people's health.

The Coastal Zone Color Scanner (CZCS) that measured ocean color for distinguishing oceanographic content and features evoked a remarkable interest in this new oceanographic tool. Scientists became capable of associating color radiance and their intensities with a wide variety of ocean life and oceanic constituents associated with oceanic productivity that affects Earth's ecological balance and climate, with applications that impact commercial fishing. The results of these diverse CZCS scientific explorations and discoveries became the basis of most of the later oceanographic-discipline satellite experiments. CZCS was a more intensive oceanographic measuring system than any previous oceanographic remote-sensing instrument. CZCS was a multispectral imaging radiometer with six channels in the 10.5-12.5 mu and the 433-800 mu spectral ranges, scanning 80° cross track with a 0.5° angular resolution. It measured the temperature of coastal waters and open ocean, mapped chlorophyll concentration and sediment distribution, detected pollution in coastal zones (including oil spills), and determined the nature of materials suspended in the water, e.g., photoplankton, phytoplankton. CZCS, which operated for eight years, was the primary oceanographic research data until the SeaWifs satellite was launched in 1997.

The Scanning Multichannel Microwave Radiometer (SMMR) was an advanced, mechanically scanned version of the earlier ESMR instruments, with ten channels operating at 6.33, 10.69, 18.00, 21.00, and 37 Gh and with both horizontal and vertical polarization. It looked conically 42° from nadir and at a constant earth incidence angle of 51° and with an angular resolution of 0.8°-4.2°. It was the first instrument to make more precise, all-weather observations of both global sea ice concentrations and type (age) and sea-surface temperatures. In addition, it measured snow cover, soil moisture, rainfall, cloud-water content, atmospheric water vapor over oceans, and sea-surface winds.

Three other new Nimbus-7 instruments, the Limb Infrared Monitoring of the Stratosphere (LIMS), the Stratospheric Aerosol Measurement II (Sam II), and the Stratospheric Aerosol Measurement II (Sam II), concentrated on making stratospheric measurements.

The Limb Infrared Monitoring of the Stratosphere (LIMS) instrument design was based on the Nimbus-6 LRIR design concept, but the objective was to study the stratosphere rather than the lower atmosphere. It measured temperature, ozone, water vapor, nitric acid, and nitrogen dioxide. The detector was cooled to 63°K by a two-stage solid-cryogen cooler. The spectral range was 6.1-15.8 mu. It scanned to 12° above the horizon.

The Stratospheric Aerosol Measurement II (Sam II), a mechanically scanned radiometer, operated at 1 um, pointing at the sun during sunrise and sunset. It had an angular resolution of 0.01°. SAM II measured and mapped aerosol concentrations and optical properties in the polar stratosphere.

The Stratospheric and Mesospheric Sounder (SAMS), developed by Oxford University, UK, measured the distribution of temperature and select gases in the stratosphere and troposphere. It had nine channels of data that operated in two spectral bands, 2.7-15 um and 25-100 um. It looked toward the horizon and scanned +/-15° about the central viewing direction that varied between 5° above the horizon to 9° below the horizon, with a 1.6° x 16° angular resolution.

The Earth Radiation Budget (ERB) was a duplicate of the Nimbus-6 ERB instrument for supporting the continuation of Earth's energy budget and energy balance study.

The standard THIR instrument provided low-resolution terminator-to-terminator day-and-nighttime cloud and water vapor global data as meteorological condition reference information. It was also used to derive cloud temperature for data products.

Nimbus-7 operated for almost fifteen years. This longevity is attributable to special orbital conditions that happened with Nimbus-7. The spacecraft was serendipitously launched in a favorable orbital plane position, i.e., the opposite side of the direct sun line from the direction in which the plane normally drifts. That gave several years of extra solar power lifetime before the orbital plane drifted to the nominal sun line plane and then started the normal drift away from the nominal sun line plane. Another contributory factor was the slower-than-normal drift away from the nominal sun line plane, such that the array cell output was not reduced significantly by the cosine of the drift angle for several extra years. The solar cell degradation rate flattened out at a somewhat lower level than normal, which was another helpful condition. The use of magnetic torquers for attitude control rather than expendable gas-jet firings, which was the normal method, was another significant factor; the spacecraft lifetime would have been shortened if expendable gas was the only means available for unloading accumulated momentum. TOMS was operable in a degraded but useful mode without the diffuser plate for several years until the end of operations; indirect means were developed to infer the TOMS's data calibration. Spacecraft operation was shut down when TOMS failed; SAM II was the only other operative instrument.

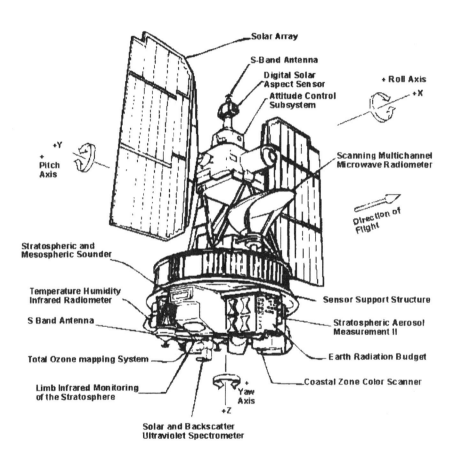

Nimbus-7 Observatory.

Footnotes, credits/references

1. The description of the effect of oil spills was taken from the NOAA National Ocean Service Office of Response and Restoration website.
2. The summary of the Nimbus contributions to science was adapted from the presentation on the contribution of Nimbus satellites to the study of Earth's radiation budget by Tom Vonder Harr of the Department of Atmospheric Science at Colorado State University.

Index

A

Abid, Geoge, 207

Abraham (patriarch), 108, 141

Abrams (veteran), 83-84

Abruzzo, Ben, 234

Advanced Vidicon Camera System (ACVS), 159

Afikomen, 77

Akiba (rabbi), 72

Alamango, Alexandra, 68

Aldrich, Josephine, 208, 213

aliyah, 79

Alpha Mu Epsilon (AME), 61

Amalgamated Cooperative, 35

Amoco Cadiz spill, 186

Amsterdam, 24

Anderson, Max, 234

Anielewicz, Mordechai, 97

Antietam National Battlefield, 107

Arlauskus, Joe, 207

Arlington Cemetery, 105-6

Around the World in Eighty Days (Verne), 189

Atlas, Pepi, 98

Atlas, Yitzchak, 98

Attitude Control System (ACS), 228

Automatic Picture Taking (APT) system, 163

B

Backscatter Ultraviolet Spectrometer (BUV), 210, 228

Baden, Ed, 207

Balin, Al, 136

Ballin, Al, 139

Ballin, Rhoda, 139

Balon, Ray, 215

Bandeen, William, 205, 209

Bar Kochba rebellion, 72

bar mitzvah, 52, 74, 110

basketball, 32, 37, 41, 44, 49, 190

Baugh, Sammy, 58

Beggs, Jim, 179

Beiber, Dave, 207

Bialystok, 32

Bialystoker Retirement and Nursing Home, 33

Bialystoker Synagogue, 32, 34

bimah, 74

Blumenthal, Sid, 120

Boeckel, John, 206

Bolton, Chuck, 207, 219

Boston, 116
boxball, 41-42
Brandy Alexander, 64
Bricha, 107
bris, 141
Broder, Sol, 207
Broome, Douglas, 205
Brown, Chester, 32
Brown, Lewis, 52
   Stranger than Fiction, 16, 52, 79
Browning, Ron, 206, 221
Bruening, Walter, 117-18
Burdette, Gerald "Gerry," 161-62, 207, 219
Butler, Dixon, 176

C

CalComp Inc., 208
Cannon Theater, 34
Carlsbad Cavern, 93
Carthey, Al, 134
Cave of Machpelah, 98
Chagall, Marc, 99
Channel Master Corporation, 12, 133-36, 138-39, 142-43, 160
Cherrix, Tom, 207
Chmielnicki, Bogdan, 23
Clancy (landlady), 114-15
Coastal Zone Color Scanner (CZCS), 173, 237-38
Cohen, Armand, 65
Connerty, Tom, 25, 32
Conservative Congregation, 74
Consolidated Electrodynamics Corporation (CEC), 159-60
control center, 202
Corlear Girls Junior High School, 33

Cote, Charles, 207, 209
Crossfield, Phil, 207
Curley, James, 116
Cutler, Jack, 84

D

Daily Mirror, 28
dance cruise, 101
Day, 28
Defense Advanced Research Projects Agency (DARPA), 190
Delio, Gene, 207
Devlin, Dick, 207
Diamond, Legs, 39
Dickey, Bill, 57
Disabled American Veterans (DAV), 67
Diskin Orphan Home, 77, 88
Dornbrand, Harry, 62
Dorsey, Tommy, 51
double-dipping, 180
Drummond, Bob, 207
Drummond, Fred, 208
Dvar Torahs, 76, 78

E

Earth globe illustration, 175
Earth Observation System (EOS), 7, 149, 176, 180
Earth Radiation Budget (ERB), 235, 239
Earth's Radiant Energy System, 184
East River, 30, 45, 47
East River Drive Park, 33
Eddington, Chester, 213
Edelson, Burt, 176
Egelstein, Jack, 92
Eikev, 78

Eisner, Herman, 74
Elderhostel trip, 6, 106-7
Electrically Scanning Microwave
    Radiometer (ESMR), 173
Ellenville, 133, 136-39, 141-42, 144, 147
Environmental Satellite Service
    Administration (ESSA), 190
Evans, Wilma, 208
ex-lax laxative, 40
extortion, 39
Exxon Valdez spill, 186

F

Fahnestock, Dale, 215
Fairchild Space and Electronics
    Company, 62
Feinberg (family physician and
    obstetrician), 142
Feinberg, Paul, 207
Fihelly, Art, 207, 223
Filter Wedge Spectrometer (FWS), 229
Finkelstein, Louis, 77
Fisher, Eddie, 94
football, 33, 41, 43-44, 61
Fordyce, Don, 206
Forman, Michael, 176, 207
Forsyth Street Park, 33
Forward, 28
Fourth of July, 47
Francesca, 22
Frankford Arsenal, 128, 130, 132
Freiheit, 28
Fried, Wendi, 75

G

gambling, 39, 118

Garber, Morris, 65-66
Garber, Tessie (née Pierce), 65
Gehrig, Lou, 57
Gellis, Isaac, 34
General Electric Company (GE), 62,
    121, 165, 167, 169
General Sportwear Co., Inc., 133
Gille gang, 48
Ginsburg, Mordechi, 98
Ginsburg, Sarah, 98, 108
Gitelman, Joe, 207
Global Positioning Satellites (GPS), 183
Goddard Retirees and Alumni
    Association (GRAA), 206
Goddard Space Flight Center (GSFC),
    148, 157
Goett, Harry, 207
Goldberg, Harold, 207
Goldstein (Holocaust survivor), 83
golf, 44, 130
Goodman, Benny, 51
Gould, Seymour, 147
Grand Canyon, 89-90, 93
Great Depression, 13, 30, 49-51, 70, 115
Green, Lloyd, 165, 207, 213
Greenberg, Carole, 129
Greenberg, Roberta, 129
Greenberg, Yetta, 129
Gunzberg, Morrie, 165

H

Haas, Sheldon, 169, 208
Haggadah, 76-77
Haley, Richard, 205
Hall, Helen, 51
Halloween, 5, 48, 120
Halpern, Martin, 75, 76

handball, 41, 43
Handler, Murray "Monis," 121
Hanel, Rudolf, 205, 210
haphtorah, 74
Harris, George, 219
Hebrew Free Loan Society, 50
Hebrew Home for the Aged, 33
Hebrew Immigration Aide Society
  (HIAS), 110
Heller, Dick, 134
Henmont Social Club, 41, 125
Herald Tribune, 28
High-Resolution Infrared Radiometer
  (HRIR), 210, 217, 225, 228, 233
Hinshelwood, George, 169
History of the Jews, A (Sachar), 53
Hitler, Adolf, 23, 28, 59, 108
Hogan, Frank, 161
Hogan, George, 207
Holocaust, 12, 24, 53, 79, 96, 104, 106
Houghton, John, 211, 229
House of Sages, 33
Hughes STX Corporation, 13, 149, 152
Hui, Peter, 207, 219-20, 222
Hunter College, 60
Huston, Wilbur "Bill," 207

I

Image Dissector Camera System
  (IDCS), 227
Interrogation, Recording, and
  Location System (IRLS), 226
In Those Days, 16
Iron Horse. *See* Gehrig, Lou
Isaac (patriarch), 98, 108
Islam, Frank, 150, 152-155

isolationism, 72
Israel, State of, 53

J

Jackson Park, 33, 47
James, Harry, 51
Jeffrin, Hal, 96
Jew, 77
Jewish Agricultural Society, 129, 133
Jewish Educational Alliance
  Settlement House, 33
*Jewish History: 4,000 Years of
  Accomplishment, Agony, and
  Survival* (Shapiro), 53
Jewish Social Service Agency (JSSA), 82
Johnny on the Pony, 46
Johnson, Art, 207
Johnson, Dave, 206
Johnson Act, 22
Joseph, Jacob, 33
Josiah (king), 78
Journey to the Center of the Earth
  (Verne), 189

K

Katz, Irving, 132
Kaveeshwar, Ashok, 149-50
Keigler, Jack, 208
kick the can and hide, 46

L

LaGuardia, Fiorello, 39, 71
Landsman, Jack, 96
Layman, Jonah, 75-76

Lehman, Herbert, 71-72
Leibowitz, Seymour, 169, 207
Lesko, John, 207
Levin, Gershon, 76
Levy, Saul, 48
Levy, Seymour, 25
Lewis, Jerry, 94
Limb Infrared Monitoring of the
    Stratosphere (LIMS), 238
Limb Radiance Inversion Radiometer
    (LRIR), 235
Lincoln Memorial, 105-6
Loeb, Fred, 147
Louis, Joe, 51
Lower East Side, 88
Luckman, Sid, 57
Ludmir. *See* Vladimir Volynsk
Luiz (Cuban American), 134
Lynch, Jim, 207

Meyerson, Herb, 158
mezuzah, 53
Michelson, Lou, 208
Mikulski, Stan, 48
Miller, Brice, 207
Miller, Glenn, 51
Miller, John, 220
minyan, 28
Mittleman, Herb, 207
Moishe (iceman), 34, 37
Monitor of Ultraviolet Solar Energy
    (MUSE), 227
Morning Journal, 28
Moscow Mule, 222
Moyer, Earl, 207
Muller, Ron, 207
Multidisciplinary Engineering
    Development Support (MEDS),
    153

M

N

Machzikei Talmud Torah, 51
MacKenzie, Charles, 176, 207
Manasseh (king), 78
marijuana, 39
Markwell Manufacturing Company,
    12, 124
Martin, Dean
    "Sway with Me," 63
Mason, Ed, 207
Matthews, Charles "Chuck," 206
Matzah of Hope, 77
Meehan, George, 169
Meehan, John, 207
Meteorological Data Handling System
    (MDHS), 163-64, 208, 212, 215,
    221, 227, 231

Nagurski, Bronko, 58
National Advisory Committee for
    Aeronautics (NACA), 62
National Aeronautics and Space Act, 190
National Aeronautics and Space
    Administration (NASA), 190
National Museum of American Jewish
    History (NMAJH), 11, 53
National Oceanic and Atmospheric
    Administration (NOAA), 13-14,
    152, 156, 171-74, 176, 190-91,
    200, 205, 231, 233-34
National Weather Service (NWS), 173
Naval Research Laboratory (NRL), 190
Nazism, 62

Network Operations Control Center (NOCC), 202
New Era Social Club, 41
Newman, Helen, 207
New York Giants, 57
New York Times, 28, 51, 124, 142
New York Yankees, 57
Nichols, Harry, 207
Nimbus Control Center (NCC), 14,159, 163, 166, 167, 172, 173, 212, 223, 227
Nimbus Program, 11, 14-15, 159, 161, 166
   benefits of, 182-83, 185-87
   Nimbus-1, 168-70, 202, 204, 206-7, 212, 216, 218, 221, 224, 226
   Nimbus-2, 168-170, 208, 224-225
   Nimbus-3, 168, 172, 188, 206, 223-26, 228, 232
   Nimbus-4, 206, 228-230, 237
   Nimbus-5, 230-32
   Nimbus-6, 199, 232-33, 235
   Nimbus-7, 15, 167, 173, 199, 209, 221, 229-31, 233, 235-36, 239
   overview of, 204-6, 208, 212-13, 215
Nordberg, William, 14, 205-6, 209-11, 220-21, 223
NY Daily News, 28
NY Journal American, 28

O

Obenschain, Rick, 207
O'Loughlin, Bill, 128
Ormsby, Dick, 164, 207, 213
Orthodox Young Israel Synagogue, 32

Ostrow, Harvey, 207
Ott, Mel, 57
Owen, Ralph, 220-21

P

Painted Desert, 90, 93
Palmer, Bennie, 14, 165, 172, 176, 212-13, 223
Passover Seder, 76
Patrick, Lynn, 58
Patrick, Muzz, 58
Petrified Forest, 90, 93
Peulio, Tony, 32
Peyser, Hedy, 85-86
Pierce, Amy, 77
Pierce, Harold, 65
Pierce, Manuel, 65, 111
Pierce, Pauline (née Locks), 65
Pine Bush, 136
Pluchino, Joe, 134, 136
Pluchino, Rose, 136
Powell, Bill, 215
Powell, Luther, 179
Press, Harry, 14, 158, 164, 169, 206, 223
Press, Sylvia, 206
Pressure Modulated Radiometer (PMR), 233
Princess Lines, 101
Prohibition, 13, 37-38
prostitution, 39
Protes, Abe, 69
Protes, Elayne (née Shapiro), 33, 69
PS 147 Elementary School, 33
punchball, 41-43

R

Rabbi Jacob Joseph Yeshiva, 33, 79
Radiation Inc., 208
Redisch, Bill, 207
reefers, 39
Republic Aviation, 62
Resnick, Harry, 133, 135, 142
Resnick, Joseph, 133
Resnick, Louis, 133
Revere Beach, 116
Rexite, Seymour, 132
Richmond Museum of the
    Confederacy, 108
ringolevio, 29, 46
roller-skate hockey, 41
roller-skating, 41, 43, 49
Roosevelt, Eleanor, 72
Roosevelt, Theodore, 71
Rossette, Ed, 160
Ruth, Babe, 57

S

Sachar, Abraham, 53
    History of the Jews, A, 53
Sandler, Helen, 147
Sargent, Jack, 174, 224
Sargent, Mickey, 224
Satellite Infrared Spectrometer (SIRS),
    172, 226
Scanning Microwave Spectrometer
    (SCAMS), 233
Schacte, Doris, 208
Schardt, Burton, 205
Schlachman, Ben, 207, 219, 223
Schmeling, Max, 51

Schnapp, Jerome, 155
Schnapper (retired economist), 82
Schneebaum, Moe, 158, 160, 206, 211
Schulman, Joe, 207
Schwartz, Edith, 139
Schwartz, Fran, 139
Schwartz, Jerry, 139
Schwartz, Martin, 136
Schwartz, Marty, 139
Scott, Sheila, 234
search and rescue (SAR) system, 183
Seder, 77, 130
Selective Chopper Radiometer (SCR),
    229
Seward Park, 33
Seward Park High School, 33
Shaare Tefila, 67, 74, 75, 81, 82
    Hebrew School, 67
Shapiro, Beckie (née Teitelbaum), 24,
    26-29, 31-32, 74, 87, 89, 116,
    123-24, 131-32, 139, 147
Shapiro, Bianca, 69
Shapiro, Carole, 110
Shapiro, David, 52, 67-70, 139, 177
Shapiro, Debbie, 67, 111
Shapiro, Ecille (née Pierce), 63-65, 67,
    139
Shapiro, Frances, 26-27, 38, 49, 61,
    106, 139
Shapiro, Grayson, 69
Shapiro, Irene, 26, 33, 41
Shapiro, Irving, 28
Shapiro, Leila, 69
Shapiro, Louis, 22-35, 37-38, 73-74,
    88, 109
Shapiro, May, 26
Shapiro, Morris (cousin), 28

Shapiro, Morris (Ralph's brother), 27, 66-67
Shapiro, Nathan, 22, 32, 69, 109, 177
Shapiro, Raful, 26
Shapiro, Ralph, 26, 161
  academic education of, 56, 58-60, 62
  coping with the Great Depression, 49, 51
  cultural exposure in senior years, 105, 107-8
  experiences of the Lower East Side Web, 88, 99-102, 104
  experiences of volunteerism, 81-83, 85
  fifty-sixth wedding anniversary, 63
  growing-up environment, 30-32, 34-35, 37-41, 44-47
  interest in Zionism, 11, 79
  involvement in charities, 88
  postretirement work as independent consultant, 155
  religious affiliations, 74-76, 78
  religious education of, 51-52
  significant experiences as youth, 70, 72-73
  travels of, 90-94, 96, 98-102, 104
  work at Channel Masters, 134-36
  work at Frankford Arsenal, 128
  work at General Electric Company, 112-16, 118-23
  work at Hughes STX, 148, 150, 152, 154, 180
  work at Markwell Manufacturing Company, 124, 126
  work at NASA, 158, 160-61, 163-64, 166-68, 170-71, 174, 176, 178, 180
  work at QSS, 152-53, 155
  work at US Industries, 143-44, 146
  Jewish History: 4,000 Years of Accomplishment, Agony, and Survival, 16, 53
Shapiro, Raphael. *See* Shapiro, Ralph
Sharon Springs, 123
Shatske, Jules, 48
Shaw, Artie, 51
Sheehan, John, 215
Shema prayer, 54, 72-73
shtiebels, 32
Silver Spring, 16, 74, 78, 105, 121, 143-44, 157
Sinatra, Frank, 51
Siry, Joe, 219
skiing, 44, 122
Skirball Cultural Center, 107-8
Smith, William, 172-73, 211
Smithsonian Air and Space Museum, 105
softball, 33, 44, 119
Solar Backscatter Ultraviolet (SBUV), 237
Sputnik, 190
Staats-Zeitung, 28
Stampfl, Rudy, 176, 205, 219
STDN Tracking and Data Network, 8, 215
Stein, Irv, 208
Steinhorn, Harriet, 82
Stengard, Ed, 207
Stephenson, Dick, 213
Sternberg, John, 160
stickball, 41, 43
St. John, Robert, 130
Stokes, Maurice, 94
stoopball, 41, 43
Stranger than Fiction (Brown), 16, 52, 79

Stratospheric Aerosol Measurement II
(Sam II), 238
Stratospheric and Mesospheric
Sounder (SAMS), 239
Strong, Jim, 207
Stroud, Bill, 158-59, 161-62, 171-72,
205-6, 223
Sunday Blue Law, 116
"Sway with Me" (Martin), 63
swimming, 45
System Z, 176

T

Tammany Hall, 39
Taube, Herman, 82
Taylor, Jim, 207
tefillin, 33
tennis, 44, 129
Terry, Bill, 57
Thienel, Chuck, 207
Three Coins in the Fountain, 103
TIROS, 161, 205
Toczalowski, Joe, 207
Total Ozone Mapping Spectrometer
(TOMS), 210, 229, 237
Trachtenberg, Sid, 128
Tracking and Data Relay Experiment
(T&DRE), 236
Triangle Shirtwaist Company, 25
Tropical Wind Energy Conversion and
Reference Level (TWERLE), 234
Trudell, Bernie, 164, 207, 222
Trupp, Austin, 68
Trupp, Darryl, 68
Trupp, Debbie (née Shapiro), 67-68, 139
Trupp, Jenna, 68
Tucker, Richard, 52

Turtill, Joe, 208
Twenty Thousand Leagues Under the
Sea (Verne), 189

U

Uemera, Naomi, 234
United Jewish Appeal of Greater
Washington, 88
United States Marine Corps Women's
Reserve (USMCWR), 66
US Industries Inc., 12, 142-43, 147,
157
USS Arizona Memorial Museum, 102

V

Van Cortlandt Park, 39
Vanguard, 190
Verne, Jules, 189
Around the World in Eighty Days, 189
Journey to the Center of the Earth,
189
Twenty Thousand Leagues Under the
Sea, 189
Versatile Information Processor (VIP),
228, 230
Vladimir (prince), 23
Vladimir Volynsk, 23-24, 98, 109

W

Wald, Lillian, 51
Walla Walla, 90
Wark, David, 172, 211
War of Independence, 79, 97
Warsaw Ghetto Uprising, 97
Weiland, Stanley, 174, 206-7

Weinreb, Adelle, 129
Weinreb, Leo, 129
Weiser, Sid, 146-48
Westrex Corporation, 163, 217
Wilson, Lou, 207
World Zionist Organization, 109
Wright, Ed, 169

Y

Yad Mordechai, 96
Yad Vashem, 96
Yale University, 120
Yiddish, 59

Z

Zionism, 6, 11, 79

CPSIA information can be obtained at www.ICGtesting.com
Printed in the USA
BVOW071248181212

308546BV00001B/5/P